DATE DUE

GAYLORD   PRINTED IN U.S.A.

The Theatre Student

PLAYWRITING

 THE THEATRE STUDENT SERIES

The Theatre Student

PLAYWRITING

Peter Kline

PUBLISHED BY

RICHARDS ROSEN PRESS, INC.

NEW YORK, N.Y. 10010

Standard Book Number: 8239–0196–3
Library of Congress Catalog Card Number: 78–107596
Dewey Decimal Classification: 371.897

Published in 1970 by Richards Rosen Press, Inc.
29 East 21st Street, New York City, N.Y. 10010

First Edition

Manufactured in the United States of America

CONTENTS

INTRODUCTION

Most books on playwriting are concerned with what the play should be. This book is more concerned with what the playwright should be. The interaction between a writer and his materials is a complex one and differs with each writer. The play that finally comes out of that interaction is an entity unto itself, and although it will necessarily resemble other plays in certain respects, there is no "rule" it may not break. Indeed, one generation's dogma may be another's anathema. One thinks of J. B. Priestley's statement only a few years ago that if dialogue alone could make a play, then *Waiting for Godot* would be a good play.

Playwriting is usually regarded in its opening stages as a solitary business. The writer closets himself with an idea, and gradually, by some mysterious process, a play is born. Some modern theatres have belied this concept of playwriting by creating plays out of improvisational work, reducing the playwright to a stenographer. On the other hand, I have found that people can work together on their plays in a way that preserves the individuality of the writer but allows him to find help and inspiration when he needs it. A group of playwrights, each with his own play, but each taking a lively and continuing interest in the plays of others, can rise above competitiveness and genuinely inspire one another. An improvisation, when it is needed, can open up new ideas. An honest comparison of one another's writing experiences can build confidence. A genuine audience reaction to what has been accomplished can help the writer to see his work objectively. A common agreement that what is being accomplished in a playwriting group is somehow related to what has been accomplished by Shakespeare and Ibsen and Strindberg and O'Neill and George S. Kaufman helps to develop a feeling for tradition and a respect for technique.

John Holt has written of the importance of "messing around" with the materials associated with a concept before you learn the concept. Youngsters can "mess around" with the materials of playwriting, probably at any age. The exercises in this book (there are more of them than could be used effectively in a single year of teaching, and they are therefore to be chosen from) can all be performed by high-school students. Some of them could be used as they are by very young children. Others might be adaptable for use by older children. Probably no adaptation would be necessary for use by more mature groups (college students or adults), although I have found that the older one gets, the more difficult become exercises depending on a flexible imagination. If these materials are used with older groups, more patience may be necessary.

This book will not teach anyone how to write a play. In the final analysis, only the playwright himself can do that. Perhaps it will help some people get more interested in writing plays. What is needed in generous supply is faith, both on the part of the student and the teacher, that something will result. Faith of the kind that Budd Schulberg had when he taught creative writing in Watts should be enough to help just about anyone write just about anything. Read the introduction to *From the Ashes* and believe that you can teach or learn writing anywhere you want to.

Playwriting is the best kind of writing to teach to a group because its efficacy is so readily measured by a group response. You cannot really be sure you are doing the right thing in slapping critical standards on a poet or a novelist—he may be seeing something that you are missing. But a play must work in the theatre, and you can be sure if it does not. Playwrights have to learn humility, and a playwriting class is a good place to teach it.

Despair, disillusionment, even fear may find their place from time to time in a playwriting class; but the end result for everyone concerned can be a satisfaction that is ordinarily a stranger to the classroom. Playwriting is supposed to be difficult to teach, but no other teaching that I have done has gone so well.

TO THE STUDENT

You might be interested in how a small group of eleventh-graders who studied playwriting as their English course for the year reacted to the experience. They were students in a private school who chose to take playwriting because it interested them, not because they had previously demonstrated any talent.

I

I really enjoyed the playwriting class. I totally immersed myself in a course that was entirely new to me, a completely new medium, playwriting. I discovered for the first time that one cannot understand playwriting unless one can write his very own play. I can now understand the real task of writing a play. Also, from writing a full length play, I discovered a satisfaction that I have never attained before.

II

Even though I'm somewhat bored, and even more discouraged by my writing (the jerkiness, the unevenness, the unreal parts, etc.), I am inspired to try again at playwriting. Maybe not this particular play, but a new idea that I might be really excited about.

III

The main drawback to this course is work. All other problems stem from it: unfinished plays, unrevised dialogue, frustration, depression, and similar maladies. With enough work, however it is distributed, most of the problems of writing a finished play can be surmounted by an average Sandy Springer. And this is where the main problem lies: it is difficult to work. If the prospective playwright is willing to work for the satisfaction of finishing a play—or even writing an act with some degree of quality— then he should get much out of the course.

IV

The playwriting course is a hard course, but very rewarding. Extreme discipline is necessary to obtain material. You will probably find a great use for "thinking" throughout the course—that is, concentrated effort to produce and create.

Now to come down off the pedestal after I've scared you to death— when I went into the playwriting course I had very little self-discipline, very poor study habits, and I found out after I got in there that I had never been made to really "think" before. Halfway through the year I decided that the course was too hard for me, but I kept on. By the end I had half finished a play that I am proud of, and by the end I could understand. So now I've gotten over the mountain of frustrations and I can really go places with a play. I've said all this simply to say that it is fantastic *training*. That part of the course was actually more valuable to my life in the long run.

Now on the other hand the study of plays and writing is the most fascinating and enchanting area of study. The depth that one can go into a play is not something obvious and around for you to have experienced much of.

Here again you really have to think. Everything means something and there's never an end to values to be found.

V

The playwriting course takes discipline most of all. I found it much more difficult to write a play than I had thought. The most important thing is to learn how to set a goal for yourself and keep to it. This is a very free course. If you are interested in educating yourself and discovering your capabilities on your own terms, take the course.

VI

I think that by the time a person is a junior, he should know, to a sufficient extent, what his writing capabilities are. He should be informed that this is by no means an escape from work. On the contrary, I think it is the hardest English course, if taken seriously.

The course should not require a person to finish a play, but to seriously set up his own goals and fulfill them—or realize during the course that he can't.

VII

The work that I put into playwriting class was about the amount of work that I expected. That is, there were many stretches of time when I worked thinking in class and taking incidental notes about my play, when I spent only about an hour a week in the actual writing. Then there were many times when I found myself sacrificing hours and hours of my free time when I was inspired or motivated to write. I do not feel that playwriting class made me weaker in any of my other studies unless it was for a short period of two or three days. In that case the work in the other classes was made up fast enough.

Out of a total of fifteen students taking the course, these are the complete statements of those who expressed an opinion about it. At the end of this book you will find parts of some of their plays. That will give you an idea of what can be achieved by an eleventh-grader who devotes a year to the study of playwriting.

The exciting thing about a playwriting class for a high-school student is, as some of the students pointed out, that you learn you can do something that you might have thought would be too difficult for you. The purpose of this book is to help you get started on some of the thinking you will need to go through in writing a play.

If you pursue the art of playwriting for any length of time, you will eventually find your own way with a play. There are nearly as many ways of writing plays as there are playwrights. However, one's way with a play is, indeed, something that must be found, not something that simply happens. This book contains many suggestions and exercises that may help you find your way. Use the ones that help you the most and forget the ones that do not. Above all, do not let the book make you feel guilty for not following its every suggestion. Feeling guilty will only keep you from working on your play. Playwriting, though it requires great effort—and often some pain— should also be fun. The joy of discovering what one has to say, of seeing a character come to life, of seeing a mystery begin to unravel—those are the joys of creating, and they are well worth whatever they may cost in pain and effort.

Read this book quickly and then put it aside. Come back to it only when you feel the need to review specific points covered in it. You should let it influence the workings of your unconscious mind rather than memorize it and let it force you into patterns that may not be right for you.

There will be times when you will be stuck because no new ideas seem to occur to you. At those times you may wish to reread portions of the book and try some of the exercises in it. They may help to start your mind working again. If you are in a class, your teacher may use some of those exercises or others like them. You will need to tell your teacher whether the exercises are helping you. If you are working on your own, you can get groups of friends together and do some of the exercises with them. Perhaps you can organize your own playwriting club.

You are about to begin a fascinating new adventure. You will discover many things about yourself and about other people and about the world that you did not know before. Whatever the outcome—whether your play is a success or not, or even gets finished or not—the experience will have been valuable to you.

TO THE TEACHER

A book designed to teach playwriting to students below the graduate school level may seem something of an anomaly. Good playwriting requires skill and maturity. What, then, can students on the college and high-school level hope to gain by studying it? One remembers George Pierce Baker's recommendation that instruction be delayed until graduate school and then be taught only to carefully selected students. I disagree. Playwriting can and should be taught at almost any age level. My own interest was whetted when in the eighth grade we adapted *Evangeline* for the stage as a class project. Since then I have found that even young children enjoy writing plays and seeing them performed. This book is based on my experience in working with eleventh-graders. I found that although they might not have developed the mature philosophy of life that many older people have, their creative energy was at a high level. Although beginners at any age cannot usually produce "mature" plays, they are capable of learning fundamentals on which later writing can be based.

But the hope that one may develop professional playwrights should not be the teacher's prime motivation. There is no better way to learn about an art than by practicing it intelligently. Students of playwriting can in a given time learn more about literature (though their knowledge is not as formally organized) than can the same students approaching literature analytically. At the same time those students will become more critical of their own lives and more conscious of what is happening in them. At a time in life when one is prone to rail against the injustices of the world, and particularly one's parents and teachers, those students will be trying to understand their elders as human beings. Antagonistic feelings about people can be transmuted into objective and even benevolent attitudes. The kind of growth that is possible is exemplified by the following comment from one of my students: "I think the main problem is that I started to write a very sarcastic play, and I started growing out of my sarcastic stage while I was writing it. Therefore it's much stronger in some places than others. Maybe in a few months I'll be totally grown out of the sarcasm—then I'll be able to look more objectively at it." Perhaps growth of this sort occurs because one is continually asking of his characters, why do they behave as they do? and his characters are likely to stem from his own deepest concerns. Playwriting class thus becomes a place in which the anguish and frustration of growth can be transformed into creative energy. In the process students learn basic literary concepts, not by being told about them, but by experiencing them, and to a certain extent evolving them out of their own expressive needs. .

If we agree that playwriting can and should be taught, we still need some vantage point from which to teach it. What are the rules? Fortunately or unfortunately, as the case may be, the most frequently uttered statement about playwriting by those who have studied the art is that there are no rules for writing good plays. This has led some people to believe that there is nothing to teach, and in one sense that is true. One cannot give instruction in playwriting the way one would give instruction in tennis or in the playing of a musical instrument, by saying that there are certain specific ways of doing things without which no good play can possibly be written. Choose any general statement you like about plays, and you will find some good play that has been written in defiance of it. Plot, character, conflict, theme, dialogue, unity of action, scenery—all are considered more or less naturally to be ingredients of good drama, and all have been effectively done without.

How, then, is one to teach playwriting? Primarily, I think, by developing a sense of theatrical values. The person who knows, in terms of theatre, what is valuable, has one of the first requirements of the playwright. True, he may be only an intelligent playgoer, or he may be a critic, an actor, a director, or a designer. He may not be temperamentally inclined to express himself through the writing of dialogue; if he is not, then playwriting is not for him, though he may learn a great deal that will help him to understand the other aspects of drama from attempting to write a play. Thousands of people, however, are inclined to express themselves through dialogue, and of those thousands very few write good plays. The poor playwright has not found a means of giving a moment of theatrical time sufficient value for those who witness it. I like Peter Brook's distinction between the good play and the poor one. He says: "A play in performance is a series of impressions; little dabs, one after another, fragments of information or feeling in a sequence which stir the audience's perceptions. A good play sends many such messages, often several at a time, often crowding, jostling, overlapping one another. The intelligence, the feelings, the memory, the imagination are all stirred. In a poor play, the impressions are well spaced out, they lope along in single file, and in the gaps the heart can sleep while the mind wanders to the day's annoyances and thoughts of dinner."

Value—intense, complex, and concentrated. That is what the playwright should seek to breathe into his dialogue. If he succeeds, no matter how it is done, no matter what the content, it should find a way to live for audiences.

But how are values learned? How does one first feel the importance of value? I think, only through experience. One who wishes to teach playwriting must make his classroom a place where experiences can happen. They may be vicarious experiences—the sort that come from a good teacher talking thrillingly about his own sense of values in such a way that his pupils absorb that sense and make it the basis of their own thinking. The two best teachers I have had taught in this manner. Or the experience may be more direct. Through doing things together, pupils learn some of the things they need to know to build a sense of theatrical value. Most basically, they should be exposed to good plays. They should see them, hear them, read them, talk about them, get to know the characters and situations in them as part of a basic vocabulary of craftsmanship. One is on dangerous ground talking about the unities of time, place, and action; but one can certainly say that in *Oedipus Rex* much of the intensity is achieved through the use of these unities and that this intensity is much like that in *Ghosts*, in which the unities again are used. One can then say that in *Hamlet* variety, rather than intensity, is achieved, and that a similar kind of variety occurs in *Peer Gynt*. One learns, then, to think in terms of cause and effect. If I wish to write a play that has a certain kind of effect, I can learn from the study of plays that produce similar effects and determine for myself how those effects are achieved. Thus, if a student tells me he wishes to write a play that combines farce and tragedy, I may tell him to read *Juno and the Paycock* or *Cyrano*. If he wishes to treat serious subjects in a farcical manner, I may tell him to read *The Bald Soprano* or *Luv*. I certainly would not tell him that it is impossible to achieve the effect he is after, though I often say that a particular kind of effect seems too ambitious for a beginner.

Since the study of classic plays is very time-consuming, and class time needs to be spent on the problems encountered by the students in writing their own plays, much of this study can be accomplished outside of regular class time. Students may individually read those plays most related to their own development. They may join in trips to the theatre or gather of an evening to listen to some of the many fine recordings of plays now available. They will learn from these plays without explicit discussion of them because they will see in them much that they are encountering in their own work. If the class can arrange to meet regularly from time to time to listen to recordings, that ensures that they will have a common experience of several plays that can then be referred to as various problems of playwriting arise in class.

Secondarily, students should read and experience other forms of literature and art. Good novels, poems, and short stories on the one hand, good movies and television programs on the other, not only give them a clearer sense of the specific needs of the dramatic medium, they also expose them to additional literary and human experiences. Good photography, painting, sculpture, and music have something to offer as well, if one has the time to explore them.

But the raw materials of the artist need not necessarily be good in themselves. My students, having listened to recordings of several very good plays, began to get discouraged and asked to hear something bad. I played them a tape of a student-written play, which they found very bad indeed, and they subsequently developed more confidence in their own work. Never forget that Shakespeare read mostly bad literature and that he used as raw materials for his writing works that in their original form were not very satisfying. Success breeds success, and Shakespeare must have increased his feelings of confidence by realizing that he could improve everything he touched. The moral is that it is wise to be exposed to things one feels he can improve on. That implies a number of possible exercises. One might try rewriting plays that have failed. One might try developing newspaper stories into plays. I asked my students to read *Genesis* and decide what the most dramatizable stories in it were and how they should be handled. It is instructive in this connection to study the miracle plays performed by the guilds in England during the Middle Ages. One can see both how they have added dramatic interest to the Bible stories and how they might be made more dramatic by being rewritten for modern audiences.

The main thing, however, is to write and to have one's work evaluated. A student is likely to find rather early a dramatic situation that interests him and then to have difficulty developing it in a way that satisfies him. This is a situation in which class discussion proves fruitful. Many students may offer suggestions as to how it might be handled. The teacher can then coordinate and evaluate those suggestions and offer additional ones of his own. I try to make my suggestions a little inadequate and to suggest several mutually exclusive ways of treating a situation. That will encourage the student to think for himself rather than rely on me to write his play for him.

Another way to develop ideas for the treatment of a dramatic situation is to have several students improvise a scene based on that situation. Many ideas will evolve that will stimulate a writer to continue his work more productively.

Many of the above suggestions may tend to give pause to the teacher schooled in traditional classroom techniques. Some people feel it is very important to be able to measure the knowledge imparted in the classroom by frequent testing. Anxiety may arise from time to time: Since one does not know specifically what is being learned, it may be that nothing is learned at all. I sometimes experienced that kind of anxiety as I taught my eleventh-graders. What would outsiders make of a course in which only one assignment was given for the whole year, and in which what was learned depended almost entirely on what individual students chose to learn? What, too, would other teachers think of the fact that I was teaching a course for which it was literally impossible for me to prepare any of my classes, since the classes were based on the problems students were having at any given time? My fears proved to be groundless, as the only complaints offered by anyone were complaints from the students that they were spending too much time on their English course. If one simply accepts the fact that one is teaching people, not facts, one can be fairly comfortable with the apparent lack of direction that such a course necessarily takes. The more the student is made responsible for his own individual development, the more successful the course can be. Moreover, a precise measurement is available as to what has happened: the quality of the play the student finally writes.

Even that measurement should not be taken too seriously, however. Some students quickly find what they prefer to work on. Others must try several subjects before they find one that is congenial. Some of my students worked on three or four separate plays, but did not finish any of them. Some wrote rapidly, others very slowly. I gave deadlines for completion of acts, but the deadlines could not be taken very seriously, as it might be far more important for a student to drop what he was working on and try something different than for him to complete an act by a given date. It is important to realize that in writing their plays most students are making significant decisions about their own values. They should feel free to regard those decisions as tentative, not to commit themselves too strongly to a given piece of work. So long as teacher and student deal honestly and in good faith with each other, the teacher is likely to have a good idea of what kind of progress is being made.

In some ways creativity is therapeutic. In giving form and structure to their dreams and fantasies, people help to structure their personalities and achieve greater maturity. When their hopes and antagonisms are carefully articulated, they are in a better position to act intelligently in dealing with their problems. Budd Schulberg has written of his experiences teaching creative writing in a workshop which he started soon after the riots in the Watts district of Los Angeles. Although interest in the workshop was slow to develop, the success that Schulberg ultimately achieved beautifully illustrates the need for creative outlets for people who are angry and frustrated. Schulberg's work demonstrates that creative writing should be taught among disadvantaged people. But one need not stop there. To a certain extent all adolescents are angry and frustrated, or should be. The goals of maturity do not come easily, and reaching for them breeds frustrations that traditional teaching of literature does little about. Large numbers of adolescents who like to write can benefit from disciplined writing instruction. Those who like to write dialogue can get the best discipline of all, for drama is by its nature the most disciplined of literary forms, and that discipline is something the student can discover for himself through classroom production of, and reaction to, his work.

I found that the playwriting class I taught to eleventh-graders was substantially more satisfying for everyone concerned than any other class I had ever taught. What was the secret of the difference? Certainly not the excellence of the wisdom I imparted. I believe I lectured once the entire year, and that was not for a complete period. Most of the time I observed what was going on, and often I had little to say that went much beyond what the students said to one another. By some standards I was less effective than I should have been. I didn't spend nearly as much time as I should have in consultation with individual students outside of class. I was really not sure how good their plays were or how they should change them. I led relatively few discussions that would serve to set standards of criticism. Probably my performance in the classroom could have been substantially improved in many ways.

But there was a kind of reality about the course that one seldom finds in the classroom. The students were trying to do something that most of them eventually decided they really wanted to be able to do. Perhaps because I did not choose to be a strong leader and fountain of wisdom, they learned to turn to one another. They did this first of all through improvisations, then through various kinds of affirmation of one another's work. I think part of the secret was in the enormity of the demand. To ask an eleventh-grader to write a short story or a poem is not to ask too much. Many students will have already done such a thing. But by and large eleventh-graders do not think they can write full-length plays; there is something a little preposterous about expecting them to. Since the task seems so enormous, not much is to be lost by failing at it. That group of students saw themselves as having a mutual plight, and they sensed that they would need one another's maximum assistance to complete the task. Every forward step seemed a tremendous thing gained. When it became evident that some of them would complete their plays, those people earned genuine respect from their classmates. Furthermore, everyone felt a vested interest in everyone else's play, since each person had contributed something, either through improvisation, through offering critical suggestions, or merely by affirming the value of what was being done. That class learned communication and mutual respect. They learned to believe in the validity of what they were doing by having it accepted and in certain ways acted upon by others. They learned to respect others' ideas because they needed those ideas in order to be successful in what they were trying to do. They learned to take joy in the personal experience of drama, and to understand the nature of excellence in drama by trying to achieve it themselves. They also could see the difference and relation between what the professionals could do and what they could do. The experience produced both ambition and humility.

Many playwriting manuals make frequent reference to existing plays in order to clarify concepts of technique. Since I have found that high-school students tend to be irritated and discouraged by frequent references to works they have not read, I have avoided doing this. Although a few plays, particularly *Hamlet* (which is standard fare in the high-school curriculum), are referred to, I have tried much of the time to work with hypothetical plays that the reader may imagine himself writing. At other times I have simply allowed a concept to remain abstract, leaving it to the student to find examples of how it works as he does his own reading. Examples from existing plays have the advantage of making clear what concept of technique is being referred to. However, they also have the disadvantage of suggesting how that technique should be handled. Inasmuch as there are infinite possible ways to give many of the concepts of playwriting expression in actual plays, the student may learn far more if he tries to apply them himself without seeing how they are handled by others. For example, when I refer on p. 69 to the fact that a kiss may be an expression of hatred as well as love, I have in mind *A View from the Bridge*. There, a man kisses his daughter's fiancé in order to suggest that he is a homosexual. A student, given this example, would probably find it more, rather than less, difficult to think of another kind of situation in which a kiss could be an expression of hatred. It seems better for him to think of his own ideas first and then find examples in professional plays. That will tend to stimulate his imagination rather than give him the impression that everything that can be done already has been done.

I offer this book in the belief that with its help many teachers can make the exciting discoveries I have made of unsuspected creativity in their students. The book is designed to be used as an adjunct to the class, a set of resource materials, to be referred to and cited when needed. The teacher should have students complete their reading of it early in the course, perhaps without specific discussion of it. Then he might draw upon its ideas as they seem relevant to what is happening in class. Students are as likely to mention it as the teacher, and will do so if they feel that a particular problem can be solved better by a discussion of particular ideas in the book.

Part I: YOU AS A PLAYWRIGHT

Chapter I

THE JOY OF CREATIVITY

Writing a play can be one of the most exciting and joyful activities you will ever undertake. If you are a creative person (and most people find that they are, once their creativity has been stimulated), you have an inborn need to communicate—not facts and figures, not dry "information," but something of yourself. Writing a play gives you an opportunity to show other people what the world is like, as you see it.

As you read this book you should come to realize that one of the most exciting things about writing a play is that there are no rules. Every good play is good in a different way. Following rules for writing plays only leads one to write bad plays. True, there are guidelines, things to consider, problems the solution of which should make your play a better play, and you will find some of these discussed in this book. But a good play is itself, and no more to be compared to another play than you, who are yourself, are to be compared to another person.

If you have been taught in school that there is always a right and a wrong way to do everything, you will have to get over that feeling as you learn to write a play. Writing a play is discovery. It is discovery of something that has never existed before and will never exist again in the history of the world —that unique relationship to the world that is yours and yours alone.

Perhaps you think you are no good at discovering things. That only means that you have never tried. Many persons decide early in life that all the important things have already been discovered, and nothing is left for them to do except learn about what has been discovered. But discovering is something that you *can* do, and once you begin to do it you will be amazed at the richness and ingenuity of your own thoughts.

Let us not pretend, however, that one need merely look inside oneself and an endless array of masterpieces will march forth as at the rubbing of an Aladdin's lamp. If writing plays were as simple as that, the world would be filled with masterpieces, and everyone would be a successful playwright. It is not only *inside* oneself that a play lies, but also in one's relationship to others, to society, and to the whole world. That relationship includes, among other things, other plays that have already been written. As you continue to write plays you will want to know more about other plays. That is important because you will want to avoid writing plays too much like the plays that have already been written.

Another thing about writing plays is that it requires a great deal of discipline. For most people discipline is a nasty word. It suggests punishment for misbehavior of some kind. But to the serious artist disci-

21

pline is a beautiful word. It is the means by which he discovers what is special in himself. Most of the things we see and most of the things we think about are not ours at all. They grow in us as a result of other people's ways of seeing and thinking about things. Discipline is the means by which an artist unlocks the world that is his own, the world that has been hidden from him by the thoughts and words of others. If you are afraid to think except as other people have thought, then writing plays is not for you. But if you are interested in finding your own way of seeing and feeling and thinking about things, writing plays is one of the best ways of doing it. Just as we never know what we are going to say until we have said it, so we never know how we feel about the world until we have expressed it in some artistic way; and playwriting, of all the ways of expressing oneself, is the clearest in its statement of just exactly what we mean and how we feel. Why should that be so?

The play is the most public form of art that exists. Other literary forms, such as poems and novels, are read by one person at a time. Pictures are looked at in silence by people in art galleries who roam about as they please and spend as much or as little time looking at a picture as they feel moved to. Even music, though many people listen to it together, is somehow more private and more mysterious than a play.

A play does not achieve its fullness until it is performed for an audience. The audience responds to the actors continually, by laughter, by silence, by restlessness, by spontaneous applause, and by many more subtle ways that actors and audiences both know but no one can express in words. Although individuals in the audience may have varying opinions about the play as it is performed, there is also a strong feeling that an audience is a unit—a single thing that feels and thinks and expresses itself. A play can grab an audience or it can lose them. When the audience is with the play, feeling strongly the power of what it is seeing, the playwright is communicating fully.

But the playwright does not communicate directly. His message is passed on to the audience through the minds of actors and a director and other people, such as the scenery and lighting designers. His message must be clear to them before they can make it clear to the audience. It is out of this working together to create a public performance that theatre people learn to understand one another and to make themselves as clear as possible.

When he has said something so clearly that all of his actors can understand it and all of his audience can feel its power, then the playwright knows the supreme joy of life: feeling that his own point of view is important and meaningful to others. It is worth a great deal of effort to attain such joy, and discipline makes that effort possible and meaningful.

Therefore you should rejoice as you learn discipline. Reading this book will help. Getting criticism from teachers and friends will help. Having your plays performed will help. But what helps most is the experience of writing itself. You must practice it regularly. Gradually you will discover your own specialness and learn the value of what you have to say. The more writing you do, the more you can be sure that one day you will understand what you have to say that is important.

Has this given you the impression that what you have to say will be an idea or a series of ideas? On the contrary, what you have to say will be a kind of picture of experience. It may be sad or it may be funny. It may be the joy of playing with words or the excitement of creating lives. Whatever it is, it will be something that cannot be separated from the total effect of the play you write. It will be a complex series of feelings and thoughts and visions, all adding up to a single feeling that all of your audience will experience as your play.

Chapter II

THE WRITER AS A HUMAN BEING

Perhaps the most ancient and important piece of philosophical wisdom is expressed in two words: "Know thyself." It is extremely important for the writer to know himself well, because it is only through himself that he can know others. Each individual has characteristics that set him apart from others, yet all people have the same underlying human tendencies. Differences result from the exaggeration of some of these tendencies and the suppression of others. If you have ever wanted to kill a fly, you can know what it would be like to strangle your wife. That is why when a character is very well portrayed in a work of literature we feel that there is something universal in him. He has been given qualities that we all recognize in ourselves, though in us they are not expressed in the same degree. Students of abnormal psychology usually experience in themselves all the symptoms they read about, even the most extremely abnormal. That is because the abnormal is an extension from the normal rather than completely different from it. Thus, if you understand yourself well enough, you can understand the feelings of almost anyone who has ever lived.

Yet it is difficult to achieve understanding of oneself as one really is. This is so for several reasons. The most basic reason is that each of us sees himself as the center of the universe. To yourself, you are the most important person who has ever lived. The fact that you are at the center of everything that happens to you means that you do not look to yourself as you look to others. You do not see the many unflattering things in your personality that others see. You do not see yourself without that sense of your own specialness that colors everything you do.

Furthermore, you probably have illusions about your own freedom. You may think that as a citizen of a free society you can be said to belong to yourself. You may think that there are few restrictions on what you can do with yourself. You may be surprised to learn that this is true in only a very few ways. Much of the human action dealt with in the theatre is based on man's restriction by his environment and by the people around him. Indeed, drama often measures the degrees and kinds of human freedom and gives us a sense of how limited they are. If you possess a thing, that means that you may deal with that thing more or less as you like, provided you do not use it to harm someone else. But you would probably like to do many things with yourself that you cannot. Therefore, there are many ways in which you cannot be said to possess yourself. Every time you experience frustration, you are experiencing an example of the way in which this is so. If you are young, your parents may prevent you from staying out late at night, or may place other kinds of restrictions on your behavior. If you are an adult, you have many legal obligations that prevent you from doing with yourself as you like. The opportunity to sell or to destroy one's possessions does not legally extend to one's self. The government, which only under extraordinary circumstances will seize your personal property, places many restrictions on your personal liberty. It may require you to serve on a jury or in the army, for example. If you are married, you are legally bound to your husband or wife in various complex ways. If you have children, you have obligations to them that the law can force you to honor. In addition to your legal obligations, you have many moral ones that do not involve the law. You must honor and try to love your family. You must be faithful to your friends. You must be considerate of strangers and help them when they are in need. You must be concerned about the social issues of your time. In all of those areas you may make many important choices, but you are not free not to choose.

Your failure to possess yourself goes much deeper, however, than any of those things. From the moment you are conceived until the moment you die you are a part of the world and cannot be separated from it. If you were cut off from the rest of the world, you would die almost instantly. You are truly the product and the property of many things and influences that lie outside of you, and you must appreciate those things before you can begin to know yourself.

Furthermore, you have not one self but many selves. That means not merely that you change from day to day in your interests and character traits, but also that at any given time there are many different selves that make up you. Let us look at some of them.

THE INHERITED SELF

Well over a billion years before you were born you began to come into being. That is, some of the characteristics found in every stage of the evolutionary development of life are still to be found in you. From the first one-celled structure that could be called life you have received some of your most characteristic traits—your need for food, for example, and your need to grow. During the billion and more years that preceded your birth, countless experiments were made, all of them seeking the solution to the problem: what is the best way for life to conduct itself? You have benefited from those experiments. Almost everything in your life goes well. The few things that do not go well represent problems that still remain to be solved. Drama is concerned with many of those problems. It is concerned, for example, with what happens when people who have not learned to get along well together must deal with one another. It is concerned with the failures that threaten the well-being of a social or cultural system. It is concerned with the mistakes people make, based on false or inadequate self-knowledge.

A small part of your inherited self comes to you from your immediate family. Their strengths and weaknesses (some of them hidden beneath the surface) have been passed on to you. You must make the best of what you have inherited. Many people experience great difficulty in coming to terms with themselves because they are unable to come to terms with their parents. Instead of seeing their parents as ordinary human beings, they exaggerate both their virtues and their faults. Thus, a man who has a very successful father may have trouble achieving success in his own life because he idealizes his father's success beyond all reason. By comparison, his own efforts will always seem to him very poor indeed, and he will come to think of himself as a failure. It is important for such a person to know just how much of his father's ability to succeed he may have inherited. If his ability is equal to his father's, then he should be able to achieve the same degree of success, provided he can view that success realistically and has the same opportunities that his father had. If he has not inherited all of his father's ability, then he must learn to content himself with those accomplishments of which he is capable.

THE PHYSICAL SELF

You have a body, and nearly all of what is characteristic about you may be explained in terms of the nature of that body. If you are naturally very strong, it may be that you have developed into a leader of men because of your power to control them physically. If you are somewhat sickly and weak, you may have become an intellectual to make up for your physical limitations. Those things are rather obvious. But in far more subtle ways the rhythm of your life is determined by the rhythm of your body. The way your muscles are coordinated determines the degree of skill you have in doing many things. The way the chemistry of your body is balanced determines the amount and kind of enthusiasm you have and the way in which it rises and falls from time to time. The quality of your nervous system determines your reactions to things and the kind of thinking and feeling you will do. Your size affects the way you see yourself in comparison with others. Your physical appearance may help or hinder you in dealing with others. All of those things work together to help you decide in what ways you are unique as an individual and how you can use that uniqueness to benefit yourself and others.

THE PSYCHOLOGICAL SELF

Partly in relation to what you are physically, partly in relation to experience, and partly in relation to certain inherited qualities of mind that are not yet fully understood, you have developed a psychological self. Most of this psychological self is unknown to you because it lies beneath the surface of your awareness. It is very significant, however, in determining how you will react in a given situation. One of the most important things in the life of any person is the extent to which his activities lie within his conscious control. Some people do almost everything without knowing why they do it. Others carefully plan most of their important actions. No one can plan all that he does, but we tend to be more successful in life as we gain control over the unconscious forces that drive us to do the things we do. To a large extent those unconscious forces stem from the primitive needs our ancestors had to meet in order to survive. Some of those were the needs to kill or dominate or receive sexual gratification from others. As we grow up in a civilized society we learn to prevent ourselves from acting on our immediate impulses. Sometimes our frustrated impulses express themselves in subtle ways that we do not understand. A momentary desire to kill someone, for example, may be expressed in the form of an insulting remark. If you did not know that you wanted to kill someone (because you had thwarted the impulse so completely that you had disguised it even from yourself), you might make a remark that would seem perfectly reasonable to you but insulting to the other person. You would then be surprised when he took offense at what you had said.

THE HABITUAL SELF

As we grow up we learn to do many things so well that we can do them without thinking about them. They become the skills we rely on in order to survive, such as the ability to walk or to speak English. Some of those skills are shared by almost everyone; some of them are unique in a given individual. They include not only obvious things such as playing a musical instrument, but more subtle ones that we do not even realize we are learning, such as how to inflect the voice in a way that makes others feel good. We may become so reliant on our habitual skills that as we grow older we do almost everything from habit. The person who is completely closed to new experiences is relying almost entirely on his habitual self to live his life for him. In order to live a meaningful life it is important to keep on having new experiences and developing new skills. One might say that the most important habit is the habit of developing new habits. Most little children have this habit, but very few adults do.

THE PRIVATE SELF

Everyone has a side of himself that he would not reveal except to his closest friends, and perhaps not even to them. Although he lives with his private self all the time and is conscious of it, to have it revealed to others would be terribly distressing to him. The private self may contain feelings of guilt or fear. It may contain secret loves and joys. It may harbor ambitions, both realistic and absurd. Everyone attaches great importance to his private self, and most people tend to be unaware that all other people have private selves as fully developed as their own.

It is interesting to note that the degree to which the private self may be revealed varies from one group to another. Some groups would consider shocking the mere suggestion that private feelings exist, and other groups would like to believe that they never have any secrets from one another. Probably no group exists in which total revelation of the private self is possible, although the closest thing to it is the relationship that develops between a psychoanalyst and his patient. Drama is at its greatest when it allows an audience to see its characters as a psychoanalyst sees his patients, that is, with full knowledge of their private selves.

THE SOCIAL SELF

This is the self you show to the world in your daily life. It is what others would call

your "personality." It is much less well known to you than your private self, because for many reasons you cannot see yourself as you appear to others. The first time you hear your voice on a tape recorder you will be shocked by the sound of it and find it hard to believe that it is really yours. The acoustics of your head make your voice sound different to you than it does to anyone else. Much the same is true of your personality. Because you are seeing yourself from the inside, you cannot be aware of how you appear to others. Nevertheless, people vary greatly in the degree to which they are aware of the effect they have on others. That has something to do with their ability to perceive others' reactions to them.

THE PUBLIC SELF

This is the side of you that is known to the strangers and institutions with whom you deal more or less impersonally. It includes the way you appear when you make a public speech, or when you apply for a job, or are under arrest. The disparity between the public self and the social self differs from person to person. Some people "freeze up" when they are among strangers and show very little of themselves. Others reveal themselves more fully. If, however, too little disparity exists between the public and the social self, it is a sign that the individual always feels himself to be among strangers. Sometimes people with very outgoing personalities are so isolated from others that they never drop the mask of personality and allow themselves to be among friends.

THE EMOTIONAL SELF

This aspect of the self cuts across all the others in that it affects all of them. It begins with the inherited self and extends all the way into the public self. It is determined by the amount and quality of emotion a person can feel. The emotion is not always communicated directly, as we spend much of the time concealing our true feelings from others; but emotions always leave their marks, and one can sense when one is dealing with a person whose emotions are always shallow or with one whose emotions run deep. The emotional self should not be confused with the experiential self, as emotions can be very strong in people who have had relatively little experience, and weak in those who have had a considerable amount. What is done with experience, not the experience itself, determines the emotional self. The emotional self may, however, be changed either by a shocking experience, which makes a person want to cut off his emotions, or by a beautiful experience, which makes him want to live them more fully.

The Experiential Self

Everything that ever happens to you is a part of your experience. It interacts with all the personality traits you have inherited in order to determine what you will become. If you have a tendency to seek out and mold your own experiences, you will be largely an independent person. If, on the other hand, you are a victim of what happens to you, you will be dependent on others. Experiences can enhance a person, or they can cripple him. That has something to do with the experiences themselves, but much more to do with the quality of the person to whom they happen. Even the worst experiences, such as life in a concentration camp or submission to slavery or torture, can be tremendously enhancing if they happen to a person who is willing to grow as a result of them. Much of the greatest literature deals with just such growth as a result of terrible experience. One sometimes hears that in order to be a great artist one must suffer. That is not necessarily so, but it does suggest that the more profound an experience, the more one can grow as a result of it.

The Spiritual Self

Perhaps the most mysterious side of a person is his spiritual side. It defies analysis. It has to do with the totality of the way he relates to himself and to others. If all aspects of his life seem to be working in harmony with one another, we are likely to feel that he has a great spirit. If, on the other hand, he is so deeply involved in his own personal problems and pursuits that he cannot become concerned about the well-being of his friends or his fellow man, then we are likely to feel that his spirit is not so well developed. A person with a great spirit need not be religious, though such people usually are, in some sense. Nor does a person's claim to religious fervor necessarily indicate greatness of spirit. Many a playwright has delighted in proving that an atheist can be more deeply religious in spirit than a deacon of the church.

As a playwright you will want to get to know yourself as fully as you can. That means examining all the various aspects of self that we have discussed above, and as many others as you can think of. Through understanding yourself, you will come to understand others. But, you may ask, how is this understanding to be achieved? Most assuredly it is not to be achieved through long hours spent meditating upon one's soul, though meditation in the light of action is of great value. One can observe himself best through seeing himself in action. To be human is to be involved in a multitude of ways with the world in which one lives. Failure to be involved merely leaves one's true nature open to question. Involvement may be achieved both through direct and vicarious action. Every time one does something, he learns that he is capable of doing it. If the thing one does is something new and radically different, the knowledge of being able to do it is very important. One has learned that he is a person who can do that new thing.

One can also learn about oneself by observing others, both directly and through artistic experiences. Whenever one sees another person in action, he can think, "What would it be like for me to do that?" Gradually one learns to imagine what his life would be like under other conditions.

Let us make this more specific by giving an example. We shall consider the experience of running the eight-minute mile. One can understand this experience best by doing it himself. Once is helpful, but repeated runnings of the mile will be even better, as one then learns what it is like to run it again and again—how the experience changes with time. The next step is to watch other people running the mile. One asks, "How would I feel about it if I were fatter? or thinner? or had a heart condition? or a sore leg?" One tries to gather other people's feelings about an experience he has had by watching them closely. One then wonders about extraordinary individuals, and how they have experienced the running of the mile. One reads about them in the newspaper (in which one must use his imagination very fully) or in a novel (in which one is helped considerably by the novelist's imagination). One watches races on television. Gradually one builds up a tremendous fund of knowledge about how it feels to run the mile under varying conditions. In relation to this experience, one then knows himself in depth, because he knows not only what he is, but also what he could be or might have been. It is that observation of others and of the world that most deepens one's self-knowledge, provided he is observing an experience about which he already knows something.

But, you will say, plays are likely to deal with very unusual sorts of experience. How am I to write a murder mystery if I do not myself commit a murder?

Conveniently enough, the great experiences can nearly all be understood through close examination of lesser ones. If you have ever contemplated the murder of a fly you have some knowledge of the urge to kill. If you have ever raided the cookie jar you have some knowledge of guilt. If you have ever tried to prevent someone from finding out what you bought him for Christmas, you have some knowledge of what it is like to try to cover your tracks. Many great writers have been, in a worldly sense, extraordinarily inexperienced people. The converse may also be true: Great adventurers are not necessarily great writers. The important thing is not so much to have a large number of experiences as to look closely at the ones you do have. With practice, the time should come when you can imagine being anybody and doing anything.

As you examine your experiences, try to keep in mind the ten facets of personality that we have discussed, and try to see how these facets interrelate to form a system. To make clearer how the interrelationship works, let us trace a single tendency through all of them. Suppose that a person has inherited a tendency to become physically exhausted quite easily. Psychologically he has feelings of insecurity for which he compensates by hoping to achieve superiority in some area other than the physical. Privately he indulges in dreams of glory about the great intellectual accomplishments he will someday be capable of. Socially he has consistently attempted to present himself as a wise and well-informed person who looks down on physical activity as beneath his dignity. His records in school indicate that he has always achieved good grades and sometimes won prizes for intellectual ability, but has never been outstanding in athletics. His emotional ups and downs stem both from his physical weakness, which makes it difficult for him to find the energy to fulfill his ambitions, and from the extremely high goals he has set for himself, goals he can seldom satisfy himself that he has met. Also, he feels himself unworthy of the affections of women and so is very shy, and at the same time romantically idealizes women. His experiences have been primarily vicarious ones. He has read extensively, but he has had few associations with people, few friendships. As a result he has come to feel very sorry for himself and has grown so self-centered that he never opens himself to any kind of spiritual experience. As his life continues, his self-centered fear grows, and he tends increasingly to become a mind without a body.

Thus we see that each of the facets of the self is related to the others. As one changes, the others must change also. When you sense yourself as a whole person, or when you sense anyone else as a whole person, you have a feeling for the way in which all the facets of self are interrelating, so that they are merely different sides of the same thing. If you will examine yourself carefully in terms of each of the facets of your personality, you will see better how you fit together as a whole person. You will then understand the wholeness of other people much better.

The important thing for your development as a playwright is that you learn to carry over these perceptions to the characters you create. Only when you sense the interrelationship of all the different facets of one of your characters will you be able to conceive of him as a human being who will seem real to an audience. It might be wise for you actually to write down a character sketch of each of your major characters before you begin to write about them. In the character sketch, mention each of the facets of personality we have described, as well as any others you can think of.

The great thing about being a playwright is that no part of you is ever wasted. Every experience, every desire, every problem you have ever had, whether good or bad considered by itself, is valuable raw material out of which your plays will be constructed. You will end up using only a small part of it, but what you do use will always surprise you. Therefore, to the extent that you come to know yourself, you will also come to know your characters and your plays.

Part II: GETTING STARTED

Chapter III

STARTING OUT ON YOUR PLAY

In school you have probably learned the orderly approach to any task, which consists of starting at the beginning and proceeding through the middle until you come to the end, where you stop. You had better forget all that when you write a play.

To begin with, it is probably best to start at the end and work back toward the beginning, but more about that later. The important thing is that writing a play does not occur rationally. You are not going to be able to just sit down and do it. You will have to learn to tease it out of yourself by bits and pieces, often at times when you are looking the other way.

One tries to present in a play something that seems to be true from an artistic point of view. That is, given the characters and the situations and the style in which the play is written, the characters should do and say things that seem appropriate to them as characters. That means a playwright must learn to see people as they really are. But almost no one sees anything as it really is. It has something to do with the fact that as young children we are told what to think about things rather than allowed to experience them in our own way. Often we are led to believe that naming a thing is equivalent to understanding it, and that once we have named it we can stop looking at it. Whenever our experience conflicts with an authoritative judgment, we are taught to trust the authority rather than our own ex-

perience. Gradually we lose the ability to see things as they really are. That may sound like nonsense, but it is not. To prove it to yourself, try this simple experiment. Select some room that you are in every day. Your classroom, perhaps, or your room at home. Now, while you are out of the room, and without previous preparation for doing so, try to describe a small section of that room with absolute accuracy. After you have written your description, look carefully at the things you have described. How much have you failed to observe? How many of the details are wrong? How much more interesting is that part of your surroundings that you have seen every day than you have ever before realized!

You have just seen how inaccurately it is that you look at life. You are missing many of its most interesting details, many of its most important subtleties. You do not look at things, because you think you know what you will see there. This idea is beautifully developed by Hughes Mearns in his book *Creative Power*:*

Your real plagiarism is with the world of feeling, the human world of which you are a part. When you write of that you miss the shouting evident beside your very ears. You think fear is expressed by trembling and excited running about

---

* Hughes Mearns, *Creative Power*. New York: Dover Publications, 1958, p. 145.

33

when it is often masked by cool silence. You think weeping is a sign of weakness or defeat. You think that downcast eyes are a confession of guilt. You think cowards are white-faced. You think indignation is an expression of boldness or even of anger, whereas it is often only a revelation of timidity. You think good-natured, laughing, merry chaps are free from worry or depression. You think—but really you do not think at all.

The fact is that you really do not know very much about what is happening between people. You do not even know much about what happens between you and the people you are closest to. If you work on your play in the proper way, you will discover a lot of things about people that you never realized before.

You will have to accept the fact that you may need to change your play a great deal at first. You may have to start over with a completely different play several times until you have found the one you want to write. It is also possible that during much of the time you are working on it your play will seem, and indeed will be, very badly written. What is more, when your first play is finally completed, it may turn out to be a truly bad play. That does not sound very encouraging, but it is better to accept the possibility in advance than to be so disappointed that you give up altogether. Nearly all of the greatest playwrights wrote many bad plays before they started to write good ones. All refused to give up, somehow sensing that they would someday do much better, as indeed they did. Writing a bad play can be a very valuable experience, if it is done right.

What is the right way of writing a bad play? It is allowing yourself to make the kind of mistakes that you need to make. Do not try to copy some other writer's successful play; write your own. If it is bad, it will be because you have not yet learned sufficient control over what you have to say.

Just as every professional baseball player at one time had to learn to throw a ball, so every playwright has to learn how to spill out his soul, however crudely he may do it at first. Cheer up, there is always the chance that you will be an exception and start off with a very good play. No harm in that, certainly, if you can manage it.

Where to begin? You must take inventory of the ideas for plays you already have. It may be that many rather vague ideas occur to you; it may be that you can think of none at all. The world is full of unwritten plays; you have only to look about you to see them. But finding *your* play is another matter. You must write about characters you care about intensely and yet can be objective about. This does not mean you must like them. You may hate them, or think they are ridiculous. But one cares about his hatreds, and one enjoys the ridiculous. In some sense (if only very abstractly), the experiences of your characters must have a reality which grows out of your experience.

You will note that we have been discussing "characters" and not "plot." It is from its characters that a play derives its main interest. When you know your characters well, they will tell you much about what your plot should be. It is very common for beginning writers to want to put into their plays much more exciting or unusual plot ideas than they have observed in the plays they have seen or read. The beginner is in search of novelty because he is not yet sure of his ability to portray dramatic truth. However, dramatic truth is what he must learn to value.

Let us suppose that you have heard a story that excited you because of what you think are its dramatic possibilities, and you would like to make a play of it. Here is the sort of news story that might possibly inspire you to want to write a play:

A young woman of marriageable age, whose parents have always restricted her excessively, has failed to come home one night. When she returns the next morning she reports to her parents that she was out on a date and spent the night in the man's apartment. The parents respond by taking her and her pet dog out into the desert. Here she is handed a loaded pistol and told to shoot the dog as punishment for her immoral behavior. Instead, the girl shoots herself.

That story has obvious dramatic possibilities because of the ironic way it ends. In attempting to correct the girl her parents have caused her death. It is out of such misguided attempts to achieve a goal while actually achieving the opposite that great tragedy can be made. Subjected to dramatic treatment, the story would quickly lead us into basic questions about the characters and the conflicts between them. Why did the girl tell the parents so openly what she had done? Why, if she wished to declare her independence, did she not simply leave home? She had the legal right to do so. Why was it so important to the parents to restrict the girl? Why did they choose that particular form of punishment? Why did the girl regard the dog's life as more important than her own? Those questions and many others like them would have to be answered fully by a play based on the above story.

But we are going too fast. Is it *your* play

presence of the sensational? Do you wish to know more about the characters than gossip would tell you? Are they the characters that you in particular have strong feelings about?

A good playwright works from his own personality, as we have seen. He has certain likes and dislikes in people and in events. What moves one person to tears may leave another cold. Some people worry about the starving multitudes of other nations, some about their pet parakeets, some about their children, some about movie stars. The difficulty is that we are not always willing to admit what is *really* important to us.

As a writer it is important for you to know what you really care about. Not what you think you ought to care about, or what you think other people would admire you for caring about, or even what you would like to care about. Deep down inside you really do care about certain things, and you will have to find out what they are.

If, for example, you are a very motherly type of person who has always liked babies, you should probably find a way to use your strong feeling for babies in a play. The feeling might conceivably be linked in your mind with any number of other feelings not necessarily logically connected with it. Here is an example of how this might work:

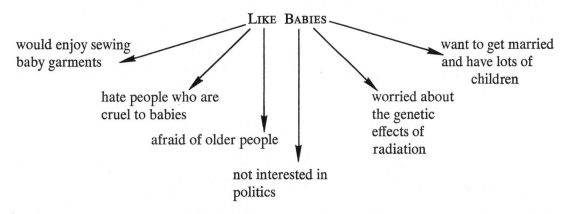

we are discussing? What specifically attracts you as an individual to that particular story? Is it not likely that your interest in it goes no deeper than that of anyone else in the

If these feelings should happen to characterize you, you would have a much better source for a play than the story we considered previously. Your play may be centered around a conflict between two people, one of whom likes babies, the other of whom does not. If you are a girl and you make your central figure a girl who likes babies, however, you are likely to have trouble. Your central character will probably turn out to be very similar to you, and you will find it hard to be objective about her. You will have to make enough changes in her character to keep her separate in your mind from yourself. Perhaps, instead, you should make her a woman who does *not* want to have children. You will have strong feelings about such a woman. You will have to keep these feelings under control and discipline yourself to see her as a whole person, but you will find it easier to keep her different from yourself. Then you can make her husband the one who is fond of babies. You will be able to understand the husband's reactions because they will be close to your own, but the fact that you must translate your feelings into terms natural to a man will help to keep you thinking objectively about those feelings.

Because babies are so important to you, you will often have wondered about people who do not like them. You will want to understand what motivates such a person. Perhaps you will believe that such a condition is unnatural and can be changed. During the course of your play the husband might persuade the wife that she really wants to have a child. Or you may prefer to make the play a tragedy and have the wife, because of her hatred of babies, destroy her marriage or herself.

Perhaps your play will begin to take on a rather melodramatic aspect. You might have visions of a final scene with a woman standing over the body of the husband she has just shot, about to commit suicide. Do not be afraid of such tendencies; many a great play has had just such an ending. The important thing is to know why your characters end up as they do—and this is where your exploration of character begins.

Beginning to explore characters may be done in many ways, but one of the best is simply to begin writing dialogue. Let the husband and wife begin speaking to each other about anything that occurs to you. Do not worry yet about whether their conversation will fit into your play—you are just getting to know who they are. Let's try a little dialogue between them:

WIFE: I'm home, dear.
HUSBAND: Where have you been?
WIFE: Shopping.
HUSBAND: Spending more money, huh?
WIFE: I've been buying groceries so *you* can get fat.
HUSBAND: Oh, excuse me.
WIFE: Why do you always pick on me?
HUSBAND: I don't always pick on you.
WIFE: You do. Yesterday when Mrs. X was here you were making fun of me right in front of her.

That is pretty sketchy. The situation is rather commonplace, and the characters have not yet discovered much individuality. Let us try making a few changes in the situation and see whether it produces more material out of which a play might be built.

WIFE: I'm home, dear.
HUSBAND: It's about time, I'm hungry. Where have you been all this time?
WIFE: Well, you know that wonderful sale on men's shirts I told you about yesterday?
HUSBAND: I've got enough shirts.
WIFE: Oh, dear, I was *certain* you said you needed a couple of new ones.
HUSBAND: Come on. That's not all you bought.
WIFE: Oh, dear. Well, I must admit that while I was there I couldn't resist a stunning new dress—oh, wait till you see me in it, darling—

HUSBAND: I knew it! When will this spending ever end?

WIFE: Why do you always pick on me?

HUSBAND: I don't always pick on you.

WIFE: You do. You don't care how I

There might be many false starts, but each one gets us a little closer to the play on which we shall finally settle and spend several months—or perhaps even several years.

To make the process of starting a little clearer, let us run through it quickly once again.

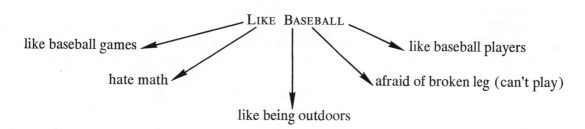

look. I could dress in rags for all you care.

Things are getting a little more interesting. The conflict is more specific. The wife spends too much money, and the husband worries about it. Let us explore some of their possible motivations that we might pursue and develop further in future drafts. The husband wants to start raising a family. The wife is trying to evade the husband's desire for children, not by the obvious means of telling him she dislikes babies, but in the much more subtle way of making it financially impossible. That is because he is so domineering that she thinks he will never take her private concerns seriously. She is forced to deal with him as if she were a child rather than a mature woman. Her technique is made plausible by the fact that she seems to be acting in her husband's interests.

Already a play has been begun. These two characters should go on for a while conversing on a variety of subjects before specific details of plot are worked out. As they continue to develop, plot ideas will grow.

So far what we have done has taken a very short time, yet a play has been started. It can easily be scrapped if it does not seem a good one, and another started in its place.

You begin to have a play when you begin to see a conflict. Let us put these feelings into people by creating a math teacher whose son wants to go into baseball. Just for a starter, let us suppose that at the climax of the play the father will break the son's leg and the son will then shoot the father. Now let us try some dialogue between these characters:

FATHER: You failed the test.

SON: I'm sorry, Father.

FATHER: You're not sorry. You have your head in the clouds. You want to be out there with those stupid sports all the time. You deadhead!

SON: Sports are not stupid, Father. Good ball requires as much intelligence as doing math problems.

FATHER: I'm going to speak to the coach. I'm going to get you off the team.

SON: Oh, no, Dad, don't do that!

FATHER: Why not?

SON: It would be horrible. I couldn't stand it.

FATHER: I'll tell you what you can stand.

Let us explore the possibilities of this scene in a slightly different way in our second draft:

SON: Hey, Dad!

FATHER: What is it, Joe?

SON: Dad, I've got bad news. Real bad. Look, don't take it too hard.

FATHER: Good lord, Joe, you look as if your best friend had died. What's the trouble?

SON: I just found out I flunked math for the semester.

FATHER: You *what?*

SON: I flunked math. For the semester.

FATHER: I don't see how that's possible.

SON: It's true, Dad.

FATHER: Did you speak to the teacher? Are you sure there isn't some mistake?

SON: I'm sure there isn't, Dad. My mind just kind of went blank on the test.

FATHER: We went over all your homework together. I was sure you understood all the problems perfectly.

SON: I guess math just isn't something I want to be interested in, Dad.

FATHER: Joe, I don't see how you can do this to me.

Although there is still stiffness here, primarily because the characters say almost exactly what one would expect in this situation, there is a more gradual working into the situation, more chance for the characters to react to what is happening.

As you listen to your characters talk that way, are you really interested in what they have to say? Do you care about them? Do you want to know what is going to happen to them? If you really care and want to know more, then someday you will be able to inspire an audience with those same feelings.

A very effective way to explore your ideas

further is simply to write down in sentence form whatever comes into your mind. If you will write a number of pages as quickly as you can without stopping, you will find yourself exploring plot ideas that may later be worked into a plot outline. Such writing might proceed as follows:

"I am thinking of a play about a brother and sister who quarrel, and a mother who dies. The brother reminds me of my friend Bill because he is very angry all the time. The mother has somehow caused his anger. How has she done this? Perhaps by siding with the sister too often. . . ."

In other words, just let the ideas flow uncensored onto the page. You will rapidly become interested in what you are writing and begin to experiment with and mold your plot in a fascinating way.

Perhaps you are beginning to see that playing with words is a little like playing with clay. At first you keep trying various things, seeing what shapes and feelings appear, seeing if anything comes out that you like. Only after you have tried a number of things do you find something that you want to develop. The habit of playing with words in that way can be very valuable to you. Sometimes a few jottings made quickly and hidden away can spring to life years later and become a fully developed play. The most important thing in getting started on your play is to have fun. If you are feeling businesslike about what you are doing and determined to get something "good" down on paper in a certain length of time, the chances are you will freeze your own spontaneity. Only when you relax and start exploring yourself and your doodles will you begin to see the first dim possibilities for a play.

Chapter IV

WORKING TOGETHER
ON YOUR PLAY

Some of the most exciting entertainment in the world happens spontaneously. When a group of friends get together and make up stories, acting them out as they go along, the effect can be unforgettable. If you have never tried improvising a story, you may have no idea what your imagination can do.

An interesting parlor game is one called "Personality." One player is asked to leave the room; meanwhile, the others will supposedly make up a story. When the first player returns to the room, he must try to guess the story that has been made up by asking questions that can be answered "yes" or "no." Actually, the other players do not make up a story at all. They simply agree that all questions ending with a vowel will be answered "yes," and all questions ending with a consonant will be answered "no." As the first player questions the others, he begins to put together a story that is in reality the product of his own imagination —and what a wild, bizarre story it is likely to turn out to be! The mere fact that he does not know he is making up a story may lead the first player to flights of fancy he would otherwise be incapable of.

That is one example of how group activity can stimulate the individual to be more creative. You can profit greatly when working on your play from associating your-self with other playwrights with whom you can exchange ideas.

At this point we need to make a few observations on the subject of competition. For some reason artistic people have a strong tendency to regard other artistic people as their competitors. That may be true not only among beginners, but among advanced artists as well. It is a completely illogical attitude. Art of any kind depends so much on the personality of the individual artist that it is very hard for one artist to steal another's ideas, as one businessman might steal another's customers. It is not the particular idea, it is how you develop it that is important. The same plot could be dealt with by a number of playwrights, and all of them could be successful. Indeed, there was a time in the history of the theatre when no one ever invented an original story; all writers based their plays on stories that had already been told many times before. Shakespeare was a frequent borrower of other people's ideas and was in turn borrowed from. Even today one sees many examples of successful plays based on earlier plays or stories. The hit musical *West Side Story*, for example, is a retelling in modern terms of Shakespeare's *Romeo and Juliet*.

If a fellow playwright were to steal an idea from you, he would have to develop it in his own way. He could not use your way; his play would be his own and quite unlike yours. But you need not worry that your friends will be anxious to steal your ideas; they are probably far too interested in developing their own and, if anything, only concerned that you might steal theirs. It would be best if everyone agreed that all ideas were common property and might be used by anyone who chose to develop them. Then we should have the emphasis where it properly belongs—not on the plot, but on the way the plot is handled; not on the good lines, but on the way the lines are interrelated; in short, upon the total effect of the finished play. If you will discuss your ideas freely with your friends, and lend and borrow ideas as seems beneficial, everyone will stand to gain from the experience. Of course you cannot use in your play material that has been copyrighted by someone else. If, for example, you choose to dramatize a book or a story that has been copyrighted, you must have the original author's permission to make any public use of what you have done. Plagiarism is a serious offense and should be avoided. When the copying of material is agreed to by the author, very successful results can often be obtained.

Another thing: You must not worry too much about whether your friends are better playwrights than you. No matter what eventually happens, there will always be better playwrights somewhere in the world. Even if you managed to write the best play ever written, you could not be sure that someone else would not later write a better one. The question of who is best is really unimportant. The only question that should concern you is, how fully are you developing your potential as a playwright? If you have something to say in dramatic form that will interest an audience, no one will care whether some other writer's play is better. The only valid concern is, how well did a particular writer do what he set out to do? You will certainly realize your potential better if you develop active relationships with other writers and communicate with them about your work.

Let us see, then, how a group of playwrights might work together, whether as a class in school, or as an informal gathering that meets on a regular basis.

One useful device is for the group to divide into a number of smaller groups, each maintaining a notebook in which its members communicate with one another. It would be passed around daily from one person to the next, and each in turn would write in it. Such a writing experience supplements the give and take that occurs in class discussion. Playwrights can consider one another's ideas and develop their own slowly, thoughtfully, and carefully. They will find themselves far better able to control their written words than their spoken ones because they can reconsider them after they have been written, and because they naturally tend to express themselves better in writing anyway: that is why they wish to become playwrights. The notebook provides an additional dimension to the writing experience of a playwriting class. Also, it is something to which the writer can turn with relief when he feels unable to work on his play. By writing in the notebook he can feel that he is accomplishing something, as indeed he will be.

Entries might be something like the following:

#1

I would like to write a play defending religion against atheism, but I can't find a good plot. I keep coming back to a situation in a church in which an atheist interrupts the sermon, and the preacher defends himself against this attack, but I can't see how to develop it.

#2

Your hang-up is that church. You've got too many other people onstage to handle successfully. It would be much better if you could put the preacher and the atheist alone in a room together and let them fight it out.

I'm stuck on my plot right now, too, but it isn't anything I can put into words.

#3

I disagree, #2. I think the scene in church would be very exciting. Crowd scenes are difficult to handle, of course, but worth the effort in my opinion. Of course the scene would have to come at the climax of the play, and there would have to be events leading up to it. Maybe the atheist is an escaped prisoner who has been trying to provoke the preacher to turn him in to the police, and maybe the preacher has been trying to get the atheist to turn himself in. Then the atheist in this big scene could shout that there is no God because he himself is a murderer. At that point, the police move in, and the atheist, having finally gotten the punishment he wants, could say, "But I see God is willing to punish me after all!"

I've got a big murder scene in my play, and I'm having lots of fun writing it, but I'm bored with the situations that lead up to it.

#4

You certainly are melodramatic,

#3

You can't be sure that #1 is trying to do this kind of thing with his play at all, yet you give him all sorts of specific suggestions about plot and even hand him a line of dialogue. No wonder you can't write those scenes that lead up to your murder scene. You can't see the drama that lies under the surface of ordinary life. You want blood and thunder everywhere. Relax, man! I much prefer #2's suggestion about #1's play.

For myself, I'm writing some rather good dialogue, but don't know where it is going at the moment.

#1

Thanks, kids, but I've decided the whole religion thing was a bit of immaturity on my part, and I'm going to try something a little more personal, like a boy-girl conflict. #2, you *should* be trying to put that thing that's troubling you into words. Maybe that would help get it unstuck. I know that writing about my problem in here helped me a great deal to think about it further. Incidentally, I think #3's ideas are great, and I'd use them if I were going to write that play. That's a really terrific scene you have imagined there, #3. #4, I'm glad to hear you're writing good dialogue. I thought the stuff you read in class was really neat.

A notebook of this sort will quickly become repetitious if it is not worked on in the light of other experiences that are being carried on simultaneously. An excellent one is the face-to-face conference between two students. It should be fairly extended, lasting at least an hour. Students can pair off, one listening as the other tells about his play. As A continues to talk, he will become more aware of his play and what its problems are. B will clarify A's thinking further by injecting suggestions, disagreements, and uncertainties. It is important that as these student conferences progress A and B do not reverse roles, but rather form new partnerships, so that one person avoids being both student and teacher to the other.

One of the best ways for playwrights to help one another is through improvisations. An improvisation is simply a scene that is spontaneously formed by the actors as they are acting it out. Inasmuch as improvisations are a powerful and complex means of communication, we shall deal with them separately in the next chapter. Here we are concerned only with the basic setup.

Let us say that A is working on a scene and is having difficulty developing it properly. He calls B, C, and D aside and explains the basic content of the scene to them. He may do so with all of them together, or with each one separately. If he chooses the latter method, he may disguise from each of the actors what the other actors' objectives in the scene are to be. That will help to make the scene even more spontaneous, as the actors are then in the position of real people, who do not know one another's thoughts. B, C, and D then perform the scene until the basic material that A has outlined has been covered. The teacher or group leader will then conduct a discussion of the scene, pointing out its values as well as its limitations. Some of the limitations will stem from the way the scene was originally thought out, some from the way it has been handled by the actors. After the discussion, it may be desirable to have the actors repeat the scene, trying to improve.

As a result of the experience, A will probably find that many new possibilities have opened up in his mind and he can write the scene more effectively than he could before. It is just as well if the improvisation has not been too polished and there have been many dull moments in it. When an improvisation is too good, the author may try to remember what was actually said, rather than letting it stimulate his own ideas. Possibly, though, he will remember actual lines that the actors used and retain them in the scene.

Another important group activity is the reading and discussion of a particular play written by a member of the group. That may be handled in two ways. The author may read the script to the class, or he may have copies made that are then read or acted out by various members of the class. In the former case, reactions to what has been written are likely to be rather general. However, during the early stages of work on a play it may be useful for an author to read a few lines that he has written to find out whether the class likes them. If they do, it will build his confidence in what he is doing. If they do not, a discussion

can center around the problem of writing spontaneous dialogue.

After a first draft of an act or a scene has been completed, having duplicated copies available to all members of the class makes possible very specific discussion of how the scene has been handled. Individual lines can be criticized, and perhaps the class can work on rewriting some of them. That activity will help the writer see more clearly how his work will stand up under detailed analysis and will give him ideas about what to work on in revising his play.

Group discussions should be so conducted that conflicting points of view are freely expressed. The writer should see clearly that his work has different effects on different people. When he has heard and evaluated in his own mind a number of points of view, he will have a better idea of what he must contend with in his audience. It is not necessary that such a discussion arrive at any conclusions—better let the author draw his own conclusions from it.

When a group is working together, the activities discussed above are likely to take up most of its time. Occasionally, however, the group may wish to try some exercises that will stimulate its thinking. Here are a few that may help groups to work together to develop their writing skills:

1. Bring an animal into the room. Try to list on the blackboard descriptive phrases that seem to contradict themselves but are nevertheless revealing, such as "gentle ferocity," or "furry sharpness." This literary technique is called oxymoron, and it is a good way of getting at the underlying contradictions in character and action that are so often found in good drama. Begin by describing the animal physically; then try to perceive qualities of personality that set this animal apart from others of his species. Observe closely any actions that the animal performs. Much of character is expressed in action. It will help you, in observing action, to try to restrict your descriptive lan-

guage to verbs, avoiding adjectives and nouns. (An animal is suggested rather than a person because it involves no potential embarrassment for the subject under discussion. Discussions of the characters of actual people should be avoided both because they may become too personal, and because in the attempt to avoid being too personal the class may cease to observe the person fully and accurately.)

2. Tell a story, each member contributing a part of the story as it develops. That can be done in two ways: One is by making up the story as the group goes along; the other is by telling a story already known to the group, but trying to elaborate on it so that it becomes more interesting. When this activity is undertaken as a game, the attempt is frequently made to make the story as good as possible, keeping it unified, and developing a single story-line. With practice, a group can greatly improve its skill in this activity. Members of the group will become more conscious in the process of their individual approaches to story-telling.

3. Select a well-known fairy tale or Bible story and discuss the means by which it could be turned into a play. Develop a plot outline for it that places it within the limitations of theatrical performance. Discuss how the characters might be developed, and how subordinate parts of the story might be given greater importance.

4. Imagine an unusual setting, such as the inside of a cave or a palace on the moon. Have each member of the group contribute something to the description of that setting. Then discuss what actions might take place in such a setting that would be dramatically exciting. (The more unusual the setting, the more the imagination is likely to be stimulated. Once a group is good at the exercise, however, it should try working with more ordinary settings, placing greater emphasis on the relation between the setting and what occurs in it.)

5. Have one of the group select a story from the newspaper. Perhaps the story is picked completely at random. Members of the group then discuss in detail the feelings the chief people connected with the news story might have. Emphasis should be placed on trying to imagine feelings that seem unusual and yet might really occur. For example, if the news item is a story of bankruptcy, one might speculate on the feelings of relief experienced by the bankrupt person now that his struggle is at last over. Or perhaps he has been deliberately trying to bankrupt himself because he does not like the business he is in and wants to be free from it. If, as the discussion continues, the characters in the news story seem to come to life, then the discussion is good. If, on the other hand, what is imagined turns into an exercise of wit and nothing more, it indicates a lack of real feeling in the group for the characters they are developing.

6. One of the skills a playwright must develop is switching from one character's point of view to another's instantaneously. Seat the members of the group in a circle. Select a hypothetical character, such as a murderer under cross-examination. The first member of the group asks the second member (who is to play the murderer) a difficult and embarrassing question. The second member, in the role of the murderer, then answers the question, putting into his answer as much feeling for the character as he can manage. Having completed his answer, he then shifts to the role of the questioner, and the third member takes on the role of the murderer—and so on, around the circle. Members of the group should come to associate with the exercise an internal, a visceral adjustment, that comes with switching from one role to another.

7. Have one of the members of the group perform an action in pantomime. It may be a simple action, such as sweeping the floor, or a more complex one. Other mem-

bers of the group then take turns outlining a story-line in which that action could occur. The object is to make the action as central to the story-line as possible. As a result, each member of the group should come to feel that a play should be focused around a single action.

8. Ask two members of the group having reasonably distinctive, contrasting voices to engage in a conversation, while the other members of the group take notes on the conversation. The object is to take down those words and phrases that most characterize each of the speakers. Then, using the notes they have taken, other members of the group attempt to reconstruct the original conversation, placing more emphasis on the characteristic speech of the two original speakers than on the actual subjects they talked about.

9. A conversation such as the above is written down verbatim. Members of the group then offer suggestions for making the conversation more dramatic—by eliminating certain phrases, by adding others, and by changing others. A discussion should ensue as to what is involved in sharpening up dialogue in order to make it clearer as to character and situation, and more dramatic.

10. Ask a member of the group to tell a story of something that occurred in his life that he considers especially dramatic. Other members of the group discuss how the story should be changed in order to make it more dramatic. The purpose is to get the group to realize that incidents should not occur in plays merely because they occurred in real life, but rather because they effectively support the dramatic action of the play as a whole.

11. It is important to realize that the characters in a play live in a physical environment and that that physical environment has a significant effect on their relationships with one another. Let the members of the group improvise, portraying the properties and pieces of furniture in a room. They are to react to human characters and events in the room and tell the story of a scene taking place in the room by their reactions. They should emphasize their individual roles in the action of the scene, so that they are participants rather than observers. Such an exercise should help the playwright to visualize his action in terms of the environment in which it happens.

In the process of working on their plays, the group will discover other exercises similar to the above that they can perform in order to help solve the problems that occur in writing their plays. They should be alert to the possibilities for an exercise in a problem, as a well-chosen exercise may save weeks of painful work in finding a solution.

In addition to solving the specific problems that arise in writing, members of the group will find that the process of working together and getting to know one another as creative artists will enormously enhance their knowledge of human nature and their understanding of themselves in relation to others. Such a result of group effort may in the long run prove more important than any of the many more specific gains that result from their working together.

Chapter V

THE ART OF IMPROVISATION

At many times in the history of the theatre, improvisation has played an important role. It has often been used by primitive peoples in the creation of folk plays of a religious or a comic nature. In Italy at the time of the Renaissance it came into vogue in the form of the commedia dell'arte, in which slapstick comedies on domestic themes were improvised. This practice influenced the development of the art of comedy throughout Europe. In Russia the great Stanislavski used it to help actors reach new heights of feeling in their performances. In the twentieth century it is finding an increasingly important place in serious theatre both as a means of teaching actors and as an entertainment in itself. Indeed, some theatres have begun to dispense with playwrights and depend on improvisation for their performances. Improvisation has also on occasion been used either in the conception of a play which was later to be written down and performed, or in the reworking and further development of a play already in progress. It is with the latter use that we are concerned here.

If improvisation is to be used purely as a means of stimulating the playwright's imagination and not as a form of entertainment or actor training, it need not, and indeed should not, become as polished an art as would otherwise be necessary. An improvisation that is perfectly entertaining in itself either should not be written down at all, or should be written down exactly as performed. It is the product of a group mind: Each actor contributes his share, but always by responding sensitively to what other actors are doing. The addition of the playwright's imagination is not needed.

What, then, can the individual playwright achieve that the improvised performance cannot? In the answer to this question lies the key to how improvisations should be used by playwrights. An improvised play, which is the product of very skillful and sensitive actors working together creatively, will place a great deal of emphasis on characterization. Each of the characters will be fully realized, not in terms of words, but in the total array of communication devices available to the actor, including such things as gesture and tone of voice. In improvisational theatre the words become of secondary importance, as words in themselves are but a small part of the total communication system a person uses. As the actors work together, a feeling of unity will grow out of their interaction. One will see an improvisation as a single experience with a profound impact.

Take away the sensitivity of the original actors and replace it with the humdrum work of other, poorer actors, and what is left? The good improvisation is so dependent on the total interplay of emotional effects that the words alone may seem hollow and feeble. A great play, on the other hand, may still seem good even if the acting is relatively poor. So much more emphasis is placed on the words by the individual playwright that they will seem significant and powerful even when they are not supported by skillful acting. Indeed, some great plays may actually be weakened by acting that draws too much attention to itself. Shakespeare's plays present an interesting case in point. Many of his characters are extremely memorable and lend themselves to great acting. But moments occur in all of his greatest plays when language alone must be the center of attention. Lines such as Othello's "Keep up your bright swords, for the dew will rust them," would lose much, if not all, of their effectiveness if the actor drew attention to anything but the line itself as he spoke. Many passages in Shakespeare demand that the words be spoken clearly and beautifully and without too much characterization. The actor who surrounds the words of such passages with other communication devices may actually detract from the total effect. One of the greatest actors of the nineteenth century, Sir Henry Irving, was at his best in plays that have today been forgotten. His performances of Shakespeare were often criticized because he spent so much time acting between the lines that he had to leave out large portions of the play. We must remember that one contribution of a playwright to the theatre is the high caliber of the words he uses—words that can be more expressive when carefully thought out by an individual mind than when improvised by a group.

Another thing the playwright can provide that the improvisation cannot is a special, individual way of looking at things. Without coming right out and saying it, a playwright subtly lets the audience know what he thinks of the situation the play deals with. Actors cannot do that, for no matter how well they work together, they always retain their individual points of view and can agree on a point of view only generally.

Because of those two things that the playwright adds to the theatrical experience, improvisations must be used by playwrights in a way that will support, rather than detract from, what the playwright is trying to do. It is the purpose of the improvisation to spark the playwright's imagination, to open up new possibilities, to suggest qualities of characterization he has not thought of. Those he will develop later in his own manner.

How, then, should the playwright use actors in order to help him? The first thing he can learn from them is whether his idea is one that will spark dramatic action. Let us suppose that he selects four actors and instructs them as follows:

"You are two couples who are getting together socially. You, Mr. A, are a very mournful person. Mrs. A, you are frustrated and hypertense. Mr. B, you are jolly, but you always make cutting remarks. Mrs. B, you are very withdrawn and stupid. Your evening together starts out to be friendly, but gradually the tension builds until you find yourselves hating one another."

The trouble with such an improvisation is that the actors have no specific goals. They will constantly have to make up topics of conversation and develop new situations, and in the process they will tend to pull apart from one another, each becoming so absorbed in his own characterization that nothing jells. The author of such a scene will have to rethink it, providing more specific material for the actors to work on. The following instructions will probably work much better:

"You, A, are secretly in love with B. You find him in the student lounge, and you try to get him to ask you to the dance. B, your roommate has put you up to finding out whether A likes him. You will engage her in conversation to get at this without ever coming out and saying what you are driving at."

In this situation the actors have objectives, and they can measure their progress through the scene by how close they are getting to the stated goal. Note that no characterization has been suggested. The actors will rely on their own personalities and out of the situation gradually develop characters that may be more interesting than those the playwright originally had in mind. If what they achieve is good but completely wrong for the characters he has imagined, he can have them do the improvisation over, thinking in terms of different characters.

Another thing a playwright can learn from improvisations is what sorts of things need to be added to a scene to give it the richness of reality. He can find that out by observing what the actors add and by observing what, in addition, seems unnatural in what they are doing. He should thus discover much about the interrelation between characters and situation.

Finally, an improvisation should help the playwright to visualize his characters. It should help him to see them as total human beings and not abstractions or one-dimensional figures. He will become aware of some of the things people in plays must do and some of the things they cannot do. He will observe, for example, that if a character is onstage he must participate in the scene in some way, and he will avoid such howlers as having a character sit down and read through a whole book when he is onstage by himself.

Even though we are considering improvisations that should not be too polished, we are still concerned with maintaining enough semblance of reality and genuineness of experience so that what is performed can be of use to the playwright. A group that is going to use improvisations to help playwrights may wish to engage in a few exercises that will help them work sensitively with one another. Those listed below are designed to increase spontaneity and awareness of others:

1. The actors sit in a circle. Each of them in turn says one word of a line of poetry, such as "The quality of mercy is not strained; it droppeth as the gentle rain from heaven." The object is first to make the sentence sound like a sentence at all, and second to give it an interpretation that varies from reading to reading. As the actors begin, they will speak haltingly, getting mixed up about who is to speak next and failing to maintain the proper rhythmic flow. After a while they will begin to forget themselves as individuals and sense the movement within the group. Their object is to say the sentence in such a way that it reflects a single different mood each time it is said. One time it may sound happy, another time sad, another time ridiculous, and so on. Each member of the group contributes to the developing mood of the sentence, but the contribution must always look back to what has gone before and be clear enough so that it guides the next player in how he will speak.

2. The actors sit in a circle. A recites "Mary Had a Little Lamb" or some other well-known rhyme. He repeats the rhyme over and over in a clearly established mood. The mood is gradually changed to a totally contrasting one. The instant A stops speaking, B must speak the next word and continue the exact mood with which A ended. The process is repeated several times around the circle. Gradually the actors become more adept at sensing one another's moods and reproducing them.

3. If two actors in the group are particularly insensitive to each other, they can both increase their sensitivity and broaden their acting style by mirroring each other's actions exactly. First one leads, and then the other. They switch at a cue from some third person. Each should try in the process of mirroring to find out what it feels like inside to be the other person.

4. Rather dramatic results can be obtained if two people who have watched the above exercise imitate what they have seen. They must not only mirror each other in the way described above, but must also try

to do it in the style of the two whom they have observed.

5. If the original pair now try to imitate their imitators imitating them, it may be possible to achieve real depth of insight into the differences between people's internal feelings about themselves.

6. This one is based on a modified version of the tomb scene in *Romeo and Juliet*. It is designed to teach the coordination of opposites, rather than similarities, as with the above. A is lying dead on the floor. B enters the room and discovers A. B has just been poisoned. As B dies, A comes to life. They should time their action so that A is fully alive at the instant B dies.

7. Using numbers rather than words, two people carry on a conversation. They are meeting for the first time. They go from friendship to anger to friendship to hatred. All this happens between the numbers of one and one hundred.

8. Two who have watched the above enact the same scene, except that they use words rather than numbers, and their words must make good sense. In no other way may they change the scene.

9. One of the problems in improvisation is that discussion of relationships often becomes too general. An improvisation can be built out of the way in which two people relate to each other in terms of a single object. It may begin with as simple a thing as two people arguing that they are both the rightful owners of the only remaining coat in the cloak room. It may move into areas as complex as a couple who are about to be divorced deciding who gets to keep the house they have always lived in. The latter will probably not be successful until many much simpler scenes have been tried.

10. This final exercise is not an improvi-sation, but a way of making people more sensitive to one another's thoughts. A group discussion can take place in which the rule is that every speaker must begin by rephrasing in his own words what the previous speaker has said. He cannot go on to make his own point until the previous speaker agrees that he has been fully understood. This kind of exercise will be most revealing if the topic of discussion is one on which the members of the group have strong and conflicting feelings.

One of the advantages of spending some time with the above exercises is that inevitably the playwrights working with them will begin to get ideas for plays out of watching them, ideas that would never have occurred to them if the improvisations had been strictly limited to the acting out of the playwrights' preconceived ideas.

If improvisations are to be successful, it is important that they be conducted in an atmosphere of freedom. Each improvisation presents a single problem to be solved. The objective should be only the solution of a particular problem in a given improvisation. Suggestions for solving the problem should be avoided, as they will cause the actors to begin the improvisation with preconceptions that will limit the free operation of the imagination. At the same time, whenever something particularly good develops in an improvisation, it should be praised. It is generally true that any negative criticism other than "You didn't solve the problem in this particular respect" will tend to discourage creativity. But pointing out and praising what is good not only encourages creativity, it also helps to develop good taste.

Chapter VI

GETTING THROUGH
A DRY SPELL

While you are working on a play there will almost certainly be times when you do not feel very much like writing. If at the same time you feel under tremendous pressure to finish the play, you are likely to get yourself so tense that you only make it more difficult for yourself to write. We need to understand first why these dry spells occur, and then what, if anything, can be done about them.

All learning occurs in three stages: input, integration, and output. Input is the gathering of information. Integration is the process of relating that information to previously gathered information. Output is the new performance based on the newly integrated information. Sometimes when information is gathered very rapidly, a period follows during which the mind is not particularly receptive to new information. So much has been learned so quickly that the learned material must be integrated within itself and with other material that has been learned previously. When this process happens subconsciously, the learner experiences a dry spell, or plateau, as it is sometimes called. He has the illusion that he is not learning, but the fact is that the learning is continuing on a subconscious level. After a time the dry spell will be over, and he will then gather new information again.

Writing a play is a learning process. You are gathering experiences, a process that involves discovering new things in yourself and the world you live in. A time comes when all those experiences must be integrated with one another. Then you feel that you are not making any progress with your play, and you become disgusted and bored with it. Actually, you are doing work that can be done only by your subconscious mind. When these periods of integration occur, the best thing you can do is forget about your play and think about something else. The more completely you can do so, the more effectively your subconscious mind will be able to work. It may be that you are having a plateau because you are insisting on doing something in your play that is detrimental to it. When your play is completely out of your mind, you may be able to forget whatever it is you are trying to do to the extent that your subconscious can try out something new.

Unfortunately, it is sometimes difficult to tell when one has hit a genuine plateau and when one is just being lazy. If one has been working very productively for quite some time and then suddenly nothing seems to work any more, it is likely that a plateau has been reached, and it is time for a little vacation from the play. But if one has done very little and done it reluctantly, then probably the difficulty is laziness. In that case, sit down and start writing. After you have been working for about forty-five minutes, you should begin to write something that you can find interesting. During a plateau no amount of writing will produce that result. If one is lazy, the habit of writing must be developed, and enjoyment will increase as the writing continues.

If you wish to continue working during your plateau, some things can be done that may help your subconscious mind along. What you must do is to break down, rather than reinforce, your present thoughts about your play. One of the best ways to do that is to find ways of making your play seem strange to you. Write some scenes that are not properly part of your play, placing your characters in other, unfamiliar situations. Imagine one of your scenes as it would work with totally different characters, and then write it that way. Change your play into a myth and people it with gods and goddesses. Have the characters in your play reverse their roles, the hero becoming the villain, the innocent wife the conniving virago. Fill out a questionnaire about your characters from their own point of view. (You will find a questionnaire you can use for this purpose in Chapter IX.) Turn your play into a narrative and use description rather than dialogue to tell your story. Shift the action of your play into some time in the past or the future: It may be that you are really trying to tell the wrong part of your story. In all of these exercises, you are trying to get as far away from your play as possible so that you can see it differently and shake loose whatever obstructions are blocking your imagination.

As time goes on and you continue to write, you will begin to discover your individual approach to working. Most professional writers have idiosyncrasies. Thomas Wolfe, who was very tall, always wrote standing up with his paper on top of the refrigerator. Jean Kerr claims that she writes in parked cars. Some people like to write on buses and trains. Some people write anywhere, jotting down an idea when it comes on the back of a gum wrapper or on a napkin. Others cannot write except under very specific conditions and must always work in the same place. It might be important for a writer to have plenty of sharpened pencils in front of him when he writes. It might be important to have the smell of sour apples around. Those things are not as ridiculous as they sound. One needs the collaboration of one's subconscious mind when writing, and those are all ways of signaling the subconscious that one is ready to begin work. It is also true that creating a slight but steady distraction, such as the noise of a fan, helps to screen out other, more irregular distractions.

Writers also differ as to when they write. Some people like to write during a particular part of every day. That might vary from the middle of the night to between 9 and 12 in the morning. Others work only when inspiration hits them. Some people like to work continuously on a thing until it is done, with interruptions only to eat and sleep, and as few of them as possible. They will then avoid writing for some time until another project is started. Others write a precise amount regularly every day. Anthony Trollope was so conscientious about this that when he finished a novel, if he had not completed his allotted number of words for the day, he would simply draw a line and start another. Once he was on a ship and got seasick. He nevertheless completed the prescribed number of words that day. The passage he wrote on that occasion stands as a blemish on his usually flawless style.

Because plays require more discipline than do novels, it is a good idea to begin writing them in a disciplined way. A certain amount of time set aside every day will in the end produce results. If one is having an off day, he should simply write what he intends to throw away rather than avoid writing at all.

If you find that writing is very difficult for

you, and you constantly have to force yourself to do it, cheer up. Most professional writers have the same trouble. Christopher Fry, whose plays give the impression that words flow effortlessly from him with almost unavoidable brilliance, has said that writing is for him about as pleasant as eating ground glass. Other writers complain in other ways about the work they do. The important thing is that they continue to do it because their need for meaningful communication in dramatic form is so great that they cannot stop. If you enjoy writing, so much the better; but if you hate it, don't let that discourage you. You may very well end up loving what you have written.

Part III: SHAPING YOUR PLAY

Chapter VII

THE ELEMENTS OF DRAMA

In one sense the title of this chapter is a contradiction in terms, for drama properly has no elements. A good play is a total experience, and to separate it into various parts is to destroy it. But just as your body has a head and arms and a circulatory system and the ability to move and a tendency to grow and repair itself (although none of these can be properly separated from the totality that is you without destroying them and you), so the drama can be thought of as having various parts or elements. If you are experiencing a problem in writing your play, understanding these elements, and how each contributes to the totality, may help you to decide where the problem lies and what to do about it.

In reality there are many approaches to talking about the elements of drama and of deciding what they are. There is probably no end to them since all plays are different. But certain common factors occur in one way or another in nearly all plays, and we shall try to decide what these are and examine each in turn. Remember, however, that what is said about each one is meaningless until it has been related to all the rest. You can never have one element of drama by itself, though you may think about them one at a time.

The first great critic of the drama, Aristotle, decided that the drama involved six elements, and named and described them. He also pointed out other features that

might have been called elements and described them as well. Since his time, critics have argued with him on various points, and modern critics have described many additional elements of drama. A great deal of thought has gone into trying to decide which is the most essential element. But it does not really matter what is *most* essential, if we understand that a given drama must have many things, some of which it will have in common with other dramas.

The elements we shall describe here are not the same elements you will find in other books, as each critic has his own ideas as to what are the most important. However, once you have read and understood the discussions in this chapter, you will be prepared to think of other possible elements on your own, and to understand various elements that may be described by other writers.

You should understand, also, that you must be flexible in your thinking about the various elements. The same part of a play might be considered as many separate elements, depending on how you are thinking about it. For example, a scene in which a king is crowned might be thought of in the following ways: The king is a character. The crowning of the king is an action. The crowning of the king is a part of the plot. The crowning of the king is an event. The crowning of the king is symbolic. The crown is an image. The crown is a property.

And so on. You might think that all these ways of looking at the same thing are redundant, but they are not. Each of them refers to a different system that runs through the play, and the crowning of the king will relate to each of these systems differently. If all of the systems in a play were functioning perfectly, the play would be an incredible masterpiece, much better than any actual play ever written. It is enough if many of them are functioning well so that the play can work on several levels at once. Some popular dramas succeed only on one level—the level of plot.

Let us consider four main categories under which the various elements will be grouped. In order to help you visualize these four categories more effectively, we shall discuss them first in relation to a painting. They are background, pattern, structure, and entity.

BACKGROUND

As you look at a painting, you will sense that your eye is drawn toward certain parts of the picture as most important. Other parts fade into the background, and if you look at the picture as the artist intended, you will examine them last. You might not think the background of a picture is important, but it is, for it determines how you will see the main objects toward which the artist is drawing your attention. In subtle ways it influences your thinking about those objects.

PATTERN

The shapes in the picture relate to one another to form a pattern. If they did not do so, the picture would not seem to be one picture, but rather many pictures. You can understand that concept better if you imagine yourself about to take a photograph in the middle of a crowded city. You could take many thousands of pictures, even standing in a single place. How do you select what you will take? What makes a picture? Somehow, you will select through the viewfinder out of all the possible scenes one with a pattern, or shape, that seems to tie it together. Perhaps, for example, you will select a pattern of rooftops making zigzags across the sky.

STRUCTURE

You might think pattern and structure are the same thing, but they are used here to mean dissimilar things. Pattern refers to the particular shapes made by objects in your picture. Structure refers to the general, abstract considerations that govern the selection of patterns. The pattern is limited to a particular picture. When one speaks of structure, one speaks of things that relate this picture to other pictures. To put it another way, we might say that structure is what holds together or relates the various elements that form a pattern. It is an unseen organizing influence. Look at a building and you will see the pattern that the building makes, the interrelation of shapes, colors, and textures that make it pleasing or unpleasing to the eye. You will not see the structure, which keeps the building from falling. The structure has been worked out in terms of the physical forces that interact within the building. It has been conceived largely in terms of mathematical formulae.

ENTITY

Although the relationship between the objects in a picture is crucial, we at first tend to see each of the objects by itself. When we do this, we are examining the entities that make up the picture. Those entities stand out from the background, and if we are not careful we shall come to think of them, rather than the total effect, as being the picture. But we must realize that the entities are only part of the picture and cannot properly be considered separately from it. For example, to speak of the *Mona Lisa's* smile, while forgetting about the relation of the lady to her setting and the color scheme and pattern in the picture, is to talk about something altogether different from the picture.

Those, then, are the four main categories within which the various elements will be classified. We shall now consider the elements within each category in turn. We shall speak of the elements of the background first, because that is the soil in which the rest of the play must grow. Although the background is that side of a play that an audience is least conscious of, it is also what most definitely determines how the audience will react to everything in the play.

The elements of the background are: world, atmosphere, conventions, spirit of the audience, sound, and scene.

World

Every individual who has ever lived has lived in a world uniquely his own. The world is something constructed in the individual's imagination out of his total life experience. China takes up a large part of the globe, but in the world of a 5-year-old American it may be no more than something to dig to. The world we construct in our imagination is not merely a place; it is something that behaves toward us in certain ways. Perhaps it allows us to vote, and we call it a free world. Perhaps it is always tripping us up, and we call it an unfair world. Perhaps it makes us happy, and we call it a beautiful world. Perhaps it makes us sad, and we call it a cold, cruel world.

Every play has a world that the playwright has constructed out of his imagination for his characters to live in. It may be a tragic world in which a leading character, having risen to great heights, must inevitably encounter misery and death. It may be a bowl of cherries in which sweet young things fall in love with handsome men and get married and live happily ever after. It may be a world in which animals talk like people. It may be a world of the future, with spaceships and visitors from distant planets, or a world of the past peopled by knights or cavemen. Whatever it is, it must be a single world. It cannot be a world of the future and then become a world of the past (unless, of course, we understand that it is the kind of world that can jump around in time). It cannot be a tragic world and suddenly become a bowl of cherries. It cannot be a world in which animals talk and then become one in which they do not. The playwright is free to select any conceivable world that he likes for his play. Once he has done so, however, he is stuck. He cannot change to some other world. He will let the audience know what the world of his play is, and they will come to expect it to behave according to its own laws. To make this point a little clearer, let us give a brief summary of the kind of play that should not be written because it mixes two worlds.

John and Bill are roommates at a boarding school. They are both in love with the same girl. The girl, Mary, loves John and cannot stand Bill. Bill tells Mary's roommate, Anne, that he loves Mary, and asks her help. Anne is secretly in love with John, so she is willing to help Bill win Mary's affections. She proceeds to make Mary believe that John always cheats on his chemistry tests. Mary, in despair, starts going around with Bill. John, wondering what has happened, has a heart-to-heart talk with Anne. While they are talking, Jupiter soars down out of the sky on a flaming eagle and tells John that Anne has been telling lies about him. In a rage, John kills Anne and goes off to Mount Olympus with Jupiter.

Such a play would not be acceptable to an audience because it clearly establishes a realistic world of high-school dormitory life which is meant to be taken at face value, and then introduces into that world something that is not properly a part of it. It would, however, be possible to construct a fantasy world in which gods and goddesses could come and go in boarding-school dormitories. Such a world would have to be represented as nonrealistic.

Atmosphere

Atmosphere is closely related to world, and is, in a sense, a part of it. But atmosphere can be changed from scene to scene. One scene can be gloomy and the next happy and gay. Indeed, atmosphere should not be unvaried in the play or the effect will be monotonous. Perhaps you can sense what is meant by atmosphere best by listening to music. As the music changes, your mood changes. The tone of the instruments, the tempo, the melody, and many other things contribute to the mood. Mood is less obvious in a play because we tend to notice plot and characters first, but it is just as important as it is in music. The general emotional impact of a scene is determined not only by what happens and the kind of people it happens to, but also by production factors, such as the colors used in the lights, the costumes, and the scenery, or the tempo and spirit with which a scene is played. Thus the director sometimes has more control over the atmosphere of a play than the author has, and he may even contradict the author's intentions by playing seriously what is intended to be comic, and vice versa.

For his part, the author can subtly contribute to the atmosphere by suggesting lighting and sound effects and by having things happening that are not directly related to the main action. A hawker walking through the streets selling his wares might open a scene on a rather somber note and set the stage for a scene of personal tragedy to follow. Some of the best examples of the use of this kind of atmosphere are to be found in Puccini's operas. Crowd scenes in those operas include many highly individualized minor actions that form a background for the main action and are interspersed with it from time to time. An effectively staged production of *La Bohème* will offer the opportunity to observe nearly every kind of atmospheric effect that is possible in the theatre.

Conventions

Every play uses conventions that are subtly communicated to the audience within the first few minutes and maintained thereafter. A convention is anything in a play that differs from real life. If the characters speak in poetry, that is a convention. If time passes unusually rapidly, that is a convention; if the characters speak directly to the audience, that is a convention. The audience will accept any set of conventions the playwright chooses to adopt, provided he uses them consistently.

Spirit of the Audience

Most Broadway plays are subjected to "tryouts" either out of town or in preview performances in New York before the official opening. During those performances the author and the director pay close attention to audience reactions. The play is then rewritten so that it will control these reactions better. An audience feels the need to know how it must take a play. Once it has decided what kind of play it is seeing, it must be allowed to forget that the play could possibly be of any other kind. Now suppose that during a tense, dramatic scene something happens that strikes the audience as funny. Laughter will ensue, but the audience will feel the wrongness of the laughter. It will feel annoyance at the production for having caused a reaction that seems out of place. This is the sort of situation that the author must prevent through sensitive rewriting. The spirit of the audience is determined by the consistency of certain other elements, such as "world" and "convention." But it is an element unto itself, for no matter how carefully the production may have been worked out beforehand, it is never quite predictable. Even the most experienced theatre people are constantly taken by surprise at audience reactions to what they have done. Skillful playwrights develop a pretty good feeling for what the spirit of the audience will be; but they are never certain of it, for even the best playwrights have their share of failures. In general, audiences are offended by inconsistencies, but the most serious crime a playwright can commit is to underestimate his audience. Audiences are growing more intelligent all the time, and it is increasingly difficult to get them to accept anything that will not stand careful examination.

Sound

Every good play has a particular kind of sound. It consists primarily of the sounds of the words spoken by the characters, but it includes also any sound effects that are used, as well as any music that is included. The overall sound effect of the play should be closely related to its atmosphere. If the atmosphere is fairylike or mysterious, it will not do to have the characters speaking everyday language. It is just as bad to have language that is too obviously poetic in a realistic play. In addition, the playwright should think about ways of extending the sound effect of the play by using nonverbal sounds. In a realistic play, doorbells and telephones may ring, clocks may strike, phonographs may play popular music, radios may deliver news bulletins, dishes may be heard breaking in the kitchen; and in the distance may be heard fire sirens, airplanes, motorcycles, people shouting, and so forth. In a more poetic play a church bell may be heard tolling softly in the distance, crickets may be heard chirping, birds singing, guitars strumming lazily, an old man chanting "Strawberries, fresh strawberries," the sound of an old man selling strawberries, a woman singing a low, plaintive song, or just unexplained sounds, beautiful but mysteri-ous and barely noticed. We shall consider the sound patterns of words more fully in the chapter on dialogue.

Scene

The choice of setting is very important in a play, for what the audience sees will have a great deal to do with how it feels about the play. It is too easy for a playwright to forget, after he has described his setting, that it remains present through every line of dialogue he writes. He should try to visualize it, and to visualize his characters moving about while he is writing. If this is a problem for him, he may wish to have a drawing of the set hanging above his typewriter so he can glance up every now and then and remind himself of what the audience will be seeing.

In choosing locale, it is important to decide how concretely it will be represented. Is the setting to be very realistic, or may it be merely suggestive? Perhaps it is a place that is no place, a street somewhere, or a field. Perhaps it is deliberately built out of the audience's imagination and a few meager properties, as with *Our Town* and many modern productions of classical plays. Perhaps it takes place in a character's mind, as in *After the Fall*. Perhaps it is an impossible meeting place for characters on two different levels of reality, as with *Six Characters in Search of an Author*.

But scene includes more than just the setting of the play; it includes everything that the audience sees happening in that setting. If a circus parade marches across the stage, the author must take its full effect into account. If a character wears a very strange sort of costume, the author must never forget that he is wearing it. If a character onstage cannot speak, but nevertheless contributes to the action, the author must always remember what effect that character is making. Every bit of action described in the stage directions must be visualized by the author so that he can determine whether it adds to or detracts from the total scenic effect he has in mind. The author should avoid including in the scene anything that will distract the audience from what he wants them to be looking at. If a juggler is onstage during a love scene, the audience will be watching the juggler, not the love scene, and the author should take that into account.

We have now considered those elements that provide the background for the other elements in the play. Their effect on the audience is very subtle, but it may be decisive, for it may determine the ultimate success or failure of the play as a whole. The playwright should master the elements of background so that he can prevent their distracting from those other elements that will have a more conscious effect on the audience.

We come now to the consideration of pattern. Pattern, remember, is that arrangement of various parts so that the dramatic experience will be unified, powerful, and beautiful. It includes plot, conflict, action, theme, irony, value, morality, imagery, physicality, and universality.

Plot

The sequence of events that occur in the play constitutes the story. If the events occur as a result of one another, the play has a plot. If they do not, the play has no plot. It is not necessary that a play have one, but most plays do. If there is a plot there is necessarily concern with three things: sequence, probability, and effectiveness. We shall now consider each of these in turn.

Not only what happens, but also when it happens, is important in a play. Certain things belong at the beginning of a play, others in the middle, and still others at the end. The things that happen in the beginning should pave the way for the main action to follow, and the things that happen at the end should tie together all the various aspects of the action so that the audience leaves the theatre feeling that things have

been resolved. An action that depends on a previous action should not be so widely separated from it that the previous action will have been forgotten; but the separation of causative actions from their results by other, seemingly unrelated actions helps to build suspense. The most exciting actions in a play (in terms of audience involvement) should not occur until near the end of the play. The audience's interest in what is happening must always increase until the end. Many a play has been ruined by having a terribly exciting first act followed by a second act that was not as exciting. The same second act might have been effective following a first act pitched at a lower level of excitement.

Near the beginning of a play the author indicates what standards of probability he is assuming. If the world of the play is an impossible one, they will not be the same as if it is a highly realistic one. The impossible probable is perfectly acceptable in the theatre, but the improbable possible is not. It is impossible for a duck to talk, but most of the things Donald Duck does are the sort of things he would probably do if he existed. As an example of the improbable possible, we often find that bad plays have what is called a "deus ex machina," which means, literally, "god from machine," referring to the fact that in some Greek plays, when the action got hopelessly confused, Zeus (or some other god), sitting on the back of an eagle, would be lowered from the top of the scene house and straighten everything out. If a highly improbable (but possible) event occurs near the end of a play in order to solve an otherwise difficult problem, the audience feels that the author is cheating. However, deus-ex-machina effects are acceptable in parodies that make fun of such devices.

Each action in a plotted play must be evaluated in terms of how effectively it relates to what is happening throughout the play. If a particular action does not forward the plot, it should be eliminated unless it contributes some other value so strong that the audience can momentarily forget about the plot. Furthermore, actions that do forward the plot must always do so in a way that seems reasonable, but was not expected. In a murder mystery, for example, there is usually a prime suspect who turns out in the end not to be the guilty one. If he is the guilty one, as the audience has been led to expect, the plot will lack surprise and therefore effectiveness. A playwright constructing a plot is a little like a magician doing sleight-of-hand tricks. The preparation for the surprise has been made while we were looking the other way.

Conflict

The plot of a play usually centers around a conflict, though there may be conflicts that do not contribute to the plot directly, as well as conflicts in a play with no plot. A conflict occurs whenever two opposing forces meet. They may be characters, or they may be ideas in the mind of a single character, or they may be abstract forces, such as money or love. The conflict is usually reflected in the dialogue and action of the play, but it may also be present in other elements, such as the scenery. Gigantic buildings painted on a backdrop crowding out a tiny house in the foreground symbolize a conflict between the dehumanization of the city and the struggle of the individual. When a conflict is predominantly a physical one, such as a fist fight, it tends to be resolved rather quickly and obviously. The more spiritual it becomes, the more it tends to be a source of truly dramatic interest.

Action

Whenever something happens on the stage, it is an action. Every action can be subdivided into the actions that compose it, and can also be seen as part of a larger encompassing action. A play should have a single action in the sense that all the actions that occur in it are part of the encompassing action which is the play. The difference between plot and action is that plot is thought of in terms of one action causing another, whereas action is thought of in terms of one action being like another. What do hitting a nail with a hammer, slapping a person's face, and walking off the job in protest have in common? All are different versions of the action "to strike." We shall develop this idea further in a later chapter.

Theme

After you have seen a good play, you have a feeling that it was about something. Often you can put the feeling into words. You might say, for example, that it was about the injustice that results from slavery. You have not mentioned the plot of the play or its characters. You have stated the idea toward which the play seemed to be leading you. Not that the play was necessarily written to prove anything. Most good plays do not prove anything. They merely show how things happen under certain conditions of existence. The theme of the play may or may not be stated in it. If it is not, different people may draw different conclusions, and so a play may seem to have several different themes. A great play often gives rise to a great many conclusions, and sometimes some of them may conflict. That does not mean the play is disorganized; it means that it has explored conditions of existence that are far-reaching and mysterious in their implications.

Irony

Irony occurs whenever a contradiction exists between what is said and what is meant, or between what happens and what is expected to happen. One common form of irony occurs when a character in a play says or does something that means one thing to him and another to the audience that sees it. Suppose, for example, that a man receives a letter from his girl friend telling him she no longer loves him, and that we, the audience, know the contents of the letter. Before the man opens the letter he says, "How happy I am! I have heard from my darling at last!" As we watch the man we do not share his joy, because we know that he is about to be disillusioned. As the man opens the letter, our attention is on his reaction. We know what the letter says, but we do not know what the man will do when he reads it. Irony increases our interest in the play. It is a combination of knowing and not knowing what is going to happen next. It is important because it draws our attention away from mere events and toward the spirit of man as he experiences those events. When human will and fate come into ironic conflict, tragedy is the result; and tragedy is the highest form of drama. The greatest irony is the story of a man who, by running away from his fate, runs directly toward it. Good examples of such irony of plotting are to be found in Sophocles' *Oedipus Rex* and Shakespeare's *Macbeth*. Because irony makes it possible for the drama to probe the depths of the human spirit, there are those who consider it to be the most important of the elements of drama. We shall have much more to say on the subject of irony in relation to plotting in Chapter X.

Value

Every play asserts the value of something. If it is a tragedy, it asserts the value of what is lost by the characters. If it is a comedy, it asserts the value of not behaving as many of the characters behave. Poor plays tend to assert their values directly. They are full of preaching and obvious morality. Good plays tend to assert their values indirectly.

Often by seeing what is, we know the value of what is not. That explains why serious plays so often depict actions that are in themselves unattractive. Destructive forces acting upon a beautiful thing are identified as the forces that should somehow be eliminated from the scheme of things. If tragedy does not give us a sense of the beauty that is destroyed or inhibited or prevented from coming into being, but shows us only brutality, then the effect of the tragedy is depressing. But if we sense a tremendous beauty that might have been but for the destructive forces we have seen enacted, then the effect of the tragedy is uplifting.

The death of a human being matters only to those who value his life. Tragedy enables us to care about those who suffer and die by giving us enough insight into their humanity so that we can value them. The values that tragedy asserts through the death and suffering it depicts are intensified because the loss of something makes us value it more. Perhaps the greatest difference between the newspaper and the theatre is that the newspaper simply reports facts, but the theatre develops a sense of the values that lie behind those facts.

Morality

Closely related to value as well as to the world that the playwright creates is the moral system he has in mind. In a sense little distinction may be made between value and morality, since morality is always based on a sense of values. Value, however, may be felt or sensed without being spelled out. Morality tends to be the product of training, thought, and experience, and attempts to deal with life consistently. One may sense a value and yet have no idea how to deal with it morally. It is even possible for a play to assert certain values on the one hand and argue in favor of a moral system that contradicts those values on the other. That could happen if a playwright attempted to persuade his audience that they should accept certain moral values, and yet depicted events in his play that contradicted that system of values. Suppose, for example, a playwright wished to assert that adultery was immoral and wrote a play showing the terrible tragedy that resulted from an adulterous situation. He might, in the process of portraying the relationship between his two main characters, so sensitively develop the love between them that the audience would feel the value of the love was so great as to be worth the cost of any suffering that might result from it. In just such a way people often experience conflict between their intuitive perception of value and the moral system they have worked out for themselves.

Every good play has a moral system implicit in it. It need not be the prevailing morality at the time the play is written, although it might be. Sophocles and Shakespeare asserted the prevailing morality of their times, whereas Euripides and Ibsen were in conflict with the morality of their times. The moral system reflected in a play is a product of the playwright's own morality, and he is often unconscious of putting it into the play at all. A play that appears on the surface to be completely frivolous may be either attacking frivolity or asserting it. If we are meant to feel the emptiness of the lives of the characters, the play attacks frivolity. If we are meant to agree with the characters that nothing on earth is more important than the joy of the moment, the play asserts the value of frivolity. The only way to keep a play from asserting a moral system of some kind would be to make its action hopelessly confused and contradictory. Even that might assert the morality of anarchy.

Imagery

An image is anything that arouses one or more of the senses. Many of the images in a play are physically present on the stage; many more are suggested in the language of the play. In a poem the images must all be perceived in the imagination as one reads the poem, but in a play a dimension is added in the interplay between the images perceived directly and those that occur in the language. Every time an image is repeated, it contributes to the formation of a pattern. If a character says in Act One, "Autumn will be here soon, and the leaves will begin to fall"; and in Act Two we see on the stage a tree with leaves falling from it; and in Act Three the character says, "I feel like an old, dead leaf," then a pattern of images has been formed. It is best, of course, if the images are not simply repeated, but are developed in relation to one another. Also, the pattern of images should grow naturally out of the rest of the play, not be imposed on it. It is very likely that the audience will be unaware of it, but its presence will subtly contribute to the total effectiveness of the play.

Physicality

Everything that appears on the stage is physically present there. That may seem obvious enough, but it is an element of the pattern that should not be ignored. In a novel or a poem, characters and objects may have varying degrees of reality. As we see what is happening through the eyes of one character, other characters may become progressively more shadowy until we reach a level at which their very existence is open to question. In a play, however, a character either walks onstage or he does not. If he does, his reality must be fully accounted for. Of course, fairies, ghosts, and dream figures occur in plays, and certain tricks of costuming and lighting can make them seem more ethereal, but even they, once they come onstage, are real in whatever world has been created for them. This physicality of plays is both a liability and an asset. It is a liability when the author forgets about it. If he has two people sit down and talk philosophy for twenty-five minutes, he has gotten away from the physical nature of his characters, and the audience will become bored. If he writes a stage direction such as the following, he is forgetting how things happen on a stage: "Joe enters and turns on the light. He yawns and stretches, takes off his clothes, goes into the bathroom and brushes his teeth, comes back into the room and gets into bed. He reads two chapters of his favorite book, then gradually falls asleep. Sleepily, he turns off the light. Hours pass. Light comes in the window. Joe's alarm clock goes off. He wakes up, stretches, turns off his alarm clock, and gets dressed."

That stage direction ignores the physicality of the theatre in several ways. The action it depicts covers too much time. Much of it (the reading of the two chapters) is mental action that cannot be shown physically. Some of it takes place offstage (in the bathroom), though the author has visualized it as if the audience could see it. Some of it is inconsistent (Joe did not set his alarm clock before he went to bed). It is not all on the same level of detail ("He yawns and stretches . . . hours pass."). The actions we observe neither arouse suspense nor seem surprising in themselves.

But the playwright who uses physicality effectively knows that a kiss onstage at the right moment is worth twenty pages of a novel in both the feeling and the information that it conveys. He knows that a character who is trying to convey what has happened to him after his tongue has been cut out, and who is dying in the process, can produce an impact in the theatre that could not possibly be conveyed through descriptive writing. He knows, in short, that an audience must automatically believe in the reality of the people physically present on a stage until he has done something to convince that audience that those people are not real. He knows that the physical nature of the actors will be the primary source of the emotional effectiveness of his play.

Universality

The theatre appeals strongly to our ability to sense the general in the particular. By the arrangement of his materials the playwright may convince us that what we are seeing is the very essence of young first love, or of the conflict between mother and child, or of the mingled fear and patriotism of a young man as he sets off for war. Strangely enough, this sense of the universal occurs only when the characters and events have been given individuality, for we must see the particular before we can sense the general in it. Although plays sometimes use characters who are abstractions, the danger is always present that they will appear to be tools by means of which the author proves his point. Individuality is possible in any kind of play, no matter how abstract and surrealistic it may be. Moreover, the characters need not be fully developed human beings in order to be individual. The essence of individuality is sometimes caught more effectively in a caricature than in a photograph. It is the nature and arrangement of the details that have been selected that determine individuality and its consequent possibility for suggesting the universal.

We have now examined those elements that contribute to the pattern the play forms—, the shapes and ideas that it leaves behind in the imagination. But how are those shapes and ideas interrelated? What is the emotional ebb and flow of the play? The elements of structure pull the play together, enabling it to work as an experience. Probably the audience will not be conscious of any of these elements; but if they are not handled well, it will feel that something is not quite right. The elements of structure are: balance, rhythm, tempo, focus, contrast, interrelatedness, expectation, and totality of effect.

Balance

Whenever two or more of anything have approximately equal importance, they must be properly balanced in relation to one another. One cannot have a first act lasting two hours and a second act lasting ten minutes. If the play has two characters of about the same importance, they should have approximately equal time onstage. The scenery should be so placed on the stage that the right-hand side is about as interesting as the left-hand side. If the play is a mixture of the comic and the serious, there should be enough of each so that they offset each other properly.

Balance is a matter of artistic judgment

acquired through long experience. There is no way to measure whether a play is in most respects properly balanced. One either feels it or one does not. One of the main reasons a playwright should see and read and work on a great many good plays is that by doing so he will gradually learn to sense what makes a play properly or poorly balanced. There are no easy answers. Symmetry, for example, should not be confused with balance. A symmetrical thing has sides that are mirror images of each other. Too much symmetry in any art form produces dullness. The playwright should not attempt to achieve balance through such artificial techniques as symmetry. He should allow his feeling for it to grow out of sensitive experience.

Rhythm

The rise and fall of tension in a play is like the breaking of waves against the shore, or the stressed and unstressed syllables in a line of poetry. If the tension in a play is not periodically relaxed, it becomes too great, and the audience can no longer bear it. That is why most serious plays contain moments of comedy. It is an important reason for including subordinate characters and situations in the play, and for frequently changing the subject of conversation in the dialogue.

In addition, the tension must build gradually toward a climax that comes near the end of the play. Usually several minor climaxes, or crises, precede the major one. In a three-act play a crisis usually occurs at the end of each of the first two acts. Thus, the rise and fall of tension is not a simple wave motion; it is a gradual ascent as well. The peaks of tension should usually be higher than the previous peaks; otherwise the audience will feel that the tension is dropping and will lose interest in the play.

One must learn to sense the rhythm that is individual to a play and to avoid things that break down its rhythmic pulse. One of the reasons so much effort goes into re-

writing plays is that the proper rhythmic pulse for a play is often hard to find. You may be able to learn something about rhythm by seeing some bad plays. You will notice that in them the tension will sometimes build too rapidly, and at other times the play will drag and grow boring. It might help you, also, to listen to a movement of a Beethoven symphony to see how the tension rises and falls in the music but works toward a climax at the end. Such an exercise may help you to sense the rhythmic pulse of a play in the abstract.

Tempo

Events tend to take place at a particular rate in a given play. One play may take ten lines to establish a character's presence onstage; another may do the same thing in two lines. Here is how it works:

Scene A (10 lines):

  A: Oh, hello!
  B: Hi.
  A: How've you been?
  B: So-so.
  A: I was expecting you earlier.
  B: I couldn't get here any sooner.
  A: Well, you've kept us waiting on this job, you know.
  B: I'm sorry about that.
  A: Let's get at it. What do you say?
  B: All right with me.

Scene B (2 lines):

  A: Well, it's about time you got here. I've been waiting for you. Come on, let's get down to business.
  B: Okay.

So long as a play maintains the interest of the audience, it really does not matter what its tempo is. It does matter that it have one, and that the author, having found the proper tempo for his play, maintain it. It is usually true, however, that the first draft of a play is too wordy, and that consequently the play is not able to move at the tempo appropriate to it. This is because things need to happen more rapidly in plays than they do in life. A tempo which is too "life-like" may be dull. Sometimes, on the other hand, the author has not allowed enough reality to permeate his lines to make them wordy enough. In that case, he may have to let things happen more slowly, in a relaxed and natural manner.

Focus

The author should know where he wants his audience's attention focused at any given moment throughout the play. He should also be sure that they see clearly whatever it is he wants them to. A character that is not fully realized may be said to be out of focus if that character is of central importance. On the other hand, a minor character that is too fully developed may distract attention from the main action and throw the whole play out of focus. A play should not be a three-ring circus, nor should it be a group of vague impressions seen through a mist.

Contrast

Too much repetition of anything quickly becomes boring. Repetition is avoided not only by having the events of the plot differ from one another, but by having the characters and moods differ as well. Excessive contrast, however, would be as bad as too little. Moreover, every play has its own degree of contrast. Just as some pictures are in pastel colors, others in primaries, so some plays will have very subtle contrasts, others more obvious ones. If the contrasts in a play are particularly subtle, they must also be particularly clear in the playwright's mind, for the more subtle a thing is, the more difficult it is to make sure everyone understands it.

Interrelatedness

The various parts of a play must not be isolated from one another. They must con-tinually add to one another's meaning, so that as one sits through a play he is constantly recalling and reinterpreting what he has seen earlier. The story of the boy who cried "Wolf!" is a good example. The first two times that the boy cries "Wolf!" and the townspeople come running, we are in the realm of the practical joke. When, the third time, the boy is faced with a real wolf and cries out—and the townspeople do not come—the previous events in the story take on new meaning. What first seemed a practical joke now turns out to be a tragic event. In their turn, the first two events lend meaning to the third event. As the boy is devoured by the wolf he feels himself not to be the helpless minion of fate, but the victim of his own stupidity.

Interrelatedness may be achieved through such elements as imagery and characterization as well as plot. In general, the more different ways we feel that a particular moment in a play is related to the play as a whole, the more powerful the impact of that moment.

Expectation

The events that occur in a play should lead us to expect other events to occur as a result of them. Such expectation comes to a head in what is sometimes called the obligatory scene. This is the scene in the last act that the author must write because he has caused us to expect it. If, in the story of the boy who cried "Wolf!" only the first two events were told and the third left out, we should not have the obligatory scene. A shaggy-dog story is a joke without an obligatory scene. In other words, it defeats our expectation that everything in the joke will be tied together. Nothing is more frustrating than having to sit through a shaggy-dog play, unless it be sitting through a play so dull that it does not even arouse any expectation for it to disappoint.

Expectation applies not only to plot, but to many other elements as well. A character may lead the audience to expect him to do certain things. A few ominous hints may lead the audience to expect a tragic change in mood. Colorful description of a property may lead the audience to expect that it will appear on the scene eventually. The sound of trumpets in the distance may create the expectation of the entrance of a king. Audiences, like little children, love to anticipate thrilling surprises. The skillful playwright creates high hopes and then more than satisfies those hopes.

Totality of Effect

When we finish seeing the play we must finally come around to experiencing it as one single thing. There is something biological about this; it is at the root of organic structure. An orange or an apple is a single thing, although it has many parts. When you get to know another person well, you experience his singleness, although his being has many aspects. The same thing must happen with a play. If, after seeing it, one is aware of many disparate kinds of cleverness and interesting things that have happened, but not of a single all-encompassing feeling (which cannot be put into words) of what its nature is, then the play seems to have no soul, and we soon forget it. In the rough-and-tumble of working on your play, you will probably lose sight of its totality from time to time. In the end, you must find it again. An idea that often recurs in dramatic criticism is, "Excellent as the individual elements are, somehow the whole thing never quite jells."

We have seen some of the elements that hold a play together and make it function in a pleasing manner. Last we shall examine those elements of entity that seem capable of being isolated and existing in their own right. Those are the things the audience actually sees and hears. They are the things that one who has seen the play is likely to mention to his friends, and consequently effective use of them will attract large numbers of people to see the play. They are: character, dialogue, event, effect, symbol, and property.

Character

We often talk about the characters in a play as if they had a life of their own. We should remember, however, that a dramatic character is the things he does and has no existence apart from them. The question, "What would so-and-so have done under other circumstances?" is interesting, but not really relevant, as the other circumstances do not and cannot occur unless another play is written (as does on occasion happen). In other words, it is not enough for an author to think that something is true of a character; he must express that truth through the action of the character. The identity of the character is all the more confusing because the things he does are usually only hinted at in the written text. Should the character break down and weep at a certain point? The author did not specify, but the lines seem to indicate that he would. The actor weeps and thereby interprets the character for the audience. The actor's interpretation in performance must be considered part of the play, for the character does not exist until he has brought it to life. For that reason, every time the play is performed it is a different play. Thus the author must put considerable thought into controlling and communicating the meaning of his characters.

A character is known primarily in terms of action, but also in terms of what is said about him by the author, by the other characters, and by himself. His exact nature necessarily is a matter of interpretation rather than fact, but one thing is certain: The character must have totality. Contradictions may be present (and probably should be), but these must ultimately be submerged in a sense of the character's totality.

Characters are sometimes called static if they do not change during the action, and dynamic if they do. These terms do not imply value judgments, since some of the most interesting characters in all drama are static characters. Nevertheless, the central character in a play is likely to be dynamic, because the events that occur in the play are likely to change his basic nature. That is truer of tragedies than comedies. In fact, characters who are truly comic are nearly always static and impervious to change. Some characters, such as Donald Duck and Jack Benny, may continue to entertain us in countless stories for many years without undergoing the slightest change of basic character.

Dialogue

The dialogue consists of all the words the characters say. Each time a new character speaks, what he says is referred to as a "line." The story of the play is told almost entirely through the dialogue, so it is important that the story be of a kind that *can* be told in dialogue. In addition to forwarding the telling of the story, a given line of dialogue may do many things. It may contribute to our knowledge of the character who is speaking, the character to whom he is speaking, and the character about whom he may be speaking. It may create expectations of what is to come, primarily through the use of irony. It may also contribute something to the developing theme and style of the play. It must always avoid detracting from the overall patterns the playwright is establishing.

Characters in a play must speak to and listen to one another. Constant interchange must take place between them. Never write a long speech when a short one will do. If a character is going to tell the story of his life, do not just have him sit down and tell it; have another character extract it from him bit by bit, all the time increasing our interest in what he will say next.

Dialogue is not the same as ordinary speech. It is what may be called "heightened" speech. In a later chapter we shall consider in detail how the two differ; for now, suffice it to say that dramatic dialogue always represents a selection from, and a careful shaping of, the way people might really talk. It must have its roots in reality, but it must not duplicate reality.

Event

An event is a single action that occurs in a play and can be thought of apart from the actions that surround it. A play is made up of a series of events. Each of them must be interesting for its own sake as well as contribute to the developing action of the play. In a complex play it would be as difficult to say exactly what constitutes an event as to say exactly how much water is contained in one drop. One could say that a herald coming onstage and making an announcement was an event, or one could say that it was three events: his entrance, his announcement, and his exit. If two characters have an argument, that is an event, although at exactly what point the argument begins is not always clear. But however we isolate an event in a play, we must always find it interesting in itself. That is to say, no event in a good play exists solely for the purpose of getting from one situation in a plot to the next.

French plays are often printed in what are called "French scenes." A new scene begins whenever a new character enters, or else when a character who has been important in the scene leaves. In many plays the events are about the same as the French scenes. That is because the addition or subtraction of a character is usually enough to conclude one event and start another. Obviously, the events would be unlikely to correspond with the French scenes if the play had only two or three characters, so the relationship is by no means a necessary one.

Much of what goes into the shaping of a play as a whole also goes into the shaping of an event. It must increase in dramatic tension toward a climax, all the while contributing to our knowledge of the characters involved. It must have a unity of its own that we continue to think about long after it has occurred.

Effect

Some effects are called "special effects." An explosion, a fire, a fog—all offer the technical director of the production the opportunity to demonstrate his skills. Special effects have great audience appeal and may be remembered long after the play itself has been forgotten. There have been times in the history of the theatre when audiences were primarily interested in the special effects, and other elements of the drama were regarded as insignificant by comparison. Technical ingenuity is not, however, needed to accomplish a powerful effect in the theatre. An action as simple as one character's putting his hand on another character's shoulder can produce an effect. It might work as follows:

"The lights dim until only the red sunset is seen in the distance. A pulsating sound of distant drums is heard. The hero enters, breathing heavily, and stands looking as if he is about to faint. A flash of lightning and a crash of thunder. Enter, the sheriff and his posse. The posse stand motionless, grouped about the stage. The hero turns and faces the sheriff. The sheriff walks slowly up to him and claps his hand on his shoulder. Curtain."

All of the actions described above might be classified as effects, for each of them can have a distinct and memorable dramatic impact of its own. Effects can add a great deal to a play, but they must be used with care. The more powerful the effect, the more difficult it will be for the playwright to make it fit properly into the rest of the play, since every effect must be dramatically justified or it will detract from, rather than add to, the play. Strewing the stage with dead bodies is not a good idea unless one happens to be a great poet. The audience is likely to remember the dead bodies and forget the rest of the play.

Fortunately, because the movies can achieve much more sensational effects than are possible on the stage, the theatre now contents itself for the most part with only those effects that are dramatically relevant. Learn to use them. Look for places in your play in which they can be included. When they are dramatically justified, they do more than their share toward making the play a memorable experience.

Symbol

A symbol is anything that represents itself and something else. It can be a word, a sound, a gesture, or an object. Some symbols are universal, some belong to a certain group of people, and some derive their meaning entirely from the situation in which they are used. They have much in common with images, and many images are also symbols; but images need not be used symbolically, and some symbols (such as gestures) are not images.

It is often possible to increase dramatic power by changing the usual meaning of a symbol. For example, a kiss usually symbolizes love, but it can also be used as a symbol of passionate hatred and contempt. A symbol may be explained directly, may be made clear by the situation, or may be left open to conjecture as to its meaning. In any case it should not be used self-consciously, but should fit naturally into the dramatic situation.

If the play is written in poetry, the symbols may be incorporated mostly in the language. Shakespeare's line, "Now is the winter of our discontent/Made glorious summer by this sun of York," tells us that winter stands for discontent, summer for content, and the sun for the victorious House of York. If the play is in prose, the symbolism may be expressed more through the use of properties, gestures, and special effects than through language. Ibsen's

Hedda Gabler is fond of shooting her father's pistols. This action symbolizes her subconscious dissatisfaction with being a woman and her desire for the freedom and prerogatives of a man.

The skilled actor is proficient in the use of gestures to communicate, whereas the playwright seldom visualizes the use of gesture in much detail. It may help you in understanding how gesture is a whole language unto itself to read Stephen Potter's *One-upmanship*. Many of the ploys he humorously suggests for asserting one's natural superiority involve gestures. For example, the doctor who washes his hands immediately after touching a patient suggests that the patient is contaminated. Dramatic gestures are nearly always symbolic in that they suggest relationships and judgments, and they can be made to interact by reinforcing and contradicting one another.

When an object is used dramatically as a symbol, it may derive its symbolic value from always being associated with a particular character. Once the association has been established, the symbol may then be manipulated in a way that suggests manipulation of that character. The association of objects with particular people is very common not only in the drama, but also in political campaigns. When it was discovered that Adlai Stevenson had a hole in his shoe, a facsimile of the bottom of a shoe with a hole in it was used as a campaign button. When Kennedy was President, the rocking chair became associated with him. We may go all the way back to George Washington and the cherry tree.

Property

Any object used during the course of the drama is called a property, or "prop." An object on the stage is part of the scenery if it remains stationary, but if its manipulation is necessary to the action, it becomes a property. Properties can have symbolic value and can thereby arouse considerable emotion in the audience. But a property need not be a symbol to be of great significance and dramatic interest. Some of the most famous properties in dramatic literature have no symbolic value, but they serve to bring about changes in the relationships between people. Among these are the handkerchief in Shakespeare's *Othello* and the cigarette case in Wilde's *The Importance of Being Earnest*.

A property may be without either dramatic interest or symbolic value, but be used simply to add to the atmosphere or realism of a scene. For example, many a Broadway play has a housewife preparing breakfast in it. The milk and coffee and toast and plates are necessary to the scene and in no way detract from it, but they have no significance beyond the realism they add to the scene.

It is often possible to increase one's awareness of the possible dramatic action in a scene by considering whether any properties might be added to it. Sometimes skillful use of a property can save writing pages of dialogue. The wife who suspects her husband of being unfaithful suddenly becomes sure of it when she finds a long blond hair on his collar. It is important, however, that properties be used in the scene naturally and not be forced into it. The wife should not see the hair on her husband's collar from across the room; she should find it while in the act of embracing him.

Now that we have considered numerous elements of the drama, it might be well to gain some practice in the use of them. Try writing a page of dialogue and then rewriting it once after you have reread each of the descriptions in this chapter. With each rewrite you should concentrate on one of the elements. For your convenience, let us review them here. They are, again, *background*: world, atmosphere, conventions, spirit of the audience, sound, and scene; *pattern*: plot, conflict, action, theme, irony, value, morality, imagery, physicality, and universality; *structure:* balance, rhythm, tempo, focus, contrast, interrelatedness, expectation, and totality of effect; *entity:* character, dialogue, event, effect, symbol, and property. When your attention is on the element of dialogue, you should consider those purely verbal effects that you have not considered while dealing with any of the other elements.

Successively rewriting in that way should make you more intensely aware of what each of the elements contributes to the total effect than you can be after merely reading about them. After practicing the exercise, you should begin to find that you can think about many of the elements simultaneously, which is what you need to be able to do to write a play. If you have trouble understanding how certain elements function, devote extra time to practicing those elements, and also discuss them with others who may understand them better.

Another exercise that may help you understand this chapter is to take a page or two of a good play that you have read, and identify and describe the functioning of each of the elements in it.

Lastly, listen to a recording of a full-length play. While you are listening, keep shifting your attention from one element to the next until you have covered the full list of elements. Try to hear in succession how the playwright is handling each of the elements through a small part of his play. You may wish to repeat the exercise several times, using the same play, until you find that you can shift your attention easily from one element to the next. That sort of flexibility in your thinking, once you have developed it, should be very helpful to you in writing your own play.

When you are actually working on the first draft of a play, however, you should not be thinking consciously about the elements of drama. Your subconscious may assist you in keeping them all straight. Your attention while you are writing should be entirely on your feeling about the play as a whole. If you are dividing your attention too much among the various parts, the play will not hold together properly in your imagination.

Now that we have briefly considered many diverse elements, we shall proceed to give fuller consideration to some of the most important ones.

Chapter VIII

BUILDING A PLOT

Plots are not so much invented or made as they are built. If you watch the erection of a huge skyscraper, you will see many stages in its development, from the digging of the cellar through the building of the steel frame to the laying of the bricks or stonework, before the building even resembles its final form. Just so a plot may have little apparent elegance in the early stages of its development. The playwright will have to learn to live with the ineptitude of his ideas in their first form if he wishes to be able eventually to produce a beautiful and well-structured plot.

You begin designing a plot by finding an idea of some sort. That idea may be in the form of a character you want to write about, or it may be a theme idea, or perhaps only a vague feeling of mood. You might even begin with the effect of the final curtain and work back from there. Early in the development of your plot you will want to identify it with particular characters, for a plot that is conceived without characters will quickly become contrived and unworkable. In this chapter, however, we are going to discuss plot in the abstract to show how plot ideas may be manipulated, without worrying too much about how they are related to the characterization that goes with them. You need to develop enough flexibility in your thinking about plot so that you can get it to do whatever it must do in order to give full expression to your characters.

"Plot is the first form of tragedy," wrote Aristotle 2,500 years ago. Since then, many critics and playwrights have disagreed with him, feeling that some other element of the drama was more important than the plot, or that plot could be dispensed with entirely. Conflict, said one critic, was essential. Irony, replied another. Character and theme have also been leading contenders for being considered most essential. Chekhov's plays, for example, depend almost entirely on characterization. Bernard Shaw argued that plays were better without plots, and frequently placed the emphasis in his own plays on philosophical discussion.

Although it may be possible to write a play in which nothing important happens, it is certainly not possible to write one in which nothing happens at all. The moment something is represented in fictional form, we have the beginning of a story. It can safely be said, then, that every play has a story. What is the distinction between plays that have stories and those that have plots?

The novelist E. M. Forster contributed greatly to our understanding of plot when he distinguished between story and plot as follows: If you say, "The king died and then the queen died," you have a story. But if you say, "The king died and then the queen died of grief," you have a plot. In other words, a story is a simple progression of events, one after the other, whereas a plot is a progression of events in which one *causes* the other. The key to our understanding of plot, then, lies in a single word, *"Because."*

Let us see how this applies to the making of plots. We are going, now, to indulge in an exercise designed to produce the kind of flexibility in thinking about plot that will ultimately enable one to discover and develop a plot in relation to one's own deepest impulses. For the time, however, we shall content ourselves with mere whimsy and not worry about depth. Suppose that I make at random two statements, each of which describes an action, such as, "I went skiing yesterday," and "My grandfather died at the age of 84." Separately, these statements have little more than ordinary interest. But now, if I connect them with the word "because," all sorts of interesting things begin to happen: "I went skiing yesterday because my grandfather died at the age of 84." Immediately we want to know more. Did grandfather's death occur yesterday? If so, does not my skiing reflect a callous response to the demise of the poor old man? Yes, perhaps I am a covetous wretch who has been waiting eagerly for the death of my grandfather so that I can inherit a fortune. Or perhaps my grandfather's death was a cause for relief, since he had kept the entire family paralyzed with fear and in the grip of his iron will for many years. My skiing yesterday was my first expression of freedom at the escape from his clutches. Then, again, it may be that my skiing was not a joy but a necessity. My grandfather's death in an isolated cabin in Alaska necessitated my skiing to the little church where his funeral was held.

All of these possibilities arise from the assumption that my grandfather's death and my skiing occurred within a short span of time. But suppose that my skiing yesterday occurred as a result of my grandfather's death ten years ago. Now the situation is fraught with mystery indeed. Did he command on his deathbed that I give up skiing for the next ten years? Or that I ski regularly once every ten years? Or had he commanded

in his will that a treasure he had buried in Alaska must remain buried for ten years before I could seek it out? Or did his death allow him to reveal finally that he was no ordinary man, but one who had come out of the mountains of Tibet, one of that race of near-humans known as the Abominable Snowmen?

Then, again, why is his age at the time of death important? Can it be that had he lived to be 85 he might have made good an ancient boast of his and thereby come into possession of vast regions of wasteland near the North Pole? And am I now skiing through those empty wastes, sad at heart because I have not inherited this territory on which I had hoped to erect a vast toy-making industry in fulfillment of a childhood dream that I might someday grow up to be the one true Santa Claus?

Perhaps you get the idea. Any two actions may be connected in that way. Standing alone they are dry, dismal, uninteresting; but as partners they strike fire to the imagination. That is especially true if there is no obvious relationship between them. Little will happen if you content yourself with a pairing off of "I ate dinner," and "I was hungry." But if you *must* use these two, let them read, "I was hungry because I ate dinner." Here at least some questions are raised. It is better, however, if you arrange things so that you can have no conscious control over the pairing of the statements. Let several of your friends each write down a statement or two describing actions. Then scramble the statements and pull two out at random. Perhaps you will come up with something like: "Rabbits eat flowers" and "Mexico is especially prone to producing volcanoes." That may leave you cold at first and make you want to go on to something else. Better stick with it and see what happens. Here, for a starter, is a "Just So" story of the type that Kipling wrote. Let us call it "How the Rabbit Got His Taste for Flowers." In this story we learn that once upon a time rabbits used to eat grass. On one occasion a particularly adventurous Mexican rabbit named Pedro came upon a beautiful wild orchid. Pedro, having become bored with the monotony of his diet, decided to see whether the orchid tasted as good as it looked. He took a bite and found the orchid delicious. Just at that moment steam began to issue from the ground, accompanied by a grumbling and sputtering. In the end, Pedro convinced all the rabbits that his eating of an orchid had given rise to what turned into a volcano, and persuaded them that by this device of orchid-eating, rabbits might hope to rule the world someday: Surely when enough volcanoes had been created in various parts of the world, men would come and kneel down to the rabbits, begging them to stop feeding on orchids. Therefore, to this day rabbits have continued to feed upon orchids in the fervent hope that here and there a volcano will leap into being from the crumbs of their meal.

It is really very easy, once you get the hang of it, but you must allow your imagination to work on every statement you create until practice has strengthened your whimsy. Note that you must move backward or forward from the idea suggested by your statement, imagining a variety of incidents leading up to or away from it. Whatever happens, do not give up on a statement. That is important for a very good reason. Time and again you will meet someone who says, "There is a play I want to write." Some one idea has occurred to him, and he has carried it around for years, hoping that exactly the right inspiration will come and that he will be able to give his idea birth in full glory. Often he hopes that some playwright will take an interest in his plot and do it for him, giving him half of the stupendous profits that will result from a Broadway hit. His idea may or may not be a good one, but it is absurd that a writer should have only one idea. The more ideas he has to choose from, the better are likely to be the ones he will develop. Fill your mind with a thousand plays that you would like to write and then pick the best of them. It may be that you will find several good ideas combining to form a single play. That is more likely to occur if your mind is filled with more ideas than you will ever use. In just a few hours of "because-ing" you may find you have created more ideas than you previously had in your whole life. Certainly you will loosen up your imagination and make it more flexible. Even after your mind is fully stocked, you will want to continue "because-ing" from time to time just to keep your imagination exercised.

Let us return now to the thought we considered earlier, that plot may not be the most important element of a play and, indeed, that it may be forgone altogether. It is probably best done without by those who find it easily come by. Few plays are as plotless as Chekhov's, yet before Chekhov began writing plays he had written hundreds of short stories, each with a clearly designed plot. Because plot came so easily to him, it was almost an exercise to do without it. Actually, if you examine a Chekhov play carefully, you will find it contains material enough for hundreds of plays. Almost every line suggests something that might be turned into a fully developed plot. It is the continual suggestion of unfulfilled possibilities that supplies much of the interest in a Chekhov play.

A more modern playwright, Harold Pinter, writes plays that are studies of states of mind rather than situations. Often in a Pinter play we have a continuous sense that something is happening, but we do not know what it is. It is as if Pinter had written an ordinary suspense drama and then simply removed the plot, leaving the suspense. Clearly the writing of such a "plotless" play requires much knowledge of the structure and functioning of plot.

It would seem that a plotless play is one in which plot has been thought out and then suppressed, rather than one in which plot is simply absent. If you can write a good plot, you can always do without it once you have written it. But if you are incapable of plot and find you need it, you are in a much more difficult position.

Assuming, then, that the ability to develop plot is desirable, let us turn our attention toward how it may be developed without sacrificing other values, such as character. It is often said that character *is* plot; that is, that the plot is something that grows out of the nature of the people involved in it, people who have special meaning to their author, rather than something that happens all by itself. As soon as we realize that, we have a principle of selection that allows us to choose from hundreds of possible stories the one we should like to tell. After we have accumulated a stockpile of stories, using the "because-ing" exercise, we can then begin to examine critically their possibilities. Always keep in mind that you want to devote your time to writing about people who seem essential to you. They must not be too much like yourself, but you must care about them, either lovingly or critically.

Let us return now to the dialogue between husband and wife in Chapter III and assume that you wish to develop from this germ of a play a plot suitable to it. The first step is to describe in several alternate ways the actions that are occurring in that scene. Here are some statements of action:

The wife bought shirts.
The wife bought a dress.
The husband objected to the wife's spending so much money.
The husband picked on the wife.
The wife tried to interest the husband in her looks.
The husband expressed disinterest in his wife's appearance.
The wife came home from the store.

Now let us combine these at random. Here are some combinations:

The wife bought shirts because she bought a dress.

The wife bought a dress because she bought shirts.
The husband objected to the wife's spending so much money because she bought him shirts.
The husband picked on the wife because she tried to interest him in her looks.
The wife came home from the store because she knew that her husband would pick on her.

All of these statements suggest character relationships that are potentially interesting, but they do not suggest much in the way of plot. That is because everything we are now producing stems from a superficial reading of a few lines. We are ignoring the original impulse that gave birth to these lines.

Therefore, let us go back a step: Among our original notes is one that reads: "worried about the genetic effects of radiation." Since we have so far suffered from the absence of plot, let us reverse the situation and see if we can suffer from too much plot. Here are two possibilities:

A. The wife bought shirts because she was worried about the genetic effects of radiation.

B. The husband expressed disinterest in his wife's appearance because he was worried about the genetic effects of radiation.

Let us explore plot A: A woman who has been brought up in an overprotective family has become so obsessed with reports that radiation in the atmosphere may affect genes adversely that she is afraid of having children. For psychological reasons she cannot express this fear directly, but one type of activity provides her indirect protection: Buying clothes at a tremendous rate makes her feel that she will not have enough money to afford children. Also, the clothes provide symbolic protection against the atmosphere. The more her husband protests her buying clothes, the more she fears he wants a child, and the more she buys them. The husband is in danger of going bankrupt because of his wife's spending. He forces her to do without money by refusing to give her access to his bank account. She, desperate, with the fear of radiation, tries to convince her husband of the danger. She hears that radiation emanates from television, so she destroys the television set. Finally, her husband has her committed to an institution.

Now let us try plot B: A scientist, working with radioactive materials, has become genetically damaged. He lacks the courage to tell his wife what has happened, but he wishes to avoid ever having a child because of it. The wife, intensely eager to have a child, tries to persuade her husband that they should. The husband first tries to rationalize his disinterest in a child, then simply refuses to discuss the matter. His wife decides he does not love her and turns against him. All the time the husband really wants a child, and is in despair over the situation.

Comparing the two plots, we find both of them somewhat improbable. But of the two, the second seems more interesting. That is because we are more interested to begin with in a husband's expressing disinterest in his wife's appearance than in a wife's buying shirts. The more your statements of action strike at the root of what is interesting about human life, the more powerful your plot is likely to be.

Therefore, the plot of a play should be kept as simple as the nature of the characters will allow. Too much attention to features of the environment and circumstances that are not directly produced by character tends to make a play seem artificial and overcomplicated. Keep things happening inside your characters as much as possible, and bring them into conflict with the world only as much as necessary in order to have them express their essential being. If your characters are interesting people, you will find that, even when it is kept as simple as possible, the plot will be fairly complex.

Perhaps we can make our plot idea more character-centered. If the husband's fear of having a child in the second plot grows not from radiation and the fear of its effects, but from something more common and basic in human experience, we may find it easier to make him seem like a real person. Perhaps he does not want a child because he himself was an unwanted child, and he is afraid he will not love his child. In that case the conflict between husband and wife can lead somewhere. She may be able to persuade him that he does indeed have the capacity to love a child. Or he may become so tense about this problem that he breaks up his marriage and destroys his life. In either case, the problem is of vital human significance, since each of us must decide whether he was or was not wanted as a child, and also whether he does or does not wish to have a child.

In selecting your plot you must ask yourself not only, is this story of vital and abiding interest to me? but also, will it hold the same interest for anyone who sees it? In order to answer these questions, we must distinguish between those problems that are experienced as basic and those that are essentially external. One might say that he experiences his own need for survival, love, and self-realization as basic, and that he experiences social problems as external. That might explain why few, if any, great plays have been written that are primarily concerned with social problems. Most great plays are about love, death, ambition, jealousy, pride, fear, and other deeply personal emotions.

Why, then, could one not get sufficient impact out of a plot dealing with exposure to radiation? One might, of course, but one would have to keep emphasizing that it is the character's reaction to his condition and not the condition itself that is important. Furthermore, his reaction cannot be taken for granted: It must be fully and sensitively expressed. One must be able to put himself in the character's shoes and know exactly how it would feel before he can account for the character's reactions.

You must find, then, not simply a plot,

but the one plot that will allow you to lavish upon your characters the kind of affection and understanding they need to grow into fully realized human beings. When you have found it, you must then develop it in such a manner that it can be staged effectively.

We shall now demonstrate the process of plot development, again without worrying about depth, treating somewhat whimsically the story of Little Red Riding-Hood.

Once upon a time there was a little girl named Little Red Riding-Hood. One day her mother sent her off into the woods with some cookies to take to her grandmother. While she was traveling through the woods she met a wolf. The wolf asked her where she was going, and she told him. The wolf then suggested that her grandmother might like some flowers as well as the cookies. And so, though her mother had told her not to stray from the path, Little Red Riding-Hood went about the woods picking flowers.

The wolf, meanwhile, went straight to Grandmother's house and devoured her. He then put on Grandmother's nightgown and slipped into her bed. When Little Red Riding-Hood came with the cookies and the flowers, the wolf quickly swallowed her up, and then went to sleep, snoring loudly. A passing huntsman heard the snoring and came into the hut to see why Grandmother was snoring so loudly. Finding the wolf, he cut him open, and pulled out Little Red Riding-Hood and her grandmother.

The story might be dramatized in three scenes, as follows:

Scene I: Little Red Riding-Hood's home. Little Red Riding-Hood's mother tells her to go to Grandmother's house and take some cookies. She warns her not to stray from the path.

Scene II: On the path in the woods. Little Red Riding-Hood enters and meets a wolf. The wolf asks her where she is going, and she tells him. The wolf then suggests that she pick some flowers for Grandmother.

Scene III: Grandmother's house. The wolf enters and eats up Grandmother. Then he

puts on her nightgown and gets into bed. Little Red Riding-Hood enters and converses with the wolf. The wolf eats Little Red Riding-Hood. The huntsman enters and cuts open the wolf, extracting Little Red Riding-Hood and her grandmother.

Of these three scenes, two are merely introductory, and in their present form would have to be very brief. The excitement of the story is all contained in Scene III. There are two possible solutions to this problem. One is to make the first two scenes more interesting by introducing subplots and minor characters. The other is to tell the story entirely in the third scene. Let us consider the second solution first.

As the scene opens, we meet Grandmother in her house. We must know that Little Red Riding-Hood is on her way with cookies, and that she has met the wolf and told him where she is going. How is that information to be conveyed? Part of it we might learn from Grandmother herself. Perhaps she is accustomed to receiving cookies every Wednesday, and she is annoyed that on this particular Wednesday Little Red Riding-Hood is late. What can have delayed her?

The second bit of information can be conveyed by the wolf when he makes his entrance. He can say that he met Little Red Riding-Hood in the woods and that he got a very good impression of Grandmother from her. He has, accordingly, bought cookies himself and brought them along so they can have a big party.

This second part can easily be made to work, as it is conveyed in dialogue between two characters. In the first part, however, Grandmother is alone, and that presents a problem. If the playwright is using an abstract or poetic style of writing, he may have Grandmother speak in a soliloquy. If the play is more realistic, he will have to use some other device. He might have her writing in a diary and speaking as she does so. He might have her calling Little Red Riding-Hood's mother on the telephone to find out what has caused the delay. He might make her a crotchety old woman who continually talks to herself. Perhaps she has, out of loneliness, invented an imaginary companion. Perhaps she addresses herself in the mirror.

It is also possible that another character could be introduced in whom Grandma can confide. This might be a neighbor woman who has stopped by for morning coffee, and who will conveniently leave just before the wolf arrives. It would be better, however, to have this character be one who can figure in the plot later. Who can it be? Of our four characters the wolf and Little Red Riding-Hood are necessarily excluded. That leaves the huntsman. Why not have him stop by for a friendly chat on his way to the woods? Besides, we have had a problem in the plot up till now. The huntsman has appeared out of nowhere unexpectedly at just the right moment. His appearance is too convenient and seems contrived by the author merely for the sake of a solution. It is an example of what we earlier referred to as a deus ex machina. If, however, we have already met him and half expect his entrance at a later time, that entrance will seem quite natural. Yes, have the huntsman in for morning coffee and allow Grandmother to complain to him that Little Red Riding-Hood is late. Have the huntsman upset, as he had hoped to see his favorite little girl this morning before setting off into the woods. When he leaves, Grandmother paces the floor nervously until the wolf enters with his cookies. Grandmother is pleased to see this stranger, hoping that he will have seen Little Red Riding-Hood in the woods and know why she is late this morning. Imagine Grandmother's joy when she discovers that the wolf is himself the cause of Little Red Riding-Hood's delay, but that she is now safely on her way. The remainder of the story can now proceed as originally outlined.

Now let us suppose that we decide to retain Scenes I and II. Then the problem is to make them interesting in themselves, so that they do more than lead up to Scene III. In Scene I we meet Mother, and we must get to know her. Why does she so dote on making cookies for Grandmother? What causes her to send her helpless daughter into the dangerous wolf-ridden woods carrying those cookies? Why does she not explain to Little Red Riding-Hood that friendly wolves may be the most dangerous of all? Perhaps she is a bumbling, sweet, middle-aged lady who lives only to make cookies. As we see her preparing the basket and talking about the dangers of the woods, we begin to anticipate the tragedy that may occur. Soon we are half afraid that Little Red Riding-Hood may meet a wolf in those woods. But we are reassured when Mother speaks of the hunters who roam the woods ridding them of wolves. Just then a hunter drops in for a cookie, and on learning that Little Red Riding-Hood plans to journey to Grandmother's house, offers to escort her. We breathe a sigh of relief. But Mother, poor fool that she is, fails to rise to the occasion, assuring the hunter that Little Red Riding-Hood knows the way very well, since she makes the trip frequently. The hunter, obliging, and quite sure there are no wolves where Little Red Riding-Hood is going, starts off on his way. At that moment Little Red Riding-Hood sees a wolf peering in the window. "It's only your imagination," says Mother, and sends her off on her way. Will Little Red Riding-Hood meet the wolf? If so, is the hunter already out of earshot? How will Mother feel when she hears of her terrible mistake? We will certainly come back after the intermission to find out.

In our next scene things must start off on rather a relaxed note. We have reached a peak of tension in the previous scene, so the rhythmic flow of the play will be helped if the tension is temporarily reduced. We must come to feel that after all Little Red Riding-Hood will get through the woods safely.

A new character or two would help at

this point. Perhaps two woodsmen have just felled a large tree and are congratulating each other on a job well done. Then along comes Little Red Riding-Hood with her cookies. The woodsmen are naturally interested in the cookies, but Little Red Riding-Hood does not wish to deplete Grandmother's supply. She assures them, however, that they can have all the cookies they want if they will go and see her mother. Having done them a favor, she asks for one in return. Are they sure that the woods are free of wolves? She believes she saw one. They reassure her. They have seen no wolves in these parts for five years. Then off they go in quest of cookies. Little Red Riding-Hood, who has had a long, exhausting trip through the woods, feels at this point that she has a right to just one little cookie to get her blood sugar up. She sits on the newly felled tree and looks through her basket for a small one that won't be missed. Just then the wolf peeks out from behind a tree. "Naughty, naughty!" he says.

Little Red Riding-Hood is now at a disadvantage. She had not thought of wolves as moral advisers, and she does not know quite how to take this wolf. Consequently, when he explains to her that little girls are always being told that wolves are bad only because they are so good, she is ready to believe him. "After all," he remarks, "aren't you told not to eat too many cookies, and aren't they good?" The wolf's logic is infallible, and Little Red Riding-Hood is soon won over. Now that he can persuade her to do anything he likes, the wolf sends her off into the woods to hunt for flowers to go with the cookies. At that point Mrs. Wolf appears. She is furious with her husband. The little ones have been hungry for days, and he has not brought home any nice little girls to feed them. What kind of wolf is he, anyway, letting that little girl out of his clutches like that? The wolf explains his plan to get not only Little Red Riding-Hood, but a big juicy grandmother and lots of cookies, and some flowers for the table

into the bargain. Finally Mrs. Wolf is pacified, and Scene II ends with our feeling certain that Little Red Riding-Hood is doomed.

Thus we see that in the process of translating a story idea into dramatic form, we must find the most exciting parts of the story and make them the basis for our various scenes. Other parts of the story must then be brought in, and additional material must be invented to fill out the scenes. Too many changes of scene should be avoided. Also to be avoided is the passage of time without the occurrence of dramatic action. In addition, time must pass onstage at a constant rate, though it may be considerably faster than the passage of actual time. If time is supposed to elapse between events, the curtain should be dropped to separate them.

When a story is being changed into a play, the elements of the story must be clay in your hands, free to take many forms until you have found the one that is most dramatic. You will have to consider the sequence of events, paying particular attention to the placement of intermissions. It is possible to release the audience's attention for fifteen minutes only when they have become so interested in what is going to happen next that they are certain to come back to find out. Therefore, pull the curtain at a moment of crisis—when the characters' fates are hanging in the balance.

During the discussion that follows, we shall be thinking in terms of the three-act play, since that is the most common form in which modern plays are written. However, not all full-length plays have three acts. A century ago, most plays were in five acts. When those plays are performed today it is usual to have two intermissions, with two of the act breaks being treated as scene breaks. Another kind of play might run for a full evening without intermission. All classical Greek plays are of that variety. Such plays do not usually last longer than about an hour and a half, and therefore the audience does not get too tired. Two acts are fairly common in the modern theatre; most musicals and many comedies are written in two acts. Some plays are written in scenes rather than acts, and intermissions in them can be placed wherever the director thinks best. Although Shakespeare's plays are printed in five acts, they were originally performed without interruption and are today performed with intermissions wherever the director places them. They are designed as plays written in scenes, not acts.

Most of what will be said here about the three-act play can easily be adapted to other kinds of plays. The important thing to keep in mind is the basic rhythm of the play, whatever its act divisions. We have already mentioned the necessity for rhythmical increase and decrease of tension in a play, with the tension building throughout. If the tension does not decrease often enough, the audience will be unable to stand the play. If the tension is greater at the beginning than at the end, the audience will get bored. Shakespeare's greatest weakness as a playwright is that he sometimes reaches his point of greatest tension too early, which reduces our interest in the latter part of the play. No modern playwright could be successful making that kind of mistake.

The various parts of a plot's design have been given technical names, only three of which we shall discuss here. They are exposition, climax, and denouement. The exposition consists of that part of the play that lets the audience know whatever it needs to in order to get the action started. The climax is the point of greatest tension in the play. The denouement is the working out of the action at the end of the play so that all the plot elements are tied together and no loose ends are left hanging. The denouement gives the audience a feeling of satisfaction about the play, a feeling that it is over now. It is like the final cadence at the end of a symphony.

In addition to the main climax there are many minor climaxes or crises. These are points which the tension of the play reaches just before it is relaxed.

Let us now see in more general terms how the plot of a play is shaped for presentation on the stage. Consider the three acts of a three-act comedy:

BOY MEETS GIRL (Act One)
BOY LOSES GIRL (Act Two)
BOY GETS GIRL (Act Three)

If you wish to turn the above into a tragedy, reverse the action of Acts Two and Three.

In this three-act design we have two crises before the climax. In the first crisis, the boy meets and falls in love with the girl. We become interested in what will happen as a result of this love, and then our attention should be distracted and the tension dropped. (Note that by "crisis" we mean here anything that markedly increases the audience's interest in what is going on.) In the second crisis, the boy has lost the girl, and we are concerned that he should regain her affections. Again our attention should be distracted. In the third crisis, the final climax of the play, we observe the boy's various attempts to regain the girl until he is finally successful.

During the exposition of the play we are told what we need to know to interest us in this boy and this girl. Perhaps he is just getting over being in love with someone else. Perhaps she has been forbidden by her parents to marry, and is about to enter a convent. Such facts, whatever they are, help us to understand the characters and their situation. Here is a very difficult part of the play to write, for the foundation must be carefully laid so that the remainder of the action will not crumble. Since the audience has not yet developed an interest in what is happening, various means must be used to arouse that interest. Good dramatic technique does not allow one to begin by simply having the characters state the exposition. Rather, the play must begin with a situation that is exciting in itself, in the midst of which expository information can be released to the audience gradually. Modern audiences are clever enough to derive a clear picture of the dramatic situation from passing references to it.

At the end of the play comes the denouement. Here we learn that our boy and girl will live happily ever after. So far, so good. But we must also know what is to happen to the villain who stood between them, and what will become of the girl's other, disappointed, lover. The denouement, too, can be difficult to write, for if the action has not been carefully planned, loose ends are almost certain to be left. That is the point at which you will discover whether your play is really working. If it is very difficult for you to resolve the action, you may have to restructure large segments of your play and rethink many of its implications.

Now let us examine the means whereby tension may be relaxed. Only then can we best see how it can be built in the first place. The playwright's art involves a certain sleight-of-hand. While the audience is watching one thing happening, the playwright has been busily preparing something else. The action always contains a certain number of false "leads" by which the audience is led to expect something to happen that in fact does not. If everything goes as we expect, we quickly lose interest in the play. Thus, for example, a hero may be about to sweep to his revenge by killing the man who murdered his father, when suddenly he pauses, caught up in self-doubts stimulated by his mother's hasty remarriage. The action we were led to expect is prevented, and the tension reduced while our interest is aroused in a new and different situation. To reduce tension we must create a different source of tension. Let us examine how this works:

A: We must get into the castle, but the door is locked.

B: Let's batter down the door.

A: Yes, we'll do so. (They begin to batter down the door. The tension rises. We are waiting for the door to collapse, and wondering whether it will collapse.) I can't seem to break it down.

C: Here's a window open. We can climb in the window. (Beginning of new action, moving in an unexpected but quite reasonable direction. As yet, however, there is no conflict to build the tension.)

D: Yes, we'll do so.

E: I see a huge pit on the other side of this window. (Tension heightened—what can they do now?)

C: Let's see if we can find a board that will reach across the pit. (Reduction of tension as they search for the board.)

In the above example the tension is entirely of a physical nature: The attempt is being made to overcome a physical barrier. In no way do the characters of the five people involved in the action matter, except that they must continue to try to solve the problem. Most dramatic situations, however, depend on psychological tension. Tension is built in a play whenever two forces of any kind come into conflict with each other. The more psychological the nature of those forces the better, for our interest is in the spirit of man, which is potentially great, not in his body, which is nearly always weak. (What applies to drama, of course, does not apply to the football field or war or the movies, in which tension is often most effective when it is most physical.) We must have a character with whom we identify. We must see him wanting something. We must see him prevented from getting it. That creates tension.

"Now," you may ask, "how am I to keep on building tension for two hours when my subject is a boy and girl who are in love but separated?" That is one of the commonest of playwriting problems. The answer is surprisingly simple and almost infallible —create a subplot. Two or three subplots alternating with one another in a play can keep things moving along very nicely. Their mere alternation provides dramatic rhythm, and we have no need to deflect our main characters from what they are doing. Thus, we turn our attention from one group that is trying to batter down the door to another that is trying to climb in the window. Each of the subplots may build its action directly without release. But intermixing them provides distraction, and therefore release.

As you begin to think in such terms about your plot, perhaps you can begin to build diagrams for yourself that will help you to experiment with plot. Dividing each act of the play into about eight minor crises, see if you can keep shifting our attention just enough so that the play never loses it. You can do so even if the play has only two characters. That is accomplished by thinking of their topics of conversation as plot units and having them alternate effectively. Suppose that four main topics are to be covered in a scene. You might at first cover them thus:

AAAAAAAA BBBBBBBBB
CCCCCCCCC DDDDDDDD

But you will do better to interlard them as follows:

ABACDBACBDCADCB, etc.

Note that the interlarding forms no regular pattern. The pattern will be determined by the train of thought of the characters. Let us see how this works:

A {
WIFE: I'd like a new watch for Christmas.
HUSBAND: That would be a good thing, because you're always late, you know.
WIFE: It's not my fault I'm always late. I was brought up that way.
HUSBAND: You should learn to tell time. It's very annoying to people when you keep them waiting.
}

B {
WIFE: Oh, you always pick on me.
HUSBAND: I'm just trying to reform you, dear. It's for your own good.
WIFE: I think I know what's for my own good and what isn't. I should be allowed to lead my own life.
HUSBAND: With my guidance, someday you will.
}

C {
WIFE: Someday. I wonder what life will be like in the future. Maybe we won't have to work any more. We'll just sit around and let machines work for us.
HUSBAND (Sarcastically.): It sounds wonderful.
WIFE: I think it will happen. And then we won't have to worry about money any more.
HUSBAND: Life would be ideal.
}

Now, if these ideas are interlarded, we might get the following result:

C {
WIFE: I often wake up in the morning wondering what life will be like in the future.
}

A {
HUSBAND: Maybe that's what makes you so late getting up.
}

B {
WIFE: Do you have to pick on me like that?
}

C {
HUSBAND: It would be a wonderful thing to be able to lie around all day. I suppose the time will come . . .
}

B {
WIFE: Apologize, please.
HUSBAND: What for?
WIFE: For that nasty remark.
}

A {
HUSBAND: I'll make up for it by getting you a watch for Christmas. Then you won't always be late.
}

B { WIFE: Are you trying to reform me?

C {
HUSBAND: No. I'm trying to help you become the ideal mate for the future.
}

In the first version the tension builds for four lines, and then a new subject arises. In the second version the conversation seems more life-like, since the rhythm of tension and relaxation is much more subtle. There is less of a feeling that tension is built and then simply dropped, more of an undercurrent of tension that may crop out at any moment.

The more you experiment with the design of your play, the more subtle you will learn to make it. You can do just about anything you like, so long as you keep the rhythm developing and the overall tension mounting. These two requirements can never be ignored. Someday you will discover your own intuitive feeling for rhythm. You may benefit from the study of good plays, indicating in the text of the play where the major and minor crises come. Then see a production of the play (or listen to a recording) and determine whether the director has seen the crises as coming where you have indicated them.

Once your sense of rhythm is developed, it will become one of your surest guides as to how your play ought to be built.

Chapter IX

CREATING CHARACTERS
THAT SEEM ALIVE

Have you ever read an exciting book and then seen the movie and been disappointed? Part of the reason for your disappointment may have been that the characters did not look and behave as you had imagined them. The book had created in you certain expectations that the movie, being a different art form, could not fulfill.

In the same way a character in a play creates expectations in an audience, so that after a time an impression has been formed, and there are certain things that the character may *not* do. Your job in creating a believable character is threefold. First, you must create a character from whom an audience may expect certain things. Second, you must see to it that the character does not do those things the audience has come to feel he would not do. Third, you must nevertheless arrange it so that the audience is always somewhat surprised by what the character does do.

Every time a character performs an action, he creates an impression of himself. If you do not believe this, look around you. As you meet people, they quickly cause you to form impressions of them by what they do. With the passage of time, those impressions will change and deepen, but they begin to be formed almost immediately. Little things, such as whether people smile and the

way they smile, how they shake hands, how they look at you, how they dress, all give you impressions that you take rather seriously. Just so, a character on the stage cannot do anything without causing the audience to form an impression of him. You must see to it that the impression that is formed is helpful to you. Let us see first how it might not be:

> FIRST GENTLEMAN: You do not
> meet a man but frowns: our bloods
> No more obey the heavens, than our
> courtiers
> Still seem as does the king.
> SECOND GENTLEMAN: But what's
> the matter?
> FIRST GENTLEMAN: His daughter,
> and the heir of's kingdom, whom
> He purpos'd to his wife's sole son, (a
> widow
> That late he married) . . .

Once you have figured out what these opening lines from Shakespeare's *Cymbeline* mean, you have also figured out that the characters who speak them have been put on the stage solely to inform the audience of what has happened before the play begins. Immediately all interest in them as people vanishes. How they feel about what they are saying does not matter in the slightest. They will soon disappear from the action, and the story will begin.

Contrast those unimaginative opening lines with these from *Macbeth:*

> FIRST WITCH: When shall we three meet again—
> In thunder, lightning, or in rain?
> SECOND WITCH: When the hurly-burly's done,
> When the battle's lost and won.
> THIRD WITCH: That will be ere the set of sun.

Those characters immediately tell you something about themselves. They prefer to meet in foul weather. They seem to be watching over the commotion of the world. They seem impartial and paradoxical in their feelings. They seem able to predict what will happen when. They seem to know one another very well and to have a mutual understanding of their purposes. Already we have a clear expectation that they will *not* do certain things. Shakespeare has been careful that before he tells us anything about what has happened or will happen in his play, he has aroused our interest in the character to whom it is happening. The moral is, make sure that the audience does not think your characters are saying things merely because you want them to.

What does it mean to make a character speak as *he* wants to? It means identifying yourself with him so completely that you are experiencing the events in the play as he would experience them. You will not be able to do that until you develop a feeling for his way of life that you can recognize and produce in yourself whenever you are writing a line for him.

How does one arrive at such feelings? That is a very subtle question. Each person has a style that characterizes him and that permeates everything he does, from the inflections of his voice to his handwriting. It gives a particular quality to his emotions and his thought. One person can know another's style of feeling only indirectly, through observation. As you watch another person you may note many details of his behavior, such as how he moves, how he speaks, or what kinds of things he talks about. Perhaps as you are watching him you will find that suddenly all the details you have observed fit together in a total pattern, so that you no longer are noticing anything in particular, but are having a general feeling of what it is like to be that person. The feeling you are having is called empathy. It is something you have experienced many times. As you watch a boxing match you sense how each of the boxers feels as he strikes his opponent and is struck in return. That is empathy of the simplest, most basic kind. Empathy is a skill that can be developed through practice, but it is something that all human beings experience to some degree.

Once you have become conscious of your potential to empathize with another person, you may become able to assume the styles of others at will. Perhaps you can do impersonations of friends or movie stars or public figures. When you do, you adjust your inner mechanism so that it assumes the style that typifies that person.

If you are an actor, you develop the ability to empathize with people you have not seen, but rather have created in your imagination. You say things not as you yourself would say them, but as some person you have imagined would do so. The playwright must go one step further. He must in his imagination become an actor who makes up his own lines. But he must be not one actor, but many, and he must switch from character to character as he writes. If you are merely writing words, your characters have little chance of coming to life. You must write as a result of feeling or experiencing a character. Do not think, however, that you must be able to do impersonations or act well on the stage to be a playwright. Many playwrights can hear the way a character speaks in their imagination without actually being able to speak aloud in the same way.

How is a playwright to discover the feeling a character has about himself? There is only one answer: through trial and error. As you begin to write dialogue, you will write only words. Then, slowly and in flashes, will come hints of empathy. Characters will spring to life for a few moments and then fade away. As you continue to write, the characters will keep coming back more and more frequently, but each time seeming a bit altered. Gradually you will discover your characters, and then they will begin to tell you what your play is to contain. They will want to do some things and refuse to do others. You must let them have their way, or you will only end by ruining your play.

An obstacle arises once you have found your characters, and that is that you have already written a substantial amount that has formed impressions, many of them false. Those you will have to change. That means you must know when your characters are being themselves and when they are not. Time and again in the dialogue you have written they have been lost or changed, and you must try to recapture them. You will have to learn to read with the same empathy you use when you write, and to sense when the character is behaving in a way that is wrong for him.

It may help you to understand how this works if you take a scene from a good play that you like and rewrite it from memory. Then read over your version of the scene, putting aside the original, and try to feel what is wrong with what you have written. Revise the lines, gradually trying to get them to sound as they should coming from the characters as you feel them. Then go back and compare your version with the original. What touches are particularly good in the original? Are any of your revised lines as good as, or better than, those in the original?

The exercise can be adapted for use by a group. Play a recording of a scene from a play. Then have members of the group act out the scene from memory. Record what they do and play it back to them. Let them listen critically for lapses of character and try to improve what they have done the next time. Keep working on the scene without reference to the original until it becomes rather polished. Then compare the recorded words spoken by members of the group with the words contained in the original play.

Another exercise that might be helpful would be to collect several rather poor translations of a play originally written in a foreign language. Compile a new translation of your own by taking the best lines from each version and rephrasing them even further, until you get the feeling that the characters are talking naturally and with their own individual styles.

If you read a foreign language well, you might try obtaining a translation into that language of a play originally written in English. Translate it back into English as best you can; then compare your translation with the original.

What you are doing is, again, a little like working with clay. You are discovering forms that you like and that seem to fit together into consistent patterns. Just as a character made of clay may seem as lifelike in his own way as a real person, or may seem entirely wrong and inconsistent with himself, so the character you are creating in dialogue may eventually find himself and seem absolutely right.

This concept might be applied in a group improvisation exercise. A painting or a piece of sculpture representing a particularly striking personality is shown to the group. Each member of the group then attempts to act out a solo scene, playing the character represented in the art work. The group then discusses which of the characterizations has seemed best, and why. One purpose of such an exercise is to establish a connection between physical appearance, as captured by the artist, and personality. The playwright must visualize his characters physically and must sense that character is partly determined by physical nature. He must be able to describe the physical appearance of each character, not in so much detail that an actor cannot be found to play the part, but enough so that the director has some guidance in casting the play. The more the group works with the above exercise, the more the relationship between physical nature and character will seem to make sense.

Another group improvisation exercise might be based on a musical theme that has a particularly striking character. Themes representing characters are sometimes used in films, and students of Wagnerian opera are familiar with the leitmotifs associated with particular characters or ideas in the opera. In this exercise, the members of the group should listen to a theme and then, working individually, try to base a character on that theme. Music represents the action of the spirit, and it is interesting to try to translate that action into personality.

We have observed that the playwright must prevent his characters from doing those things that the audience senses they would not do. That necessity makes great demands on the playwright as he is revising his play, since he is likely to find many lines in which he has lost his concentration on a character and allowed that character to behave in a way that is inconsistent with what has been previously established about him. It is impossible to suggest any rules for determining when a character is thus out of focus. One must develop a firm enough feeling for the character to sense when it is happening. There is a game that helps to develop that sense. Two or three members of a group read a scene from a play that is not familiar to the group as a whole. After they have read a page or two of the scene in order to establish a feeling for the char-

acters involved, they make changes here and there, making up lines to replace or insert between the ones in the play. Members of the audience try to spot the changes. If a member of the audience thinks he has heard a made-up line, he raises his hand. He then must explain why he thinks the line is not part of the original play. Other members of the group may challenge him, arguing that it is. A player who correctly identifies a changed line gets five points. A player who correctly refutes another player's argument by proving that a line has not been changed gets ten points. If a player says that a line has been changed and it turns out that it has not, he loses two points. If he challenges another player and turns out to be wrong, he loses five points. The winner is the player who has accumulated the most points by the time the scene is completed.

Let us now consider our third problem, that of making the character not only right but a little surprising as well. Consider the following dialogue.

> FIRST MAN: Hey, man, what's happening?
> SECOND MAN: Eh, what?
> FIRST MAN: Don't wig me out, man.
> SECOND MAN: Oh, I say, bloody ridiculous your talking that way.
> FIRST MAN: Say, are you ever out of it, man!
> SECOND MAN: Jolly good of you to put it that way, what?

These characters are stereotypes. Once we have caught on to the style in which they speak we know more or less what to expect, and they will never do anything surprising. If in a relationship with another person one always knows what to expect, the relationship, though it may be perfectly good in other respects, is not very interesting. One likes the feeling of discovering new things about other people. In a play, the discoveries that might take place between real people during a lifetime must be made in the space of two hours. They are much more concentrated, and not a moment may pass that does not reveal something new.

Let us make clear the distinction between making a character do what he would not do and making him do what is unexpected. Whenever a real person behaves in a way we do not expect, he does so by revealing some facet of his personality of which we had not previously been aware. Everyone has many diverse sides to his personality that are reflected in various situations and relationships. Similarly, it is important that a character in a play continually reveal the various sides of his personality. That is how we get to know him. If he is a static character, he does not change his basic personality; he merely reveals it ever more deeply. If he is a dynamic character, the changes that occur in his basic character as a result of the events in the play throw additional light on what he was like before the change occurred. Most dramatic characters are static. There is no time for them to reveal themselves in depth, and change as well. Often, however, the most important character is dynamic.

How is one continually to reveal the varying aspects of character while at the same time advancing the plot? Fortunately, the two things go together very well. If we have been faithful to the idea that character *is* plot, we shall be able to advance the plot while at the same time expressing the character's reactions to it. Let us see how this works by moving from dialogue that reveals merely plot to dialogue that reveals plot and character simultaneously.

MURDERER: I'm going to kill you.
VICTIM: Why?
MURDERER: You have seduced my wife, stolen my money, and destroyed my reputation.
VICTIM: That isn't true.
MURDERER: It is true, and now I shall kill you. (*The murderer shoots, and the victim dies.*)

There is enough plot in the above dialogue to fill a whole play, if, indeed, not more than enough; but it is totally devoid of character. Let us try to breathe a little life into it:

MURDERER: Say your prayers.
VICTIM: Why?
MURDERER: I wouldn't want you to die without a chance at heaven.
VICTIM: Die? You make me laugh.
MURDERER: You don't think I'm serious, do you?
VICTIM: A joke's a joke. Now let's . . .
MURDERER: I mean it. I'm here to kill you.
VICTIM: Why could you possibly . . .
MURDERER: You know why.
VICTIM: Of course I don't. There couldn't possibly be any reason. Why, you and I have always been best friends.
MURDERER: You're trembling, aren't you? You're afraid to admit I might know the truth.
VICTIM: Don't be silly. What? Have you gone insane? I can't believe it. Look . . .
MURDERER: You didn't count on Jane feeling sorry for me, did you?
VICTIM: Jane? Jane wouldn't . . .
MURDERER: Wouldn't what?
VICTIM: Oh, nothing.
MURDERER: You stole Jane from me, and you know it, you swine. Furthermore, it was you who robbed me of every cent I had.
VICTIM: No! No!
MURDERER: Take one last look at this face. It's the last human face you'll ever see.
VICTIM: My God! I think you're serious!

MURDERER: You didn't think I'd find out, did you? That's why you pulled the wool over my eyes for so long . . . (*The murderer shoots, and the victim dies.*)

In the above scene, the characters react to the same situation a little differently with each line. That is because both the characters and the situation have been developed more fully. Our interest lies not so much in the killing as in the changing reactions to it of the two characters. That is not to say the second version makes a good scene. The characters have not yet been found; their reactions are poorly conceived and melodramatic. The situation itself has not yet been fully thought out. But the characters do reveal new facets of themselves by revealing new facets of the situation. The characters are on the way to discovering themselves.

As an exercise, try writing a scene in such a way that only plot is conveyed. Then rewrite it in several ways as it would be acted out by several different characters. Adapting this exercise to a group, give all the members of the group a copy of the same scene, written so that plot only is conveyed. Then have the members of the group act out the scene, creating characters as they do so. Each version of the scene should be acted with characters who clearly differ from those of the previous versions. After each version is acted, the whole group should discuss the characterizations that were conveyed, trying to determine whether the actors communicated the personality traits they had in mind.

Character achieves its fullest realization when it has expressed a moment of drama that seems somehow absolutely right. Such brief moments often become forever afterward identified with the character who expresses them, as when Shylock cries out, "My daughter, O, my ducats"; or Falstaff remarks, "The better part of valour is discretion"; or Willy Loman in Miller's *Death of a Salesman* betrays his anxiety with, "The woods are burning, boys." One wishes to feel that, given the character and the situation, what is being said is not merely what might be said, but rather the best that could possibly be said. In his preface to *Saint Joan,* Shaw wrote that he had represented three of his characters as saying "the things they actually would have said if they had known what they were really doing." But of this matter of rightness we shall have more to say when we come to the subject of dialogue.

What, then, can be said of the ways in which characters interact with one another? A good play and a symphony have much in common. In a symphony the main themes and their developments are passed about among the various instruments and given a distinct character by each. There should be as much difference between the characters in a play as there is between the instruments of the orchestra. Each should have his own way of stating and relating to the action, and the various ways should be unique and not interchangeable. Just as the instruments of the orchestra are seldom sounded alone, but usually appear in harmony with one another, so the characters in a play are seldom alone, but usually in conversation with, and relation to, other characters. We shall now examine some of the unspoken things (conscious and unconscious) that occur between characters when they are together. Let us conceive of these things in the form of the following system:

I feel _____ about myself.
I feel _____ about you.
I feel that you feel _____ about me.
I feel that you feel _____ about yourself.
I feel that you perceive that I feel _____ about myself.
I feel that you perceive that I feel _____ about you.

Thus, when a character says to another, "How are you?" he might be thinking the following:

I feel like a little shrimp.
I feel he is a big bully.
He thinks I am a little shrimp.
He thinks he's pretty hot stuff.
He thinks I don't think much of myself.
He thinks I think he's pretty hot stuff.

So far, this seems simple enough. But now suppose that the other character, as he replies, "I'm fine, how are you?" is really thinking:

I'm just a poorly educated slob.
He's a snob about his intelligence.
He thinks I'm not very smart.
He thinks he's pretty hot stuff.
He thinks I think I'm a pretty good athlete.
He thinks I don't appreciate his education.

It is fairly common in real life for people's reactions to one another to fail to coincide in this way. It is out of such failure that drama is often made.

Consider the following dialogue:

FIRST SPEAKER: How are you?
SECOND SPEAKER: I'm fine. How are you?
FIRST SPEAKER: Just fine.
SECOND SPEAKER: That's good. Would you like some tea?
FIRST SPEAKER: That would be very nice, thank you.

So far, nothing has indicated that there is any tension or misunderstanding between the two characters. Partly for that reason they have not given any indication that they are characters at all. Let us try to create confusion between them:

FIRST SPEAKER: How are you?
SECOND SPEAKER: (*Sullenly.*) Just superb!
FIRST SPEAKER: Anything wrong?
SECOND SPEAKER: Oh, no! Why should there be?
FIRST SPEAKER: I just thought . . .
SECOND SPEAKER: Skip it. Have some tea.
FIRST SPEAKER: Well—all right . . .

Nothing in the language is striking as yet, but the tension in the situation is clear now; that is, the scene has become more dramatic. The second speaker has made the first uneasy and has apparently intended to do so. The first, however, does not have the courage to pursue the matter, and is drawing his own conclusions about what is wrong with the second. We will need more dialogue before we know what those conclusions are, but we already know that the first and the second speakers would not agree in their perception of each other. The first would probably say that the second was rude and insensitive, while he himself was attempting to show concern. The second, on the other hand, would describe the first as tedious and prying, and would describe himself as justifiably irritated.

Let us now consider the special language, or tone, that needs to be associated with each character if the play is to be orchestrated. We shall try to add to the scene we are writing so that our two speakers have distinctly different tones:

FIRST SPEAKER: How are you?
SECOND SPEAKER: (*Sullenly.*) In ecstasies.
FIRST SPEAKER: Anything wrong?
SECOND SPEAKER: Nary a smidgen.
FIRST SPEAKER: I just thought . . .
SECOND SPEAKER: Trouble not your thinking machine. Would you partake of some tea?

FIRST SPEAKER: Well—all right . . .

Now the two are using language differently. But the effect is a little like a duet between a flute and a tuba. The difference is too great, and not the sort of thing that can be sustained for very long. The first speaker's speech is purely conventional and the second's anachronistic. Let us get them closer, but keep them distinct.

FIRST SPEAKER: How goes?
SECOND SPEAKER: (*Sullenly.*) Just peachy-keen.
FIRST SPEAKER: You got probs?
SECOND SPEAKER: Oh no, nothing like that.
FIRST SPEAKER: Pardon me for living.
SECOND SPEAKER: That's okay. Have some tea.
FIRST SPEAKER: Sure, why not?

The colloquial way each of the two expresses himself conceals much of the feeling. It would be hard to act these lines without expressing in them considerable irony. The characters are beginning to become involved in a relationship that may challenge both of them.

You will probably not wish to analyze the relationships between your characters too closely—certainly not while you are actually writing. But if you occasionally observe in yourself and in literature the ways in which people misinterpret one another's attitudes, you will begin to sense more clearly when your characters are relating to one another as human beings, and when they are merely mouthing the words the playwright insists on giving them.

The thoughts that lie unspoken beneath the words of the dialogue have been called the subtext. It must be constructed in the actor's imagination from the clues contained in the dialogue. The actor must know at any given moment just what the character is thinking about what he is saying. It might be instructive for you to read a play in which the subtext has actually been written out. In Eugene O'Neill's *Strange Interlude* it is spoken by the characters as "asides" to the audience.

Something else lies beyond the actual spoken words that might be called the supertext. Whereas the subtext is the character's moment-by-moment awareness of what is happening, the supertext contains those things that are always true of the character, and the clues to it are in the style in which he speaks and the kind of reactions that he has. Thus, always running through a play are three separate kinds of awareness: the character's general nature, as perceived by himself and by others (the supertext), his immediate behavior in a situation, as perceived by himself and others (the dialogue), and his experience as perceived only by himself (the subtext).

In opera it is sometimes true that all three kinds of awareness are simultaneously presented to the audience. The words that the characters sing represent their actions as perceived objectively. The notes that they sing provide the supertext, and the notes that the orchestra plays provide the subtext, in addition to commenting on the situation in general. If you are sensitive to music, you might try listening to a scene from an opera several times until you are very familiar with it. Then try to write out the supertext and the subtext of the scene in words. If the words that you have written have behind them the feeling that the music conveys, and if you can relate that feeling to the experience of characters in real life, you are well on the way to understanding how much feeling a playwright must have for his characters beyond what he actually puts down on paper for them to say.

Once one has been working with a character for a while, one of the best ways to crystallize one's thinking about that character is to fill out a questionnaire, answering as many of the questions as you can from the character's point of view. In the process of thinking of answers to the questions, you will discover many new things about your character that should be useful in the development of the play. Following are sixty questions that may prove useful in this regard. Do not feel that you have to answer all of them; merely investigate those that seem most helpful.

CHARACTERIZATION QUESTIONNAIRE FORM

1. List five things you like very much.
2. List five things you dislike very much.
3. Did you have a happy childhood?
4. Describe the incident in your childhood that you think most affected you.
5. How do you feel about your mother?
6. How do you feel about your father?
7. What are your favorite hobbies?
8. What person do you think has influenced you the most?
9. How do you feel about sex?
10. What is your religion?
11. How important is religion to you?
12. What are your politics?
13. How important are politics to you?
14. What is your philosophy of life?
15. If you had a million dollars, how would you spend it?
16. What do you like to do on a vacation?
17. How do you feel about the way you usually spend your day?
18. Have you any medical difficulties?
19. What kind of education did you have, and how did you feel about it?
20. How do you think other people react to you as a person?
21. What are you proudest of?
22. What are you most ashamed of?
23. How do you feel about food?
24. What do you dream about?
25. What makes you feel good?
26. What do you try hardest to avoid?
27. How do you react to the current world situation?
28. What one person had the greatest effect on you as a child?
29. How athletic are you?
30. How methodical are you?
31. What are your chief taboos?
32. How much traveling have you done?
33. Describe a situation in which you feel you have behaved courageously.
34. Do you see yourself as a self-centered person?
35. Do you see yourself as a loving person?
36. Do you see yourself as a popular person?
37. Do you see yourself as potentially having an important influence in the world?
38. What is the purpose of man?
39. How artistic are you?
40. How do you feel about money?
41. What are your plans for the future?
42. How idealistic are you?
43. How realistic are you?
44. How successful are you?
45. Name the five things that you most often object to in other people.
46. Name the five things that you most object to in yourself.
47. How gullible are you?
48. How intelligent are you?
49. Do you believe that the end justifies the means?
50. How attractive are you physically?
51. What do you worry about most?
52. Do you know of anything worth dying for?
53. What experiences led you to this conclusion?
54. What makes life worth living for you?
55. What is the difference between good and evil?
56. What kind of person would you most like to be?
57. What ideas in the history of the world should be forgotten?
58. Which changes now taking place in the world should be encouraged, which resisted?
59. What ideas now popular in our society do you consider potentially dangerous?
60. What do you consider to be worth knowing?

Chapter X

DEEPENING THE IMPLICATIONS

Your play is not just a story, it is an experience; and the more meaning your play has, the more powerful it will be as an experience. We shall be concerned in this chapter with how the playwright goes about meaning more than he actually says.

The implications of a play may be deepened in four general areas. First, we shall consider the way in which irony adds to the superficial meaning of an action a second, somewhat contradictory, meaning. Out of the interplay between the two meanings will come a feeling that the drama has some of the complexity of real life. Second, we shall consider the need for avoiding the sentimental in serious drama, and show how this need can be met by preserving the consistency of the world the playwright must create as part of the background for the action. Third, we shall venture into the language of dreams long enough to develop the idea of symbolism, which is based on subconscious but universal human drives. Such language, which pervades myth and ritual throughout human history, is also to be found in the greatest drama; and it can be used quite consciously by the ambitious playwright as a means of deepening the psychological im-

pact of his play. Finally, we shall investigate the concept of action as distinct from plot and show how a play can be made up of a variety of related, or analogous, actions. The latter investigation will show the playwright how he can unify several apparently quite separate subplots and characters into a single well-organized play.

Let us begin by considering the function of irony in giving power to one of the greatest dramatic tales ever written.

Once upon a time there lived in the city of Corinth a young man named Oedipus. Oedipus was a very proud and rash fellow, and when it happened that he was told that he was not the son of his father, he wanted to know whether he had been told the truth. He went to the oracle at Delphi, and the oracle gave him no answer to his question, but told him instead that someday he would kill his father and marry his mother. In great fear Oedipus left his home in Corinth and journeyed to a foreign city. When he came to a place where three roads meet, he fell into a dispute with another man as to who might pass first. In anger he killed this man and those who traveled with him. Then he came to the city of Thebes. The King of Thebes had died, and Oedipus learned that whoever could guess the riddle of the Sphinx might become his successor. "What walks on four legs in the morning, two in the afternoon, and three in the evening?" asked the riddle. "Man!" cried Oedipus. "Man, who crawls when he is an infant, walks upright in his maturity, and uses a cane in old age." Having answered the riddle, Oedipus ascended the throne and married Queen Jocasta, widow of the former king.

For many years Oedipus reigned in prosperity. Then a blight fell upon the land, and Oedipus learned that in order to appease the gods he must find the murderer of Laius, the former king. His inquiries as to the murderer led him to the realization that the stranger he had killed where three roads meet had been King Laius. He further learned that his wife Jocasta had once borne King Laius a son, but that when it was prophesied that that son would kill his father and marry his mother, he had been sent off to the mountains to die. But the shepherd who had been charged with executing the child had taken pity on him, and Oedipus was carried safely to the land of Corinth. Thus Oedipus learned that in trying to escape his fate he had run directly toward it.

We have already observed, in Chapter VII, that irony results from a contradiction between what happens and what is expected to happen. The story of Oedipus provides an example of the greatest, most tragic kind of irony, for in it the finest efforts of a great man prove inadequate to deal with the demands made on him by his fate. We leave the theatre sensing the greatness and the limitations of rational man at the highest levels of his aspiration.

We shall now consider some means by which irony may be built into a plot idea so that the plot may be deepened and made

more relevant to the eternal conflict between human freedom and limitation. The key to irony might be said to lie in the imaginative use of a single word: "but." When two parts of a statement directly contradict each other and the statement is a powerful one, high drama may result:

"Oedipus tried to escape his fate, but he ran directly toward it."

"Macbeth thought he would be happy being king, but he made himself miserable."

"Willy Loman thought almost everyone liked and respected him, but almost no one did."

We have earlier said that a good plot may be originated by placing the word "because" between two unrelated statements. But a good plot does not in itself contain irony. If we find a way to combine the "because" formula we considered earlier with the "but" formula we are considering now, we may be able to make the plot much more dramatic and powerful. In considering plot alone, we are moving in only one direction. We begin at the beginning and proceed through the middle until we come to the end. We have a series of events, each of which might be diagrammed as follows:

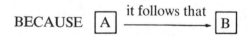

Dramatic irony, however, introduces what might be thought of as an underlying countermovement, and our diagram may now be expanded as follows:

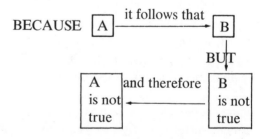

Expressing the story of Oedipus in these terms, we might get for one of its parts:

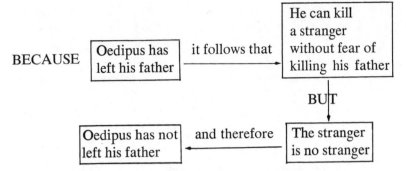

That, of course, is only one of several dramatic ironies the story of Oedipus contains.

Let us now return to our story about the husband and wife, which might be diagrammed thus:

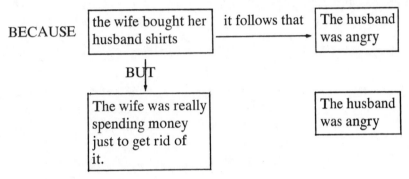

ironic set. Moreover, the two versions of the second event are again the same. If the wife could somehow appear to be turning against her husband when in fact she was not, the impact of the plot would be much greater.

Comparing the two versions of the second event, we find that they are the same. Furthermore, there is nothing to connect the ironic version of the wife's behavior with anything in the husband's, nor is there a sequence running counter to the sequence of the original set of events, as in the Oedipus story. Lack of any balancing force on the ironic level of the plot means that this version of our play is inherently weak.

Again:

We must be careful, however, not to use irony for its own sake. Dramatic irony, to be effective, must point out some subtle truth in human relations.

It is often difficult to express the dramatic irony of a play in a way that shows we really understand what the play is driving at. That is because in some plays the dramatic irony is not so much in the plot structure as in the reactions of the characters to what is happening. Suppose we try to solve the prob-

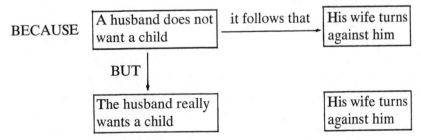

Again, there is no counter-movement between the original set of actions and the

lem with the above plot by grouping together the two events now being considered separately and developing a set of character reactions to set off against them. The result might be as follows:

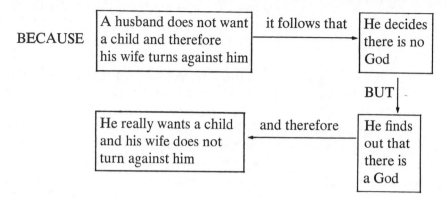

We have now established a connection between the actions in the second set, and developed a sequence there which runs counter to the sequence of the first set, just as in the story of Oedipus. Moreover the irony in our story will be more intense and perhaps more believable if the consequences of the first set of events are not eliminated by what happens in the second set. Consider what happens if the story is told in two ways:

First: A husband, having been exposed to radiation, does not want a child. His wife turns against him. He becomes morose, decides there is no God, and attempts suicide. His wife finds his suicide note, but manages to save him. He interprets this as an intervention by God, and his faith is revived. Overcome with emotion, he tells her the cause of his misery. She replies that she loves him even though they cannot have children, and had rejected him only because he had rejected her.

Second: A husband, having been exposed to radiation, decides he cannot have any children. He is a deeply religious person who loves his wife very much but does not tell her of his affliction because he cannot bear the thought of the suffering it will cause her. He therefore takes refuge in his religious commitments as a reason for not having children. She, feeling rejected, becomes pregnant by another man. When he finds out, his faith is shattered, and he murders the other man. The victim, while dying, tells him that the wife had been motivated only by a desire for children. He further says that he regards the husband as a man of little faith, and calls upon God to forgive him. The husband, filled with remorse, comes to feel that his faith had been superficial, and that he had never really trusted God. He decides to face his wife with all that has happened and to ask her forgiveness. When he does so, she says that she still loves him and has turned away only because of his apparent lack of love for her. They are reunited in love, but realize that the justice of God demands his execution for the murder he has committed.

At the end of the second version there is intense dramatic irony, since the husband's actions have committed him to one direction, whereas his understanding has taken a different direction. We find that an action that is irreversible, committed with knowledge that is later reversed, produces intense dramatic irony.

What, then, of the desire many people express for a happy ending? It might seem that deepening the dramatic irony for its own sake would be a somewhat sadistic approach to the business of entertainment. To a certain extent, that is true. When the business of the theatre is primarily to entertain, a happy ending can be very satisfying. When the theatre goes deeper and attempts to hold the mirror up to nature, the problem is not so simple. Life is full of situations that cannot be easily resolved. Within the context in which they occur, some of them are, perhaps, insoluble problems. Others might be resolved if their nature were more fully understood. When the theatre is reflecting life as it is, its purpose is to help us better understand the problems with which we live. If the theatre suggests that a problem that strikes at the root of human nature can be resolved easily, it is misleading us, and creating false dreams that are not good for us. A serious play may end happily only when the problems the characters must face really can be fully resolved within the situation the play represents. Given a particular situation and a particular set of characters, it may be literally impossible to have a happy ending. To give such a play a happy ending would be to make it sentimental in the worst sense of the word.

A play becomes sentimental whenever it asks an audience to feel emotions that have not been prepared for in the structure of the characters, the situation, or the language. Because the playwright wishes the audience to respond emotionally to what happens on the stage, it is very hard to avoid being sentimental. Every bit of emotion that an audience feels must somehow be justified through action.

You may well ask what is wrong with sentiment. Under certain conditions, nothing is wrong with it. Perhaps the most imaginative product of American theatre is the Broadway musical, which often uses sentiment in the good sense of the word. Musicals are fun to watch. They help one to escape from the harsh realities of daily existence into a world of dreams where love is always young, where older people fade adoringly into the background, and where villains, being nothing more than villains, must always lose and always be punished. The music is pretty, gay, and sometimes memorable. The plot exists for the sake of the songs, and no one expects to take it very seriously.

In drama without music, however, the sentimental is often fatal. In order to respond to an emotion, the audience must share it, or at least be made to see some reason for it. Because of their overexposure to the mass media, theatre audiences are becoming extremely sophisticated and are likely to laugh if the playwright has something happen merely for the sake of playing on the emotions.

Let us understand that a playwright has certain godlike powers. He can have his characters do anything he wants them to. But he also has the responsibility of creating a world in which they can live according to his laws. The world that the playwright creates consists of all the conditions under which his characters exist—their environment, their background, their opportunities, their kind and degree of reality. These conditions must be uniform throughout the play, and they must be communicated to the audience as quickly as possible. A sentimental ending to a serious play violates conditions that have been clearly established earlier in that play, conditions that determine the nature of the world in which that play's characters exist. A sentimental musical is acceptable because the kind of world in which the characters live is clearly understood at the outset.

Although the world of the play is created predominantly of external things, it also contains materials that lie within the characters. This is a matter partly of personal background and partly of innate temperament. The following sequence illustrates one way in which the world that lies within the characters might be inconsistent with itself.

A: Ah feel lak sich a fool.
B: Oh, that's too bad. What's the matter?
A: 'Tis some vile fiend possesses me.

A's first speech establishes an internal world represented by a particular dialect. His second speech is inconsistent because it represents a different world, or culture. He must be consistent in his use of dialect and of the cultural behavior patterns that are associated with it.

The sentimental, then, arises from the violation of established conditions. It may also arise from the failure to create such conditions to begin with. If the playwright has been careless in establishing the conditions under which his characters live, he will probably lapse into the sentimental rather frequently. Let us consider the following sequence:

A: Good evening, Mrs. X, how are you tonight?

B: Just fine, thank you.

A: You look dimly familiar. I think I've met you somewhere before.

B: Really?

A: Now that I think of it, you must be my long-lost aunt.

Such writing is very common among inexperienced playwrights. The dialogue does not violate anything in particular, because nothing has been established that can be violated. Rather, everything that happens does so merely because the playwright wants it to. It is perfectly acceptable for B to turn out to be A's long-lost aunt, but we must know many things about A and B before we can regard the discovery as an important one. The following are some of the questions this dialogue raises:

1. Who are A and B?

2. When did they last meet?

3. How did they feel about each other before they were separated?

4. Why were they separated?

5. How do they feel about each other when they first appear to be strangers to one another?

6. What, exactly, causes A to recognize B? (This must be specific, and it must be something the audience can see and recognize as clearly as A sees and recognizes it.)

7. In what ways will A's life be changed by his recognition of B?

8. What perfectly natural circumstances have brought A and B together? (We must feel that circumstance, not the playwright's whim, is responsible for the reunion.)

The above questions would not apply, of course, if the play is a deliberate parody of bad playwriting technique, and meant to be funny.

Aristotle, in *The Poetics,* the oldest piece of dramatic criticism that has come down to us, spoke of the impossible probable and the improbable possible (which we considered earlier), saying that the former is acceptable and the latter is not. An animated cartoon is an example of the impossible probable. It is impossible for animals to speak, but if they spoke as they do in animated cartoons, their conversations would probably follow the style represented in the cartoon. If, on the other hand, in a realistic play something important happens as a result of unlikely chance, one concludes that although it could happen in real life and is therefore possible, it has happened in the play only because the playwright wanted it to, and is therefore uninteresting.

In general, if you establish conditions under which your characters exist and have the characters behave consistently with those conditions, you should succeed in avoiding the sentimental. That will help you to gain your audience's sympathy and respect for your characters.

We have so far spoken of the world of the play as if it were something the playwright created entirely on a conscious level. That is true only to an extent. The world of the play establishes a framework within which the playwright can express an idea that is entirely his own and deeply felt. But often his point of view transcends that idea and goes deep into his personality, reaching many things of which he himself is unaware. The world is the world that the playwright sees. His point of view unconsciously unifies that world and, when he is writing well, focuses it upon the central idea he is trying to express.

It might seem strange to suggest that a playwright could express in a play things of which he himself is unaware. It is important to realize that that is so, and to understand something of how it works. Let us, therefore, talk briefly of the language of dreams and of myths, realizing that such symbolic language is to be found in the structuring of the world's greatest dramas.

Sometimes the ideas that pass through your dreams are clear and could be understood by anyone. If you were starving and dreamed you were eating a steak dinner, it would be obvious what desire was reflected in your dream. More often, however, dreams reflect ideas of which the dreamer is not consciously aware. Dreams are often made up of symbols—images that represent something more than themselves. For example, a house can be a dream symbol for a human body. Suppose I dream of a castle sitting between two ordinary houses. That might indicate my desire to be superior to those around me; that is, if I feel a strong sense of identity with the castle. When I awaken I may remember my dream, but unless I understand the symbolic language of dreams, I have no way of understanding its true meaning.

Much of the symbolism of dreams seems to be universal. People of all nations and all times whose dreams have been recorded have dreamed in many of the same symbols. The same symbols also are found in myths and fairy tales, though stories that are handed down through the ages may also have their origins in actual events. The same symbols can often be found, too, in works of art. Shakespeare's plays share many of their symbols with simple folk tales told during the Middle Ages in Europe, and also with stories told in lands as far away as China and Malay. It would seem that highly creative writers are sometimes so strongly influenced by their unconscious thoughts that they use the symbolism of dreams, a

symbolism whose meaning they cannot always fully understand. Let us consider an example of this.

Shakespeare's *Hamlet* deals with a prince who seeks revenge for the death of his murdered father. His uncle is guilty of that murder, but Hamlet has been unsure of his guilt. His only source of information has been the ghost of his father, who has appeared to him at midnight. Hamlet knows that the ghost may be a ruse of the devil rather than a true ghost, and he desires to put his uncle to the test. He therefore causes to be performed in his uncle's presence a play that contains the murder of a king by the same means that the uncle is reported to have used. His uncle reveals his guilt by his violent reaction to the play.

While Hamlet is gloating over the success of his detective work, a courtier named Polonius brings word that Hamlet's mother wants to see him. Hamlet's reply is a very strange one:

> HAMLET: Do you see yonder cloud that's almost in shape of a camel?
> POLONIUS: By th' mass, 'tis like a camel indeed.
> HAMLET: Methinks it is like a weasel.
> POLONIUS: It is backed like a weasel.
> HAMLET: Or like a whale.
> POLONIUS: Very like a whale.
> HAMLET: Then I will come to my mother by and by.

Hamlet has been pretending that he is insane so that people about the court will not realize he is spying on his uncle, and will not attempt to account for his actions. We can dismiss the above dialogue by saying that it is merely Hamlet's pretense of madness and his pleasure in making fun of Polonius. Or we can look into it more deeply.

Throughout the play Hamlet has been trying to make sense out of the world, but he has found that the values with which he has been brought up are not in accord with behavior in the court. On one level, then,

Hamlet is suggesting that trying to make sense out of what one sees around him is a little like trying to prove that a cloud has a certain shape. One can read into it anything he likes. Thus Hamlet's "madness" provides a clue to the problems that trouble him.

Let us go a step further. One finds, particularly among primitive peoples, a tendency to symbolize one's father in the form of an animal. The symbolism of the totem pole is a reflection of that tendency. Why is it that Hamlet sees only animals in the cloud at a time when his father is so much on his mind? It is almost as if the ghost of his father were appearing to him again, in symbolic form, to urge him on to his revenge. This idea is reinforced by the fact that Hamlet continually talks of his dead father in the play and has the feeling that he wishes him to move more quickly toward his revenge.

It is natural to wonder whether Shakespeare had all these things in mind when he wrote this passage. Probably he did not consciously think of them, but rather felt an identity with Hamlet's state of mind which was so strong that it contained these unconscious elements.

If you read Freud's *Psychopathology of Everyday Life,* you will understand that it is almost impossible to make a random remark without expressing in it some aspect of your unconscious thought. It is quite likely that when you have written a play you will have expressed in it many things of which you are not aware, but which many members of your audience could agree were there. Such an undercurrent of the unconscious in a play is an indication that the play has been sincerely written, though it must not be taken to mean that every word of the play is sacred and cannot be revised.

We said earlier that a play's point of view *may* be called its theme. Sometimes in a play a conflict exists between what a writer desires to express and what his unconscious mind desires to express. The great poet T. S. Eliot felt that Shakespeare had that sort of problem with *Hamlet,* and that the play was therefore an artistic failure. Whether or not Shakespeare had the problem, you might easily have it. It arises in this way:

Suppose I set out to write a play that demonstrates the truth of the statement, "Love of money is the root of all evil." That, I have decided, is my theme. I wish it to be my theme because I would like to believe that the statement is true. But let us say that I have a deep unconscious craving for money and power. In developing my play, I will consciously make my villain that character who most avidly pursues money. But because I secretly sympathize with him, he will grow increasingly attractive and do less and less of what I want him to in my play. At the moment when my fair damsel in distress is about to perish, I may discover that my villain rushes in to liberate her while my supposed hero is off in a church somewhere praying.

When that sort of thing happens, it becomes clear that a conflict exists between the conscious and the unconscious elements of my play, which may represent a conflict in my own personality. Somehow I must learn to know myself well enough to resolve that conflict. Otherwise an unfortunate thing will happen: My characters, held in the iron grip of my theme, will remain lifeless and inert, unwilling ever to take part in the action of their own accord. My play will become hopelessly intellectual and dull, and I will quickly lose interest in it.

I must learn to *feel* my thoughts so deeply that feeling and thinking are one. That means my play may have to go through many forms before I have found the right one. This is not surprising. Our conscious and unconscious thoughts do not work together easily. So much of what we say stems from what we think we ought to say, or what other people want us to say, that we do not easily find out what we really think. Too much rebellion is not thinking, either. The person rebelling is not so much acting on his own impulses as he is against someone else's. For example, the playwright brought up in a religious family who sets out to write a play attacking religion may be paying far more attention to the views that he is attacking than to his own alternatives to them. That can give his play a hollow, unconvincing quality. Therefore it is a good idea to make many varying plot outlines based on the same source until you have found the one that seems to you absolutely right in expressing what you are trying to say. Then, perhaps, you will have begun to feel your thoughts.

But let us not overemphasize the role of thought in a play. It must be there, of course, if the play is to have depth, but what one primarily feels in the play is *action*. The thoughts are expressed through the actions of the play. Every minute something must be happening. Yet it is surprisingly easy to write a very long play and not know what its central direction is. One can know what it is about and who the characters are, and one can have a number of diverse things happening in the play. But without an overall sense of what is happening, the other achievements have little value.

We shall see the problem most clearly if we try to state the action in the form of an infinitive phrase. The action of the play is expressed as "to _____." That means every character in the play is in some way involved in that action, either positively or negatively. The action of a murder mystery is probably "to find the culprit." Obviously the murderer himself will be trying to avoid being found, and will thus be involved in the action only in a negative sense (although in Agatha Christie's most popular plays, and in Sophocles' great thriller, *Oedipus Rex,* the murderer is, or appears to be, the one most active in his search for the culprit). What we do not need is a character who is in no way involved in the action, but is, rather, involved in some other, unrelated action. Such a character should be left out.

Before we learn to take this idea too literally, however, we must introduce the concept of *analogous action*. When a play has one or more subplots, the actions for each are not literally the same. Furthermore, we do not wish to see them duplicate one another. A murder mystery with a subplot should not contain a second murder mystery. It might, however, contain a scientist who is looking for a germ that is causing an illness. The actions of trying to find a murderer and trying to identify a germ are *analogous* in that they are similar enough to fall under the general heading of "to find the culprit." Before we develop any more fully the concept of analogous action, let us clarify what is meant by the term "action" in this context.

Action, as applied to drama, is a most abstract concept. It is a little like the spirit, or motivating force, of the drama. It moves the characters through the plot toward whatever goals they seek. Just as a body with no spirit would be a dead body, though it contain all the parts that a live body contains, so a plot with no action would be a dead plot, though it would appear at first glance to be no different from any other plot. Were we to sit through an actionless play, we should see things happening, but we should not only not know why they were happening, we should also have an almost instinctive feeling that no force was directing the events of the play, unifying them, moving them forward toward some end. The plot would appear completely haphazard.

A good example of a play that concentrates much more on action than on plot is Christopher Marlowe's *Tamburlaine the Great*. It depicts the efforts of a great warrior to conquer as much of the world as he can. Most of the play is an episodic recounting of victorious conquests. Few plot complications or complexities of character arise to draw our attention away from the main action.

That raises the important question of the difference between plot and action, for plot also concerns itself with what happens. The difference is that plot involves, as we have seen, cause-and-effect relationships, whereas action involves only a simple ongoing drive. A play that depicted a person walking down a street or reading a book would have an action, but certainly no plot, whereas a play that showed a group of characters each doing something entirely different because of something that was done to him would have plot but no action. In the best plays plot and action work so well together that they seem inseparable.

But, as we have said, action is often a very subtle thing; and it may be difficult to decide while watching a good play what the action is. Let us talk now more in terms of people.

Some people seem to drift through life without any sense of purpose, often getting themselves into trouble, often unhappy, often changing their sense of what is important. Such people seem to have poorly developed goals. One could say they have not yet decided what their main action in life is, or, to use a more contemporary phrase, what their "thing" is. Other people decide early what their goals are and pursue them rigorously and without ever wavering. These people may be said to have a clearly defined sense of the main action of their lives. But if that action is taken so literally that it is never veered from at all, the personality becomes rigid, and such a person derives little enjoyment from living.

Somewhere in between the two is the person whose life has purpose but whose actions, although all contributing to the accomplishment of that purpose, all seem very different from one another. That person has great subtlety in his thinking about the main action of his life.

Good plays have that same sort of subtlety. You feel that they are driving at something, that somehow all the actions in them are related; you feel a mounting sense of the urgency and direction of the play; but you might find it very difficult to put into words just what the play's action was.

The playwright who knows his action so well that he does not know it at all—does not ever think about it—is in a very fortunate position. He will sense what should or should not be in his play. But if your play does not seem to be going anywhere, seems aimless and purposeless, it may be that you need to think about its action. On the other hand, if it is so rigidly moving toward its conclusions that it lacks air and light and gives its characters no chance to breathe, then it is important to think about the action in more subtle terms.

Let us, therefore, examine several ways of looking at, thinking about, and transforming action. To begin with, one should be critical of the form in which the action is stated. It should not concentrate too much on particular details:

"to run a mile in eight minutes before breakfast in the presence of the Queen"

nor should it be too vague:

"to live well"

nor too narrow:

"to walk down the street" (though some surrealistic plays keep the action very narrow with great success).

But you may make it as broad as you like:

"to conquer the world" (Marlowe's *Tamburlaine*)

"to evolve into a higher species of man" (Shaw's *Back to Methuselah*)

It is very important that it strike fire to the playwright's imagination. He may wish to state it in colorful language:

"to desecrate corruption"
"to lubricate the jowls of the monster, jealousy"
"to conquer height"
"to shine through a glass darkly"

Stating the action in such a form might crystallize a feeling that one wishes to pervade the play. It is conceivable that work on a play could begin with the formulation of such a statement, but much more likely that a play that is about to be abandoned could suddenly spring to life once the action has been crystallized. That is because it is only after you have been experiencing your play for a while that you are likely to know what you want its total effect to be. An action imposed on a play from without, rather than allowed to grow naturally out of its characters and situations, would be as undesirable from the play's point of view as having to live one's life according to someone else's dictates. You need to find your play's action rather than impose it; and if your play is healthy enough, you may never need to know what it is.

But if you wish to loosen up your play, you may want to do some experimenting with analogies. State an action:

"to find the culprit"

Then list as many different forms that action might take as you can think of:

1. "to find the murderer"
2. "to identify a germ causing a disease"
3. "to find the bottleneck in a production line"
4. "to find what is upsetting my child"
5. "to find out what makes my friend dislike me"
6. "to find out why my friends are really my enemies"
7. "to find out why I am allergic to toads"
8. "to find out why we have been fighting over the very thing that draws us together"
9. "to find out why I have trouble communicating"

You would not want to crowd all of these things into one play, but in the process of making your list you will find that extending it continues to uncover possibilities, some of which will be useful to you. Shakespeare's *Hamlet*, for example, makes important use of numbers 1, 4, 6, and 9.

So far we have thought of the action in abstract terms. However, in a particular play it must have specific concrete manifestations. To make the action more concrete, you will want to work it into the materials with which you are dealing, the characters and the plot. Using the general action, "to find the culprit," try the following device: pretend that you are the culprit, and try to think of the many kinds of things you could do to upset the other characters.

poison their beer
make horrible faces at them
insult them
cut their telephone line
write anonymous letters to them

Now instead of being the culprit, be something that is associated with each of the things on your list:

poison
facial expressions
a cruel word
a strong wind
a peculiar kind of handwriting

Now go back to your original list and make the above culprits the object of the action:

1. "to find the poison used in my beer"
2. "to find the malice lying beneath a bland expression"
3. "to find what caused him to speak harshly to me"
4. "to predict the coming hurricane"
5. "to identify the handwriting used in this letter"

You will note that the list contains a number of rather specific actions, all of which are analogies to the main action. They need not be applied directly to your villain, but may relate to a number of other things in the play. Numbers 1, 2, and 3 are used in *Hamlet,* but far more specifically than the actions from the previous list. They help to define specific scenes and events.

In the process of experimenting with action, one needs to move in three separate directions. We have already considered finding additional analogous actions and making the action more specific and concrete. A third, seemingly contradictory, method is to make the action more abstract. That, of course, is in addition to the other two methods, and is used to add more dimensionality to the action. When the action is at its most abstract, we are dealing with the spirit of the play and the characters. It is in the area of abstraction that the great play is distinguished from the merely good. A good play is exciting to watch. One wishes to know what will happen next. But a great play gives one in addition the sense that what is happening somehow relates to all lives everywhere. It has what is called universality. That increases as the action becomes more spiritual, or, in other words, happens in the souls of the characters, rather than in the intricacies of the plot. Poisoning beer is a concrete action that complicates the plot, whereas poisoning someone's mind not only complicates the plot but involves complex character changes as well. Poison, facial expression, anonymous letters—these are concrete. They exist in a physical sense. Relationships, emotions, conditions of life —these are abstract. They exist in the mind.

In *Hamlet* the pursuit of the murderer is complicated by the fact that Hamlet feels "the time is out of joint." It is not only the murderer, but all the conditions of life in Hamlet's time that distress the prince. He sees the crime partly as a product of the general moral chaos in the midst of which he lives. His search, therefore, is not only for the culprit, but for the whole meaning of life. That is one of the reasons *Hamlet* is considered a great play, whereas an Agatha Christie murder mystery can be considered only a good play.

Let us look at the way in which some of the specific actions we have considered can be given abstract qualities:

{ poison their beer (concrete)
{ poison their minds (abstract)

{ make horrible faces at them (concrete)
{ make life seem ugly to them (abstract)

{ insult them (concrete)
{ make them doubt themselves (abstract)

{ cut their telephone line (concrete)
{ cut them off from love (abstract)

{ write anonymous letters to them (concrete)
{ distort their understanding of the world (abstract)

In each case the abstract action works directly upon the soul, whereas the concrete action may be responded to in a variety of ways depending on the condition of the soul. One can avoid drinking poisoned beer, but it is more difficult to avoid having one's mind poisoned. One can refuse to look at an ugly face, but there is no escape from an ugly life. Thus, with abstract action the characters are necessarily involved as total human beings, and the condition of their souls must become known to the audience.

Because drama works first on a physical level and only second on a spiritual one, it is most effective when the concrete and abstract are closely related. The relationship may be inverse or direct. It is common, for example, for a character to be blinded in a physical sense and to declare that he now has his sight, for when he had eyes he could not see (or understand the meaning of life). A character may somehow reveal his "true self" while taking off a mask or an article of clothing.

In realistic plays the emphasis will be on the concrete action, with the abstract somewhat vaguely sensed. In surrealistic and poetic plays the relationship is reversed. Characters will do specific things, but those things on a concrete level will seem to have little relation to the world we live in. On the abstract level, however, the actions will become quite precise in their meaning.

For example, if a man strangles his wife on the stage, the audience may be primarily, concerned with the characters involved and the events in their lives that led to the strangling. If the play is Shakespeare's *Othello,* one may or may not sense the abstract strangling of innocence by disillusionment. If, however, an unknown man strangles an unknown woman while crying out, "Wail, for the world's wrong!" we would see this rather clearly as an abstraction, and only with difficulty relate it to actual events that might occur.

The fact that realism gives predominance to the concrete and surrealism to the abstract in no way represents a value judgment. Each can produce works of art that are universal. Each approaches the same problem from a different direction.

It is possible that if you are deepening and enriching the action of your play, you will temporarily feel uncomfortable with what is happening to it. Do not despair. When you have worked for a while with the new actions that you are introducing, they will begin to feel at home in your play and fit into it more comfortably. As you continue working with the concept of action, you will sense more and more strongly how it makes possible diversity within unity.

We have considered four basic ways of deepening the implications of a play. They are: developing irony, justifying the actions so that the sentimental is avoided, using symbolism as a means of feeling the ideas, and considering the central action of the story. It may help to make these ideas more concrete if we now consider how they apply to the student-written scenes in Appendix A. You may wish at this time to read at least the first three of these scenes, as we shall now consider these three in turn with regard to the four techcniques we have discussed.

The first, by Sarah McClelland, deals with a young married couple who have a new baby and a nosy neighbor. The section of the opening scene that is printed here explores two basic ironies. The first is the young father's developing sense of the difference between himself and his baby. He feels the baby's extreme youth and consequently his own age. Yet he is unable to develop an approach to the baby that takes the difference into account. It is hard for him to relate to the baby except as to another adult. The second irony deals with the nosy neighbor's attempts to be helpful. Everything she does either irritates or creates a potential problem, or both. Mrs. Hackshaw is a well-conceived character whose potential for relating to the young couple in their developing lives is, in theatrical terms, enormous. That is largely because of the great difference between the way she perceives her own actions and the way the other characters perceive them. So far, we are dealing with two unrelated ironies, but at the end of the scene the author skillfully ties them together by using the first to defeat the second. The young father, realizing that he does not yet know how to take care of a baby, but that all of Mrs. Hackshaw's helpful hints will only confuse him more, uses his sense of inadequacy as a means of getting rid of her. We have thereby a third and much stronger irony, which derives from the union of the previous two.

The tone of the play does not allow us to take any of these ironies very seriously. It is a light comedy in which the father, at least, is very conscious of the absurdity of his own situation. We feel that when he says he thinks the baby is ugly he does not really mean that, but that he has seized on his feelings of frustration with the baby as a means of expressing his frustration with Mrs. Hackshaw. Several of the most basic issues of life are hinted at in this little scene, but they are touched very lightly and without malice —a welcome relief from much of the anger and intensity found so often in the theatre today.

The scene has neatly avoided being sentimental despite dealing with subject matter that might easily have been made so. It does so largely through the ironies we have already discussed, but also by the individual tone in which the characters talk. This is not just any married couple with a new baby and all the feelings that married couples are supposed to have for new babies. This is a family in which the wife is absent-minded enough to forget that she has to shop for the baby as well as for her husband, and in which the husband points this out not directly but with the humorous question as to whether "old man" rates peas and steak, a comment that goes straight to the heart of his difficulty in dealing with the baby. After only a few lines of dialogue the couple has made clear that their behavior will be their own, not behavior that is either idealized or sentimentalized.

It is in the area of feeling the ideas that the scene probably needs the most work. The play will have something to say about role playing. That is, the author is conveying her awareness that people go through life not so much doing what comes naturally to them as doing those things that their situation in life requires of them. Sometimes they do these things very ineptly, but they must nevertheless carry on with the role that life has assigned to them. This idea has been beautifully expressed in terms of character, but not so well in terms of physical action. One bit of stage business does express it, however. Jim gives his baby a pacifier and then comments on how the baby is already establishing a pattern that will continue throughout his life. The author needs to search for more such moments that will make us feel the reality of her theme.

The action of the scene might be expressed as "to do what is expected of me." In that sense the scene is perfectly unified, since all of the characters are struggling with the problem. Even the baby fits in, as the father succeeds in getting him to stop crying and then speculates on his other behavior. One reason that Jim's assertion that the baby is ugly is so effective is that he has for the moment given up the attempt to do what is expected of him and has done the exact opposite, thereby beautifully accomplishing his purpose.

Examination of the scene reveals that the most unassuming kind of writing can make extremely effective theatre. Characters need not be caught up in world-shattering problems in order to communicate effectively and importantly. The history of theatre is full of evidence that richness of theme and depth of implication are often achieved with the lightest rather than the heaviest of touches.

The next scene, by Bill Swet, introduces a play in which two patients in a mental institution and their guard reverse their states of sanity. Already, in the opening scene, we can see that one of the patients is in certain respects more sane than his guard. Pierre has begun a serious quest for meaning in the world and in his own life. He has begun to define his identity in relation to his environment. He realizes that the mind creates the world in which it lives, and that his mind is free to create a world in which it will thrive. But he has not yet made that realization firm, and he keeps slipping back into a previous state in which he was dependent upon the outside world. The guard, by contrast, is a conformist whose life is dictated by other people and by habit. But he has begun to question the validity of the habitual acts in which he daily indulges. Already his authority over Pierre has been undermined by a sense of self that is less secure at times than Pierre's. Even by the end of the first scene, patient and guard have momentarily changed places, and the guard is blaming the patient for misusing his authority.

This exchange of mental stability between patient and guard provides a powerful irony, many facets of which can be explored during the play. Indeed, the play will be built solely on that one irony, with no others introduced. It will represent a search for stability and meaning in a world gone insane. Increasingly, the institution will come to be seen as a symbol of contemporary society, and the characters, who have already shown a penchant for identifying themselves with mythological figures, will come to represent states of humanity rather than individuals. It is an allegory in which the characters gain universality without losing individuality.

Actually, more danger of sentimentality lies in Bill Swet's play than in Sarah McClelland's. Lines such as "Anne, I love you, watch the pond," depend not on an understanding of a previously existing relationship, but rather on the listener's assumptions about what such a relationship might have been. The relationship that may have existed between Pierre and Anne has not yet been made to function dramatically, the way the relationship between Pierre and the guard functions. But note how skillfully the playwright turns toast and coffee for breakfast into a means of contrasting the securely habitual behavior of the guard with the questioning, angry, and confused search for self-definition of Pierre. He has flushed the toast down the john, just as society is flushing him down the john. His mind seizes on symbols everywhere, and in its mercurial behavior leaves the guard feeling helpless and vacant. Thus, in the specific details of a developed relationship, the play avoids sentimentality, though it sometimes falls into it in developing its background. In a play that depends as heavily on symbolism as this one does, it is difficult to avoid using symbols that are not defined sufficiently in terms of the dramatic action, and thus become sentimental. It is to Bill Swet's credit that his symbols interrelate as effectively as they do, even within this one scene.

In Swet's play much more than in McClelland's, the ideas have been experienced as feelings. Thematically, the play is saying that sanity or insanity is defined largely by how one perceives his relation to society. That idea is never stated in those terms, but nearly every moment of the action represents a struggle between each character's perception of social expectation and his perception of his own mind. Thus the theme is closely related to the action, which is "to find my identity"; and as the characters struggle with each other, we find that they are nearly always struggling in terms of that action.

What gives the play its variety is its changes of mood. Pierre is like Hamlet in his ability to switch from the most playful kind of punning to the most serious consideration of the nature of life. Consider, for example, the sequence, "I know truth. I've been to the Phoenix and back. And where is your Phoenix, man? Somewhere in Arizona?" The phoenix is a mythical bird that periodically rises out of its own ashes and is a symbol of rebirth. Thus Pierre means that he knows truth because in the asylum he has been spiritually reborn. But he realizes that the guard is probably too literalminded to understand his remark, and humorously suggests that the only phoenix *he* can relate to would have to be something that actually exists, such as the capital of Arizona. In its movement from the philosophical to the silly this is a little like Hamlet's "Man delights not me—No, nor woman neither, though by your smiling you seem to say so."

In Swet's play the setting is not merely a place where things can happen, but is also symbolic of the world in which they happen. The lines are filled with references to actual things that exist in that world, and these things quickly take their part in the overall symbolism. For the most part, however, the things referred to do not actually appear in the play, and so the action of the play is not made as concrete as it might be. Relationships to physical objects present on the stage usually add dimensionality to the symbolism of a play. This play could be strengthened by adding them.

In the scene by Gwynn Swinson, which is the second scene of a play, two kinds of irony are very important. One is an irony of tone, which is established in the scene between Anna and Mary. Although these two women are intimate about things that are deeply tragic, they talk about their problems in a light, sociable manner that helps them to keep their emotions under control. That irony intensifies rather than diminishes the audience's feeling for what is going on, for the two women do not seem to be asking for pity from each other. It disappears in the scenes with George, for George makes no attempt to disguise his feelings. Indeed, he expresses them so fully that he might easily become difficult for the playwright to handle if he did not intimidate the other characters so much that they tend to be unexpressive in responding to him.

The second irony is the conflict in Anna's own mind. Living with a boorish and disabled husband, and with every opportunity to run off with a lover who appears to offer her everything, she seems unable to make up her mind to any definite action. Some kind of feeling for George, a feeling we are not yet able to identify, is holding her back. As the play unfolds, our attention will be focused on her as we seek to understand feelings that may turn out to be self-destructive.

The scene varies in the skill with which the audience is prepared for what is to happen. Notice, first of all, the natural way in which we learn about the existing relationships of the characters. They are referred to in casual conversation just as such problems might actually be discussed. In this way the author has been careful to give the audience enough information so that it is always clear what is happening. Thus we

feel that we understand the relationships and can believe in them.

Less effective is the way in which George finds the letter from Raymond. Anna happens to go out to get the mail at exactly the moment when Amy comes in with it, and also at a moment when George has demanded that she do something else. Strangely, Anna does not happen to meet Amy. Strangely, too, George shows unusual interest in the mail, seems almost to be looking for the letter from Raymond. Anna returns just in time to find him reading it. That sequence of events does not seem natural. Rather, the author seems to be arranging things so that an emotional scene can take place. In rewriting the scene the author should attempt to have George read the letter for reasons that are important to the rest of the plot.

Other minor details have been handled a little carelessly. For example, early in the scene the drinking of gin occurs far too rapidly in relation to the lines of dialogue. In a realistic play the author must scrutinize all details of that sort to make certain that they will seem natural.

Finally, it is going to be important for us to know how to judge Raymond before we can evaluate Anna's relationship to him. He may be very sincere in his love for her, he may be a scoundrel, or he may be unsure in his own mind. Mary seems to feel that Raymond's love for Anna is so strong that she herself has no chance of winning him, but it is possible that she is mistaken. Before long Raymond must be brought onstage so that we can have an opportunity to evaluate him ourselves. If we continue to know so little about him, Anna's feelings for him will come to appear sentimental.

As yet the play does not seem to have crystallized its ideas. It could be telling us that it is more important to remain loyal to someone to whom one has legal obligations than to follow one's own inclinations, it could be telling us the opposite of this, or it could be developing some other unrelated idea. It will depend on how the plot develops. There is no reason we should know at this stage of the play's unfolding what ideas the author wishes to convey, since the emotional relationships between the characters who appear onstage are very clearly and fully developed; but eventually the author will have to decide, and at that point she will have to check the meaning of the symbols the scene contains. In such a realistic play, ordinary actions may or may not take on symbolic significance. Thus, George's appearance in a wheelchair, the bringing in of the mail, and the drinking of gin might eventually be made to contribute to the symbolism of the play in a way that the audience will recognize only unconsciously.

The action of the play, even at this stage, appears quite clear. It is, "to work out my relations to the people I love." Almost every line spoken in the scene reflects that action. All the characters feel very intensely about other people, and their feelings of love and hate are interrelated in a complex way. None of them is quite sure how he stands, and thus each still has some important decisions to make about the meaning of his own life. Here is a play that will make powerful emotional demands on its audience once it has been fully developed. It may be that the author is attempting too much and should use more restraint in the working out of the action, muting some of the relationships, pushing some of the emotion into the background. Just how much it will be possible for the play to sustain will not be clear until it has progressed further.

Now that we have examined the first three scenes in Appendix A, it may be that the reader will wish to make his own analyses of the remaining three. All of the scenes are early portions of plays that had not been completed at the time this book was written. It is therefore interesting to speculate how they might be developed. A group discus-

sion could center around several possible alternative conclusions for each play. That could be followed by speculation as to the various means of deepening the implications that might be used in these scenes if each of several possible alternative conclusions were adopted.

As you work on your own play, you will have to develop skill in deepening its implications in the various ways we have discussed. An interesting and rather exciting group exercise may be helpful in developing that skill. The group is divided into two teams. A newspaper story is selected at random. The first player on the first team proceeds to describe how the implications of the story can be deepened. He may point out ironies implicit in the story, or suggest some that may be developed. He may indicate the background conditions out of which the actions in the story might arise, so that they do not seem to happen arbitrarily, but are rather motivated by clear and consistent characters. He may suggest the theme of the story and how the characters feel about that theme. He may try to indicate the story's main action and the subordinate analogous actions that it might contain. For each thing he is able to add to the story, his team gets one point. Any player on the opposing team may challenge him by attempting to show that some development he has suggested is inconsistent because it detracts from the total effect of the story. If he is successfully challenged, or if he can think of no more ideas, the story then passes to the opposing team. A group leader will act as referee to determine at what point a player has been successfully challenged, and to decide when a point has been earned.

When the story passes to the opposing team, the next player on that team may elect to continue working on the story, or else to have a new story read. If he continues with the same story, he gets two points for each idea he can add to the story (always building on the foundation established by the previous player). He continues until he has been successfully challenged, and the story passes back to the first team. The next player gets four points for his team for each addition he can suggest, if he continues with the same story. But if he elects to start a new story, each addition will count only one point. The game continues, the number of points a player may gain for each addition he successfully suggests doubling with each new player who works on that story. The game is concluded at the end of a time period agreed upon by both teams at the beginning. The team with the highest score wins.

Repeated exercise with such a game over a period of time should do a great deal to develop both the imaginations and the sense of significance of the members of the participating group. One's confidence as a playwright is strengthened by the knowledge that he is capable of developing almost any story in an interesting manner, no matter how dull it seems on first hearing. When the playwright feels that there is no end to the stories he can dramatize, he is less likely to try his hand at the first thing he thinks of. He will be better able to search for the story that really appeals to the deepest that is in him.

Chapter XI

CHOOSE YOUR LEVEL
OF REALITY

Many of the elements of drama interrelate to give a sense of the personal stamp of the playwright. We refer to that personal stamp as style. Style is a very difficult concept to define, and many not very convincing pages have been written in the attempt. Possibly the best and shortest definition was that given by Robert Frost, who said, "Style is the way a man takes himself." Eventually any play has to find a way of taking itself so that it "knows" what belongs in it and what does not. Frequently several drafts are necessary before the playwright can begin to feel that he has found the style of his play. Once you have found it you recognize it, just as you recognize an orange or a banana. You would not feel that an orange should have parts of a banana in it. No more will you feel that your play should have parts in it that do not rightfully belong there.

In a play, style is determined primarily by the level of reality on which the author has chosen to tell his story. In order to understand what this means, we must first understand what the word "reality" means when applied to the drama. By reality we generally mean those things that exist outside ourselves—objects and events that we perceive around us or believe to exist apart from our immediate surroundings. Not all of the various components of reality hold equal interest for us; we select from our total surroundings those things in which we are interested, and think only about them. The dramatist is an observer of reality who selects from all that he perceives only certain things that interest him. Let us think for a moment about how this is done.

If you were to sit concealed in a room and watch everything that happened in it, you would be placing yourself in a position like that of an audience at a play. Probably, unless the room you chose were such a place as Grand Central Terminal, most of the time it would be empty. From time to time people would come and go and do things or engage in conversation. It is unlikely that the things happening in the room would have much in common with one another, and it is extremely unlikely that they would contain any sustained dramatic interest.

A playwright tries to assume the vantage point of an audience and record for them what is presumed to happen in a given place, except that out of all that happens he selects only those things that will seem interesting and relevant to the idea of his play. His characters are always more eloquent than real people, and his events are always more condensed in time and impact than equivalent events in real life. The manner of his selection from the total reality that might take place determines the level of reality that his play depicts. Let us examine how that level can be changed in order to arrive at a variety of styles. Here is how a conversation might actually occur:

A: But—see, what'd you think?

B: W—I haven't any i—

C: (*Interrupting.*)—seems to me it was—really—uh, yes—well, it was good —course I, now we—

B: Had its limitations, of course—

C: we both agree to that—

A: Yes. It was good.

B: So. And when did you—

A: Around two w—last Tuesday, a week ago last Tuesday.

C: Didn't you—

B: You—it would have—you should have called us.

A: I—that is—I phoned several times.

C: (*Laughing.*) We're so hard to reach.

You can see that this kind of talk would have little interest if acted upon the stage. An entire play made up of such stammering could have interest only as an avant-garde experiment. Although some plays are more "realistic" than others, no play is a direct transcription of reality. Even if all the words in the text of the play were selected from words actually spoken by real people, the process of selecting the words and arranging them into patterns would reflect the thinking of the playwright. It is from the actual conversations he has heard and the experiences he has had that the playwright selects, shapes, and transmutes the dialogue of which his drama is made. It is his mind acting upon his experience that produces the style that fascinates us. Let us try to imagine how different playwrights, having heard and transcribed the above conversation, might turn the ideas in it into material for a play. For the sake of demonstration, we shall follow the trend of the original conversation rather closely in each case.

For a starter, let us imagine treating this as high comedy:

A: My dear fellow, what was your opinion?

B: I never give an opinion, except on trivial matters. Where really important issues are concerned, I remain completely impartial.

C: My darling, you know perfectly well that you spoke of it as being superb, exquisite, unparalleled. That was privately, to me, of course, so I knew you wanted everyone to know.

B: My privately expressed views are never an indication of my real opinion. Of course I felt its primary strength lay in its limitations.

C: You see, George darling? We both agree that it was splendid.

B: I always agree with everyone who agrees with me.

A: Splendid, eh? I'll record that in my diary. One should always write down everything one is never likely to forget.

B: George, you rogue, you must tell us how long you've been up to town.

C: We've missed you so much that the magic of your presence can't possibly compare with the beautiful sorrow occasioned by your absence.

A: Why, I drove up a fortnight ago, actually. It was terribly urgent. I was anxious to escape the excitement of living in the country.

B: Oh, dear me, you really should have called us before this!

A: I had Jeeves ring you up at regular intervals—

C: Darling, you know it isn't fashionable to be at home nowadays. Nobody who is anybody is ever at home, except doctors and people like that, and then only on matters of pleasure.

Now, as low comedy:

A: Well, I don't rightly know—

B: Strike me dead if I—

C: Oh, it was real good. Wasn't it, William?

B: Can't kick, I reckon—

C: William and I allus sees eye to eye 'bout most *everythin'*. William is sich a angel. Ain't you, honey chile? (*He giggles.*) Oh, he's a *angel.*

A: Real good, huh?

B: C'mon, you geezer, when did you blow into town?

A: Reckon a coupla weeks ago.

C: Why, you—

B: He should've looked us up 'fore this, Baby Cakes.

C: Lak I say, William and I sees to eye.

A: Reckon I 'most busted myself poundin' on yore door.

C: William and me, we're *never* home.

Now, let's try to make this conversation seem melodramatic:

A: I'd like your opinion on that. You know how much I respect what you say.

B: I'm afraid I—couldn't—say.

C: Please, George. It isn't easy for him to express these things. He said to me quietly this morning that he thought it was good.

B: I didn't say any such thing. I trusted you. It was bad. For God's sake, it was bad!

C: Oh, if only he could find it in him to say it was good!

B: So. When did you blow into town?

A: Two weeks ago.

B: Two weeks ago! And you didn't call? George, you and I used to be very close friends. Very close. I wouldn't have stayed in your neighborhood five minutes without picking up the phone. What has come between us, George?

A: I called as soon as I arrived, honest to God I did.

C: We must have been out.

This next is more surrealistic in its effect:

A: Well, what *did* you think? I suppose you thought it was splendid, huh?

B: I—

C: For God's sake, George! My husband never thinks. He is, you might say, thinkless. Ha, ha, ha—how did you like that, William? Thinkless. Most husbands are thankless; you're thinkless.

B: That was very good. That was—

C: All right!

B: —very good.

C: ALL RIGHT! Anyway, George, William's reaction was that it was splendid. I personally thought it *stank,* but then, you know William.

B: I told her privately that I thought it was good when actually I thought it was lousy, because I wanted her to agree with me about something for once in her life. You know? Agree?

C: So we both agreed that it was splendid.

A: Good. In that case I'll avoid it altogether.

B: So. When did you—bless—this happy city with your—

A: I came in on the 3:13 two weeks ago Tuesday.

B: Morning or evening?

A: A.M.

B: At 3:13 A.M. two weeks ago Tuesday we were here. It was the only time in the past month that we have been here. Why didn't you call us immediately?

C: Don't be silly, William. We were on that very train! My husband is always getting confused about time.

B: Of course we were. We always arrive on the 3:13. Especially on Tuesdays.

A: Perhaps that is why I saw you sitting next to me on the train.

Now a rendering in blank verse:

A: And what is your opinion of—
B: Life?
Or some dead husks of meaning unrevived?

Or time? Of these I'm sure, but not
Of what you ask.

C: It gyred in his brain
Like some huge falcon seeking out its
    prey,
Then earthwards left the heavens ten-
    antless,
Plunging to vanishment. He said 'twas
    good,
But said it fearingly, as if the words
Once out would choke him with their
ironies.

B: 'Tis true, I feared that overpraise
    would lead,
At last, to overcondemnation.

C: "It
Was good," is best of what he thought.

B: Tell us
Now, if some rude thistles threaten not
Your tongue, what brought you here to
town? And when?

A: Hitherward I stole upon the traces
Of the sun a fortnight since.

B: Two weeks?
Nay, you've stopped too long and have
not stopped
Our ears with news of your esteemed
presence.

A: Like lover banished from his mis-
    tress' eye
I panted on your doorstep hours together,
Wanting in the parching of my throat
The soothing balm of your blessed com-
    pany.

C: We seldom stop at home these har-
ried times.

B: 'Tis true.

It is a common fault among beginning
playwrights to mix styles in a play. The result, in an extreme case, might have the
following sort of effect:

A: Well, what *did* you think? I suppose you thought it was splendid, huh?

B: I never give an opinion except on
trivial matters. Where really important
issues are concerned, I remain completely
impartial.

C: It gyred in his brain like some huge
falcon seeking out its prey, then earthwards left the heavens tenantless, plunging to vanishment. He said 'twas good,
but said it fearingly, as if the words once
out would choke him with their ironies.

B: I didn't say any such thing. I
trusted you. It was bad. For God's sake,
it was bad!

C: William and I allus sees eye to eye
'bout most *everythin'*. William is sich a
angel. Ain't you, honey chile? (*He giggles.*) Oh, he's a *angel*.

A: Good. In that case I'll avoid it altogether.

B: Tell us now, if some rude thistles
threaten not your tongue, what brought
you here to town? and when?

C: We've missed you so much that the
magic of your presence can't possibly
compare with the beautiful sorrow occasioned by your absence.

A: I called as soon as I arrived, honest
to God I did.

C: William and me, we're *never* home!

In this last example all the lines relate to
the same situation and follow one another
more or less logically. Yet if one were to
read this example without having read the
others first, one would sense something
wrong. When we realize that the last example is a random mixture of distinct styles,
we can see that an adjustment would have
to be made in nearly every line if the scene
were to be made actable.

So long as one is writing a play merely
to forward the action of the plot, one is
likely to be inattentive to style. For that
reason the first draft of a play is often
stylistically confused. One must decide what
kind of play one is writing and be sure that
every single line contributes to making it
that kind of play. If that is not done, the
results when the play is performed will be

disastrous. The audience will laugh in places that the author had intended should be serious. More important, the audience, failing to know how to take the play, will lose interest in it and become inattentive.

Furthermore, each effect your play achieves must be based on a previous effect. Consistency of style is necessary to make that possible. When it is lacking, there will be no accumulation of effect, and the play will always seem to be trying to get started but never going anywhere.

We have noted that every good play has its own unique style. You cannot learn what that style should be in any other way than by writing the play and discovering it. But you can become more sensitive to style in existing plays. Let us consider some exercises that might help you to develop your sense of style.

One of the most obvious means of trying to improve one's sense of style is imitation. Many people are afraid of imitation, believing that somehow it will rob them of their individuality. On the contrary, individuality is enhanced by imitation. A writer's style is developed slowly as a result of his assimilation and synthesis of the styles of his favorite authors. To start you out, see if you can become more sensitive to an author's style by typing or copying by hand long passages of his work. Then be sure to encourage the tendency that you will have to write in that author's style.

As an exercise, try obtaining a copy of a play and a plot summary of it. Select a passage of dialogue from the play and then try to continue in the same vein, following the plot summary. After you have worked carefully on about a page of dialogue, compare what you have written with the original play and study the differences, perhaps actually revising your dialogue into the form of the original by changing specific words and phrases one at a time. Continue working your way through the play in this manner, a page at a time.

A group exercise devoted to developing a more general awareness of style is the following. The group leader selects an individual who is to begin speaking in a very distinct style of his own choice. After a few moments, the leader points to another member of the group, who must continue in that same style, and then gradually shift to a completely different style. Each player must continue the previous player's final style and then shift to another style. The players are selected at the discretion of the group leader rather than in any particular order, so that all players will constantly be listening carefully, ready to take over from another player instantaneously. As a variant, the players may wish to choose their own successors. This allows each player to develop his style as fully as he wishes before being cut off. After each member of the group has played, the group may wish to try to describe the style initiated by each. It may be that a particular word will come to mind easily, such as "eloquent," "hysterical," "pedantic," or "rustic." In that case, the player will know that he has communicated the style clearly. If the group has trouble deciding how they felt about the style, that is a cue for the player to try to clarify his stylistic concept the next time the game is played. If the group plays this game frequently, and at length, the members will become much more sensitive to slight shifts in style and will learn to take tremendous delight in the game. They will probably also improve their feeling for characterization.

Let us now consider a little more carefully the examples of style given earlier in this chapter. In each case particular aspects of communication are emphasized at the expense of others. Let us see what each kind of style demands of the writer.

In the first version, an attempt to create high comedy, the emphasis is on the speaker's tendency to generalize about his behavior from his reaction to the immediate situation. The generalization is usually an ironic one, giving the opposite of what might be the expected reaction. The characters are more interested in parading their own wit than in responding humanly to what is happening. If one were to try to improve the passage through revision, one would try to make the pointedness of the remarks more telling. The more one feels that a particular line reveals an ironic truth about human nature, the more one will feel that the author has accomplished his purpose stylistically.

In the second passage, the emphasis is on a picturesque dialect. The author is searching for phrases that will identify the *type* of character he is portraying, rather than the particular individual. The more he gives the impression that the people who are talking have exhausted the possibilities of their particular linguistic mannerisms, the more successfully he will accomplish his purpose. In comedy of that type, whether it is straight drama, radio and television programs, or comic strips, there is a tendency to use minor characters who appear again and again at intervals, always using the same catch phrases, adapting whatever situation arises to their particular vocabulary. The undertaker who at the end of every conversation remarks, "I've got to be shoveling off," provides an example of this technique.

In the third passage, the emphasis is on the suggestion of pent-up emotion. The characters, for reasons that are not always clear at first, tend to overreact to the situation emotionally. Anyone who, asked for his opinion of something, cries out, "For God's sake, it was bad!" has something more than a simple aesthetic judgment on his mind. Such overreacting tends to build suspense because it makes the audience wonder what is really happening inside the character's mind. Revision will require great skill, for the author must decide just how much his audience will accept of this type of emotionalism, and must develop it consistently. He will have to be certain that when the characters' inner conflicts finally are revealed, they will seem to justify the reactions that have been expressed earlier.

In the fourth passage we are concerned with presenting a superficially bizarre set of reactions which nevertheless reveal something essential in human nature. In the passage a shift of style occurs from one kind of bizarre effect to another. The author will have to decide which style he prefers and unify the passage to fit that style. The first half of the passage derives its effect from allowing characters to be less inhibited and more witty than real people are. Thus the underlying tensions of the characters lie nearer the surface and are more easily observed than those of real people. The characters seem to be playing a kind of game in which each allows the other to be as brutal as he likes. In the second half of the passage the emphasis is on the distortion of everyday activities. The idea of arriving at 3:13 in the morning and immediately phoning one's friends, and the idea of the characters' having been on the same train, distort reality in order to suggest the inconsistencies in more ordinary human conduct. The audience will have to "translate" the dialogue into more familiar forms, much as one must "translate" an expressionistic painting into whatever it is supposed to represent, to understand how the artist has reflected some underlying quality of his subject. In the first half of the passage characterization is very important, whereas in the second half it becomes practically nonexistent, since the emphasis is on human action in the abstract.

In the fifth selection the emphasis is on images and sound patterns. Character is important too, in that the images and sound patterns must reflect and contribute to its development. No line, however, will be acceptable if it does not contribute something to the musical richness of the play. As the writer revises this passage, he will ask himself, "Have I chosen the best possible poetic image for this situation?" Word choice will probably be considered more carefully than would be the case in revising any of the preceding selections. That is chiefly because every word chosen must fit the rhythmical design of the line before it is acceptable. Consequently there will be a tendency to think about the structure of each word much more than if a metrical system were not being used.

The author will probably attend to the patterns formed by the images he uses. Certain types of image will be repeated in different forms, and those will give structure and unity to the dialogue. The image patterns should not be too concentrated and obvious, but should be spread throughout the play. In the short passage given, however, you will notice an emphasis on images referring to parts of the human body ("brain," "tongue," "throat") and to nature ("dead husks," "heavens," "thistles," "sun"). Also you will note repeated suggestions of someone bound to something and yet separated from it ("the falcon plunging to vanishment," "I stole upon the traces of the sun," "like lover banished from his mistress' eye"). Anyone who has practiced writing poetry sufficiently to attempt poetic drama will know of many additional ways to add to the richness of his lines.

We have seen in general that one may move in a number of directions, creating different kinds of theatrical reality. Now let us consider in greater detail how one might turn a realistic play into a surrealistic one. The reason for considering this particular technique is that the theatre of our time is increasingly turning from realistic to surrealistic drama. The two styles require quite distinct types of discipline from the writer. In a realistic play the problem is to avoid violating the realities that the writer has gradually accumulated. In what they do and say, characters must be consistent with what the author has established about them. The events of the plot must never seem too unlikely.

Surrealism, on the other hand, does not place emphasis on consistency either of character or of plot. It is a difficult style to discipline, because it appears chaotic at first sight. Yet a good surrealistic play operates according to rules that it establishes for itself. These rules may be of almost any kind, and they vary from one play to the next.

Surrealism abstracts something from realism. It may be that the author wishes to give the effect of cocktail party conversation heard at random by someone not involved in it. That has its own reality, but presented on the stage without character consistency or plot, it may seem at first a strange sort of pattern. Another possible device would be to have two characters converse with one another, each replying not to the spoken words of the other, but to unspoken thoughts not actually expressed in the play. These are two simple ways of abstracting from reality. Most surrealistic plays combine several such techniques.

Let us try to create a surrealistic conversation out of a realistic one:

A: How are you?
B: Fine, thanks. How are you?
A: Oh, pretty good. Nice day, isn't it?
B: Just beautiful.

That's how two people are likely to greet each other. It has only a superficial realism, because it is so common a dialogue that it tells us nothing about the personalities of the two speakers. A surrealistic version of this might investigate how the two speakers would communicate if each spoke what he were thinking subconsciously. Let us see how this might work:

A: I'm so sorry to see you. I would gladly have walked around the block to avoid doing so.
B: Take this knife and use it on yourself.
A: It's a beautiful knife.
B: I'm so glad you like it.

A: I'm glad I ran into you. Before you gave me this knife, I would gladly have used it. Now I shall always prize it because it has made us friends.

This situation has something very real and interesting about it, though it is not one that could occur in real life. It suggests the characters and underlying motives of the two speakers. Thematically, it might be taken to suggest that a conflict amounting almost to a feud could be quickly resolved if it were openly expressed in a form that simultaneously created bonds of friendship between the two speakers. The gift of the knife vents B's antagonism toward A and creates feelings of gratitude in A that make B want to like him. A's gratitude may stem from a masochistic desire for reproach from B. Such progressions have the reality of dreams, and the surrealistic drama often draws upon the logic of dreams for its effect.

Now that we begin to understand the principles of organization in surrealistic drama, let us see how a realistic plot might be made into a surrealistic one.

Joan has been living with Bill, though she has not yet decided to marry him. Bill has a close friend named George who is trying very hard to break up the relationship between Joan and Bill. As a result of repeated conflicts with George and resulting conflicts with Bill, Joan comes to realize that she is immature because of her tendency to be excessively subservient to Bill. Feeling the need to develop greater independence, she breaks away from Bill and goes to live by herself.

Suppose that after you have been working on such a play for a while, you become bored with its characters and situations. A fully developed realism continually eludes you, and you feel tired out at the very thought of continuing to work on the play. It may be that you need to find a surrealistic plot for whatever you are trying to express. It is probable that you have not managed to convey in the style you are using some of the ideas that attracted you to this plot in the first place. Try making a list of hidden motivations associated with the characters and actions in your plot but not yet expressed in anything you have written. Such a list might include the following:

1. Joan dominates through being dominated.

2. George, though appearing to be friendly, is actually attacking the relationship.

3. Joan has never freed herself from the influence of her father, and is subtly trying to make Bill over in his image.

Now we shall invent three surrealistic plots, each based on one of the above ideas.

1. The scene is a torture chamber. Joan is bound in a straitjacket. A man enters and tries to break her down through questioning. With each question, Joan becomes more confident and exultant, and the man weaker and less sure of himself. Finally he is writhing on the floor in agony. Enter another man who proceeds to apply some other kind of torture. He, too, gradually gives in to his own technique, and is at last writhing on the floor. After that has happened several times, Joan breaks free from her straitjacket and cries out that she is free at last of all influences.

2. The scene is Joan's and Bill's apartment. George enters and proceeds to say terrible things about Joan and Bill. However, he always speaks in a polite tone of voice and phrases everything very delicately. All of his remarks are responded to by both Joan and Bill with warmth and affection. Finally, Joan and Bill kill each other. As they are dying, they thank George for his kindness.

3. The scene is an art studio. Joan is painting Bill's portrait, which we cannot see. She converses with Bill in a friendly manner about her relationship with him, and contrasts him with her father, whom she claims not to like. At various times her father enters and causes Joan to cower to

him. While Bill talks, he from time to time turns away in such a manner that he can apply some makeup to his face. Step by step Bill's countenance takes on the exact features of Joan's father's. At the end of the play, Joan shows Bill the portrait of him, which is actually a portrait of her father, and Bill comments on what an excellent likeness it is.

The above three ideas may be combined in a single play as follows.

The scene is an art studio. Joan is painting Bill's portrait in the manner described above. George is present, and talks to Joan and Bill about their relationship in the manner described above. From time to time Joan's father enters and attempts to dominate her. His attempts at domination have no effect on Joan, but they eventually reduce him to a cowering weakling. Meanwhile, Joan and Bill are taking everything that George says at face value and are beginning to express their antagonism toward each other, while remaining friendly toward George. It is George who comments on the excellent likeness of the portrait to Joan's father. George then instructs Joan and Bill in how to kill each other, and they do, thanking him as they die for his kindness.

The purpose of the above play is to express in the abstract those qualities of human nature that have appealed to the author of the more realistic play earlier outlined. The plot is deliberately confusing in order to draw attention away from what is happening and toward how it is happening. Surrealism appeals to those who naturally tend to see characters and events in the abstract. But note that the surrealism in this case has been derived from a realistic plot and is not chaotic whim. A surrealistic play derived from the author's intense perception of realism may be a highly disciplined work of art that helps its audience better understand certain universal human problems. Surrealism should be avoided by those who turn to it merely because a failure to develop intense feeling for their characters causes them to become bored with realism.

Once you have understood the problem of style and have found a style that best expresses your particular frame of mind, you will discover that other elements of the drama tend to fall into place in your play more easily. It is possible that you will at first have a tendency to be influenced by the styles of writers whose concerns are not in harmony with your own. That may cause you to make some false starts stylistically, and you may try your hand at several sorts of play before you find one that is congenial to you. If you make a few false starts, you will not be wasting your time; you will be discovering yourself.

Chapter XII

HOW PEOPLE USE WORDS

All that happens in your play is either spoken or physically performed, and nearly all of it is spoken. So you will need to give thorough consideration to how people use words. In this chapter we shall consider a number of categories of speech behavior. If you study these categories carefully, it may help you to notice many things about the way people speak that you can then use in the dialogue of your play.

A few words of warning, first, about this chapter. Human speech is an extraordinarily complex system involving interrelationships between the individual's own body and mind, his past, present, and future, and his experiences with other people. Any attempt to categorize speech makes a natural human phenomenon seem both artificial and much simpler than it actually is. Therefore you must be careful to take nothing in this chapter too literally.

Furthermore, the chapter describes some of the ways in which people use words, but by no means all of them. Many of these ways are reflected in sentence patterns. Many others are primarily psychological, and the expression that they take is subtle and varies from person to person. But to arrange the categories in groups reflecting that or any other distinction would be impossible, as they interrelate with one another in so many ways. Some categories are subheadings of others. Some overlap with others. Some may even seem redundant with others;

that will depend on the kinds of things you are already accustomed to look for in speech. As an exercise, you may wish to try grouping them in ways that seem to express their interrelationships most effectively. You may wish to debate with a friend the fine points of some of the distinctions between those that overlap. You will certainly wish to relate them to speech that you hear around you. Bear in mind that they are not arranged in any particular order of importance.

Some of our observations may seem to you to reflect value judgments. Actually, everyone has preferences for or prejudices against certain speech patterns, and tends to judge people in the light of those likes and dislikes. All of the great playwrights pass judgment on at least some of their characters by subtly manipulating the way they speak. But such judgments are personal, and each playwright should develop his own attitudes, not reflect those of someone else.

As you study the speech categories, remember that they are not mutually exclusive. We are always using more than one at a time. But as you direct your attention to the development of a given speech, you will find that the emphasis keeps shifting. After you have studied the speech categories awhile, you should become more aware of those subtle shifts. If you try to memorize the categories, you will only confuse yourself; but if you let them heighten your awareness of the dynamic processes in the conversations you overhear, you will develop a kind of sixth sense about speech that will sharpen your ear long after you have forgotten all about the categories.

Let us proceed, without further ado, to examine them:

1. *Dialect*. This category is the sublanguage that an individual has been brought up on or has adopted for personal or professional reasons. It is not the property of that individual alone, but is shared by all the members of a clearly defined group, and it is therefore inadequate in itself as a means of characterizing. "Oh, I say!" and "Ah reckon!" are different dialects, but they hardly represent individual speech. Some playwrights (notably Bernard Shaw) have prided themselves on an ear for dialect, but many good playwrights have written successfully without ever drawing attention to it. Dialect is not essential, but when it is used it must be used consistently.

Two major problems are associated with dialect. One is that a very thick dialect may be difficult for an audience to understand. The other is that overemphasis on dialect may produce stereotypes rather than characters. Melodramas of the nineteenth century often contained sailors who referred to their girl friends as "smart little craft," and who talked exclusively, repetitiously, and nauseatingly in the jargon of the sea. Such techniques always draw attention away from, rather than toward, the individuality of the character, and should be used only for parody.

2. *Vocabulary*. Everyone has his own individual vocabulary. This refers not only to the total range of words he uses, but also to those he uses most frequently. It also applies to misuse or unusual use of words. One of the greatest characters in all literature is Sheridan's Mrs. Malaprop, who has given her name to the humorous misuse of similar-sounding words. Imitations of her, however, are likely to be stereotypes.

You can acquaint yourself with the subtlety of individual vocabulary by tape-recording a conversation and making note of every unusual word that each speaker uses more than once. Some tendency will be noted for each to echo the other's vocabulary, but some words will be used by one speaker and not the other. You may also wish to try this exercise on some good plays, though here you are getting your information secondhand, rather than from direct observation.

It is probably the individual use of vocabulary by influential and popular people that gets colloquialisms started. Phrases like "Man, I dig it," and "Hey, this is a real drag," started with someone and then became the property of groups. Once vocabulary has become associated with a group, it is no longer sufficient to characterize an individual. If one of your characters is a jazz musician, he must, of course, use the vocabulary associated with jazz musicians, but he must also have his own individual vocabulary.

It is interesting, too, that a given person can provoke vocabulary in another person without using it himself. Shakespeare's Falstaff has a highly individual vocabulary, but he also provokes Prince Hal to use words that he himself does not use and that Hal uses only when talking to or about him.

3. *Length of phrase*. The length of the phrases a person uses is determined partly by his situation, partly by his intelligence, and partly by his breath control and general physical stamina. A fat man who is always gasping for breath cannot talk in long phrases. A character who prides himself on coolness and intelligence might use consistently long phrases. Instability of character can be indicated by variety of phrase length. Hamlet varies his speeches from one-word phrases to extremely long and involved ones. A long-winded person, like Polonius, is apt not only to use many words to say a simple thing, but also to crowd a great many words into a single sentence so that

it is difficult to interrupt him. His phrasing within the sentence, however, is usually in units of four to eight words. Compare this with the tendency of Hamlet's uncle, King Claudius, to speak in phrases that are usually one to three *lines* long. Long phrases are often associated with very formal situations and with people who are customarily found in those situations. Intense, powerful, deeply emotional people may often speak in words of one syllable.

4. *Continuity.* Closely related to phrasing is continuity. A person may speak with the elegance and organization of fine prose, or he may frequently interrupt himself and change the drift of his thought. He may be given to contradicting himself from one sentence to the next. The playwright should pay particular attention to the lack of logic in people's thinking, as there is a tendency when writing to want to make everything logical. Shaw, the most logical of all playwrights (all of his characters express themselves very precisely and consistently), took note of the fact that Shakespeare's characters were often highly illogical, particularly in moments of stress. This led him to say that Shakespeare's writing didn't mean anything, but was instead great "word music." Shakespeare's writing does have meaning, but it is often emotional instead of logical. People who are caught in a conflict may express opposite ideas about the same thing because that is the way they feel. "I want to stay and fight because if I run away I will be called a coward, but I don't want to stay and fight because if I do I will get killed," might, under duress, be expressed as "I want to stay and fight, but I want to run away." Shaw's characters always make up their minds as to how they feel about such things. The rest of us are more likely to feel confused.

5. *Degree of approximation.* People vary in how exactly they express themselves. It has been suggested that young people these days say "like" so frequently because they do not want to be committed to something that might prove false, since they have already found most of the eternal verities lacking in truth. Thus we have the expression "It's like 42 degrees outside," which means "It was 42 degrees outside when I looked at the thermometer if the thermometer was accurate," and also means "I feel right now as if this might be worth saying, but I might change my mind later."

Some people exaggerate constantly. Some are nearly always vague. Some are finicky about details. Some are inaccurate in their perceptions:

A: How was it?

B: Great.

A: How was it?

C: You could say it was all right, but then again—

A: How was it?

D: Absolutely stupendous, it was one of the best things I've ever—

A: How was it?

E: He made three mistakes and the sun was too hot, but otherwise I rather liked it.

A: How was it?

F: Like, man, it was a gas.

6. *Use of subordination.* People vary in their ability to control ideas. Some can have four or five things going on in a sentence and keep them all beautifully related: "One Sunday morning under the elm trees when we were young I remember Mother speaking in delicious consonants of the sunrise that day." Some try to do this and fail: "One Sunday morning, it was, I think it was back in 1943, if I remember correctly, Mother—it was under an elm tree and I—where was I?" Some string everything together with conjunctions: "It was a Sunday morning and we were very young and I remember Mother was standing there and she was speaking of the sunrise and how it came up that morning and then—" Some make no attempt to handle more than one idea at a time: "We were kids, see? Well,

Mom used to go on about the sunrise. Geez!" In general, the more mature a person, the better he can interrelate ideas in a sentence; and the more intellectual a person, the more often he will try. Shakespeare's kings usually speak in involved sentences and his common people in simpler ones. Villainous kings use devious and confusing phrases, good kings use brilliant and beautiful ones, and stupid kings use illogical ones. The more involved a sentence, the more revealing it is likely to be of the person who speaks it. That is why reticent people are so likely to speak in brief sentences. If one wishes to conceal information, however, the involved sentence maybe an excellent means of doing so:

A: Do you like this picture?
B: Well, as to that, if you really want my opinion, I'd say that in relation to certain other pictures I have seen it has a quality that would rather tend to set it apart in certain respects if you don't take into account its more common, universal elements.

A is unlikely to repeat the question because, unable to wade through B's verbiage, he is not really sure it hasn't been answered, and he doesn't want to appear a fool by asking twice. Politicians are particularly good at this sort of evasion.

7. *Use of imagery.* Some people are visually oriented, some think in terms of sounds, and some in terms of physical sensations. Thus, the imagery in a person's speech is likely to be dominated by one of the three. There is also synesthesia, which is a mixing of sense impressions: "Her voice rang out like bright orange; it had a sharp sound." The more original and spontaneous a person is, the more imagery he is likely to use.

A: Hell is a mere glass-house where the devils are continually blowing up women's souls on hollow irons, and the fire never goes out.

B: You don't say. Sounds pretty scary.
or
A: You drive me up a tree, Sam, you really do. I feel like swinging like a monkey and hooting Indian yells whenever I see you!
B: You make me pretty mad, too.

Too much imagery in dialogue can be worse than too little, though some modern playwrights, particularly Christopher Fry, have very successfully used far more of it than one encounters in normal speech.

8. *Degree of irony.* Some people never give a straight answer. Others are incapable of anything except what is literally accurate. Speech is characterized by the degree of irony one hears in reaction to ordinary things:

A: What's with you?
B: Nothing. I'm just enjoying the beauty of that sunset.
A: Well, I guess *some* people dig sunsets.
B: Why not? It makes me feel so glorious. The wonders of heaven!
A: Oh, wow, man. Like it's posing for a picture postcard maybe.

A, here, is deliberately avoiding direct statement, whereas B embraces it. These two will not continue the conversation for very long, because sentimental and ironic people are usually irritating to each other. Here is an aspect of dialogue that is very useful in creating conflict. One modern play, *The Zoo Story,* is built almost entirely on this kind of language conflict.

9. *Sentimentality.* This category is closely related to the preceding one. Sentimental people are likely to express their feelings directly and not try to disguise them. Sentimental language is likely to be conventional, but it is also sincere. The playwright who makes fun of a sentimental character's speech absolutely destroys the audience's ability to take the characters seriously. How-

ever, some very successful entertainments derive much of their humor from mocking the sentimental. Among them are *The Beggar's Opera* and the operas of Gilbert and Sullivan. The cultivation of "camp" in recent times (as in the television program *Batman*) also mocks the sentimental.

The comments we made in Chapter X about sentimentality in the drama as a whole do not apply to the sentimental character. Many people really are sentimental, and there is no reason that a truly sentimental character cannot function as part of a good serious drama.

10. *Circuitousness.* "Full thirty times hath Phoebus' cart gone round/Neptune's salt wash and Tellus' orbéd ground—" is a roundabout way of saying "Thirty days have passed." Some people always say simple things circuitously. Others are invariably direct and to the point.

A: How are you?
B: Well, yesterday I went to see the doctor and he said I had a good record, but today when I woke up I—
A: Skip it.

11. *Thinking vs. reacting.* Some people think; others react. People who think about everything, no matter what it is, have very little contact with their own emotional life. People who react to everything and never pause to think have very little control over their emotions. It is also possible for a person to react quickly to something and then think about it at length. Another person may be characterized by delayed reactions to things.

A: I'm going to get him! I'm going to kill the lousy bum!
B: Now, wait a minute. Are you sure that's wise? After all, all he said was—
A: He called me a no-good—
B: But if you examine the situation, I think you'll see that he really meant to—

12. *Sensuality.* The emotional life of a person may be deeply hidden from others, or it may be fairly close to the surface.

A: That sunset is so beautiful it makes me want to melt.
B: It's nice.
A: Can you smell the perfume in the air? It makes me feel like dancing.
B: I hadn't noticed it particularly.
A: Oh, you're a creep!

If sensuality lies close to the surface, it is likely to make use of imagery. If it is concealed, the language will be more stilted and intellectual. It is also possible to have a false sensuality that results from trying to persuade oneself that he is emotional when, in fact, he is frightened of his emotions. This is characterized by overstatement without imagery: "Oh, I think it's simply di*vine,* simply *mar*velous, oh *darling,* you're so *won*derful."

Some people are emotionally rather bland without having actually repressed their emotions. They simply have not inherited much sensitivity. In that case no attempt will be made to disguise emotion, but no very imaginative response will come, either: "That sunset is pretty, isn't it?"

13. *Sensitivity to the sounds of words.* Some people have a natural feeling for the sound of language, and their speech verges on the musical. Others are awkward and speak in sound patterns that lack rhythm and beauty. For some reason it is the Irish playwrights, particularly Sean O'Casey and J. M. Synge, who have been most sensitive to the music in ordinary speech. Among leading American playwrights, O'Neill seems least sensitive to the beauty of words, and Tennessee Williams most sensitive. Careful reading of the plays of Williams, O'Casey, and, of course, Shakespeare will help one become aware of the many ways in which speech can be beautiful and still quite natural. All of these playwrights derive their

word music from the way human beings actually talk, and not from a false attempt to create a poetry of the theatre apart from natural speech.

It would be well for the serious playwright to become an avid reader and student of poetry, so that he will learn to recognize the beauty of natural speech when he hears it. Effective sound consists of a subtle interrelation first between the sound of the words themselves, and second between the sound of the words and their meaning.

"I don't think I want to."

Here the only repeated sounds are "I" and the final consonants of "don't" and "want." (The initial "t" of "to" is likely to merge with the final "t" of "want.") In addition, the final "k" of "think" is related in effect to the two "t's." But all of the vowel sounds (except the repeated "I") are unrelated. Rhythmically, the sentence consists of words of one syllable, all of about the same importance and emphasis. The effect might be reminiscent of stamping one's foot repeatedly, but the sense does not reinforce that idea, as "don't think" weakens the aggressiveness of the statement.

" 'Twouldn't hardly be worthwhile."

Here is a much more beautiful way of saying the same thing. The ruggedness of the speaker is suggested by the tumbling sound of the first two words, both two-syllable words crowded with consonants. The vowel sounds in " 'twouldn't" and "worth" are related, and "worth" also repeats the "r" of "hardly." The most striking sound effect is the repeated "w," which gives the speaker an almost wistful quality. The double negative of " 'twouldn't" and "hardly" is not self-contradictory, but reinforcing in effect, indicating the speaker's strong negative feelings; but both words are weak negatives to begin with, so that his reticence about asserting himself is also suggested.

No playwright would consciously analyze the sounds of his words in this way. The foregoing brief discussion is merely intended to suggest that there can be a vast difference of subtly felt sound effect between even commonplace remarks, and that one of the considerations in the selection of a line of dialogue should be its sound effect. Of course our discussion would be more complex if we related the lines we have discussed to those that might precede and follow them. A line cannot be good all by itself.

Perhaps the most memorable statement about word music occurs in *Hamlet,* when the rejected Ophelia speaks of the effect of her lover's madness on his speech:

> And I, of ladies most deject and wretched,
> That sucked the honey of his music vows,
> Now see that noble and most sovereign reason
> Like sweet bells jangled, out of tune and harsh.

Speech should be beautiful or ugly as the dramatic occasion demands. If a character is under stress, his speech should be capable of going "out of tune." It is a distressing limitation of many modern plays that the characters in them never can speak "out of tune" because they are never "in tune" to begin with.

14. *Word play.* Some people are fond of playing with words. The most obvious kind of word play is the pun, usually a light, and sometimes very bad, form of humor. However, puns may also be used effectively in moments of great seriousness. One of the best examples of this occurs at the most dramatic moment in *Hamlet.* The King has concocted a plan to kill Hamlet. The latter is to fight his friend Laertes in a fencing match, but Laertes will use a rapier with a poisoned tip. If Laertes is unable to kill Hamlet soon enough, the King will offer him a cup of wine into which he will throw a poisoned pearl. Hamlet is offered this

drink, but puts it by for a moment. His mother the Queen sips from the drink and is poisoned. Hamlet, realizing this, kills the King and pours the poisoned wine down his throat while he speaks the following:

Drink off this potion. Is thy union here? Follow my mother.

The word "union" (the Elizabethan word for "pearl") refers first to the jewel that was put in the drink to poison it. It also refers to the almost simultaneous death of the King and Queen, who are united even in death. This particular word play derives even more power from the following additional connotations. The pearl is a psychological symbol for the integration of the personality which comes from a sense of fulfillment in life. The pearl, then, is associated with Hamlet's final success in killing the King, which has been his sole purpose throughout the play. It also ironically refers to the King's purpose in life, which is to deal out death in the strengthening of his own political position. Secondly, throughout the play Hamlet has been deeply concerned with the marriage between his mother and the King, a marriage he considers incestuous, since the Queen married her deceased husband's brother. The union between them has, in effect, poisoned his whole life.

Thus we can see that word play is not always a thing to be taken lightly. It is not, however, a tendency that is found in a great many people, and should not be used indiscriminately in a play. One character, or at most two or three, may engage in it.

Word play involves not only punning, but also imaginative, even bizarre, use of language for deliberate dramatic effect. Humorous metaphors and similes are very common. It may also involve the use of archaic or otherwise unusual words and syntax. It may include deliberate parody, or allusion to well-known works of literature or historical events, frequently in an indirect way.

Word play usually exaggerates the tendencies of the situation to which it refers.

Characters who indulge in word play are often characters with very serious personal problems. They have taken a step beyond grief into a kind of morbid humor that proclaims with endless variation that the world is an unpleasant joke that no one dares to take seriously.

15. *Use of clichés.* At the opposite extreme from the character who delights in word play is the one who is always falling back on clichés. He is usually a humorless person who takes himself very seriously. He identifies the cliché with something essential in his life, and regards it as great wisdom. Whenever he quotes it, it is with a didactic attitude. Because he has difficulty relating meaningfully to others, it is often particularly important to him to try to influence the young as a means of compensating for his sense of his own inferiority. Although this quality may be completely identified with a dramatic character, it is sometimes found in other characters in whom it does not predominate. The tendency to want to be serious without having to do one's own thinking is a common human weakness in which most people indulge from time to time. The writer should be careful that when he uses clichés he uses them to portray character and does not take them seriously himself.

16. *Whimsy, playfulness, and childishness.* Although related to word play, this is not the same quality. It occurs whenever a character has fun not with the structure of language but with its tone. He may lapse into baby talk. He may make innocently absurd statements. He may indulge in pseudopoetry. The character who indulges in word play is often a deeply serious, even tragic, figure; but the character who indulges in whimsy usually is not, though a tragic figure may occasionally indulge in it sarcastically. The whimsical character is likely to be both happy and imaginative. He does not feel that life can be effectively re-

lated to only in terms of what is really happening, so he likes to transcend reality just for the fun of it. He is not necessarily very intelligent, and so his whimsy may have no particular meaning beyond creating an atmosphere of play.

17. *Humorous leading astray*. One of the means of expressing dominance over another person is in terms of what is sometimes called a "put-on." This consists of giving information that is false or misleading, or at least seems to have implications other than the real ones, in order to create temporary confusion in another person. Sometimes it may consist of an elaborate fiction carried on at great length, and perhaps include practical jokes. Much of the plot of Shakespeare's *Merry Wives of Windsor* is little more than an elaborate put-on, and other Shakespeare plays are quite rich in this verbal technique. In a sense, the tragedy in *Othello* is an extended put-on conducted seriously and for malicious purposes. Usually, however, this verbal behavior consists of a few short remarks designed to make another person feel uncomfortable for a short time, and is followed by the revelation that the information given has been false.

18. *Acuteness*. People differ in their ability to relate meaningfully to a situation. For some, a few well-chosen words can sum up perfectly what has happened. For example, in a student improvisation a blind character who had spent the evening by herself while her friends went to a party was asked, "And what did *you* do this evening?" "Oh," she replied, "I sat around and had an exciting time." The girl might have said, "I was bored," or "I didn't do anything." What she did say conveys far more about her life and her relationship to the other character than either of those remarks would have. In the situation in which the remark occurred, the following ideas seemed to be conveyed:

1. I was bored.
2. Because I am bored most of the time,

I have to learn to make boredom exciting.
3. You know perfectly well what I did this evening.
4. Well, *you* certainly had an exciting time, didn't you?
5. You forget what it's like for me to be blind when you ask questions like that.

In that two-line conversation the difference in acuteness of the two characters is clear, and will be even clearer when the reply comes. The first speaker may reply with complete ignorance of the irony that she has heard. She may try to fight back or defend herself. She may change the subject and pretend nothing has happened. She may try to top the blind girl's remark with one that is even more acute.

The acuteness of a remark in no way depends on its length or its poetic richness or the imagination it contains in itself. It is entirely in response to the situation that has occurred, and it condenses into a few words an attitude and evaluation of that situation. When they are uttered by real people, such remarks often go down in history, as, for example, Sir Thomas More's remark to his executioner, "If you'll help me up, I'll see to the coming down."

Remarks of that sort always stand out as memorable moments in a play. They must be well chosen and used sparingly. If a character is always ready with the perfect reply, one begins to feel that things have been rigged by the playwright, who has more time to think than the character could have had. Even so, it may be possible to build a play around a character who is particularly skillful in this way. One such play is *A Man for All Seasons*.

This area of acuteness is one to which the playwright should devote particular attention. It may well be the most important of all the categories we are considering, because it best fulfills the drama's need to idealize human action. One feels when the acute remark is uttered that the character is saying exactly what he ought to say under the circumstances, and that he speaks not only for himself but for the whole culture of which he is a part. Genuine acuteness in a dramatic character gives the audience a sense of power, which arises from its perception of the heights of intelligence and sensitivity of which humanity is capable. It is with the acute remark at its best that the drama rises to a level that is inspirational.

19. *Cleverness*. The distinction between acuteness and cleverness is that acuteness depends for its effect on the totality of the situation, whereas cleverness can exist in and of itself. Because of the very facility of his imagination, the clever person might never penetrate deeply enough to be capable of real acuteness. Cleverness of some sort is to be found in nearly everyone's conversation at some time, but it seldom dominates a character entirely. Anyone who was clever all the time would suffer from an inability to manage genuine human relationships, since cleverness is a way of avoiding involvement in the human qualities of a situation. It is the speaker's way of declaring his independence by demonstrating his mental superiority. A clever remark might be very cruel, or it might be used to break the tension in a difficult situation. When two people engage in a contest of cleverness, both are likely to enjoy the experience; but when only one participant in a conversation is clever, the second is likely to feel uneasy because he cannot rise to the level of the first. In certain situations cleverness wins respect, and it is often a means by which a member of a group who was thought to be inferior may rise in the estimation of other members of the group.

20. *Brittleness*. Some people give the impression that they are always on the verge of a nervous breakdown. Their speech is harsh in tone and staccato in rhythm. They are incapable of receiving any kind of criticism and often see slights when they were not intended. The degree of brittleness of a character's speech is an indication of his degree of discomfort in a given situation in which he cannot express that discomfort

directly. Under such conditions a character will say as little as possible unless he breaks down, at which time he may open the floodgates of his pent-up emotion in a verbal tidal wave.

21. *Jealousy*. Jealousy is a basic human emotion, but it is seldom expressed directly. A common way of expressing it is through some form of one-upmanship. The jealous character wants to get even with the person who has what he does not, and he will resort to subtle means to make that person feel uncomfortable. When a character lacks the imagination to thus express his jealousy, he is likely to be sullen and say as little as possible to the person of whom he is jealous. Fear and jealousy are closely related, so the jealous person may behave as if he were afraid at times. The more jealous a person is, the more his superficial behavior patterns will seem to have an underlying quality of bitterness. A humorous example of how jealousy affects people's speech to one another can be found in Oscar Wilde's *The Importance of Being Earnest* in the scene in which Gwendolyn pays a call on Cecily and discovers that both young women are engaged to Earnest.

22. *Aphoristic quality*. Sometimes a character gets off a concise and pithy precept that fits the situation well enough, but can be quoted just as well out of context. That is called an aphorism. Shakespeare's plays are filled with such remarks; for example, "Sweet are the uses of adversity," or, "What's in a name? That which we call a rose by any other name would smell as sweet." *The Importance of Being Earnest* is a play built almost entirely out of aphorisms, and it is one of the finest comedies in our language. But in general, because the aphorism depends for its success on its own brilliance rather than on its relevance to the situation, it is a dangerous instrument that may detract from the play's effectiveness more than it adds to it. *The Importance of Being Earnest* has never been successfully imitated, and Shakespeare's aphoristic tend-

ency has led many fine playwrights astray. Most serious modern playwrights do without aphorisms almost entirely, though they make good use of acute remarks. Some surrealistic plays make considerable use of pseudo-aphorisms in order to mock the tendency of language to become fossilized. The ending of Ionesco's *The Chairs* provides an example of this.

23. *Symbolism.* Some people see the world as being much more alive with hidden meaning than do others. Their conversation may naturally reflect their awareness of the richness of the symbolism surrounding them, though their awareness of the meaning of that symbolism may be unconscious. A symbol may reflect the mystic qualities of life, or it may be a perfectly ordinary object, such as a piece of chewing gum. It is anything that is used dramatically to mean more than what it means when taken only literally. In other words, any object may become a symbol as soon as it acquires qualities that are attributed to it by the imagination. The speech of the characters in Tennessee Williams' plays is full of symbolism, which is largely derived from the environment in which they live. Shakespeare's characters use many symbols derived from nature or from government. Some surrealistic plays contain conversation that is heavily weighted down with symbolism.

Some objects are thought of primarily as symbols, as, for example, a flag or a wedding ring.

Here the ring is treated as an object only:

A: This ring hurts my finger.
B: Maybe you need a larger one.
A: You're right, I'll get a larger one.

Here the ring is treated as a symbol. The hurt is spiritual, not physical:

A: This ring hurts my finger.
B: I, too, feel the bonds of marriage irksome.
A: Perhaps we should separate.

24. *Abstraction.* Some people talk in language that seldom relates literally to what is happening. Others are extremely literal in what they say.

A: I'd like to be wafted away on wings of song.
B: You're too heavy.

Abstraction can reflect a religious or mystical frame of mind, or it can reflect mere vagueness. It may be that the person who talks in abstractions is so disturbed by the world in which he must live that he cannot bear to think about it, and so lives in a world of the mind. It may be that he simply enjoys flights of fancy.

Abstractions are good or poor depending on how effectively they are derived from real experiences. A person who is unable to perceive reality meaningfully will think in poorly organized, often bizarre abstractions. A person who can perceive reality, but simply doesn't wish to, may have brilliantly organized abstract thoughts. The playwright should be careful to handle both good and poor abstractions as sensitively as the character himself would handle them. Shakespeare's Richard II thinks in poorly organized, bizarre abstractions, but they are so sensitively portrayed that Richard is one of Shakespeare's most poetic and memorable characters. Insanity must be portrayed with special sensitivity, and from the insane person's point of view. Remember that whatever such a person says makes sense to him; and the playwright must at least feel that sense, even if he does not literally understand it.

25. *Multiple levels of meaning.* Occasionally a person finds it desirable to speak in a way that has more than one level of meaning. This would be likely to occur if two characters share a secret that other characters present on the scene do not know of. Sometimes a character speaks on multiple levels entirely for his own gratification, or as an indication of the depth of his

mind. Some of the categories already discussed, such as word play and abstraction, almost invariably have more than one level of meaning, but the tendency to speak on several levels is a significant category in itself, which reveals in a character either a momentary or permanent tendency toward depth or secrecy.

26. *Level of consciousness.* Consciousness is not something that either is or is not present in a person. It is always present in varying degrees. A person in a drunken stupor is operating at a lower level of consciousness than is one under ordinary conditions, whereas a person of very high intelligence or sensitivity is operating at a higher level of consciousness. Some people seem unaware of almost everything that is going on around them, even their own tendency to be the butt of a great deal of humor. Others have an awareness that seems almost supernatural. One of the first impressions one usually has of another person is of his level of consciousness. This impression is often accurate, though it may be affected somewhat by another person's shyness or his attempt to conceal the degree of his awareness. If the level of consciousness is very low, the character lives in what is called a primary sensory world. That means that most of the things he thinks and talks about are things that he can actually see and touch. To others he will seem primarily concerned with trivia. If his awareness goes beyond the obvious features of reality that surround him, it usually takes the form of a rather vague admiration of certain people or ideas that have been influential in his life. A character whose level of consciousness is very high can shift easily from concern for everyday things to concern for things that affect the whole pattern of living. He will tend to relate to other people more or less in terms of their level of consciousness, picking up the tone of voice of the person with whom he converses and adopting a different style with each.

If you wish to study the conversation of people whose level of consciousness is varied but generally low, read the plays of Chekhov. If you are interested in how people with a very high level of consciousness talk to one another, read the plays of Shaw. Shakespeare's characters range through all the levels of consciousness. It is interesting that often an ironic contrast is found in Shakespeare's plays between level of consciousness and station in life. For example, compare the level of consciousness of Polonius with that of the Second Gravedigger in *Hamlet*.

27. *Exclamatory quality.* Some people's reactions to exciting events are immediate and intense, like the steam rising from a pan of boiling water. Whenever anything arouses them, they express a full reaction to it. Others react immediately but far less intensely, radiating a little warmth like a pan of lukewarm water. Some are like a pressure cooker, feeling intensely but holding the feeling inside, perhaps exclaiming only long after the event. The more intellectual people are, the more they tend to temper and delay their reactions. It has been observed that in our culture a much higher percentage of profane words are spoken by lower-class people than by higher-class people. Many obvious exceptions to this exist, but in general the exclamatory tendency drops as one becomes more thoughtful. Because this is true, the most dramatic moments are often the quietest ones. Think, for example, of the last line of Robert Frost's poem, "The Death of the Hired Man": " 'Dead,' was all he answered." Contrast that with an outburst like, "Oh woe, oh woe, oh woe, alack the day."

28. *Repetitiveness.* The repetition of words and phrases may point to a childlike quality in the speaker, for it is characteristic of children to love to hear the same sounds repeated over and over. It is important to observe the form that the repetition takes. It may induce boredom: "I was saying to myself only last week, I was saying, well yes, what was it I was saying, oh yes, it was only

last week that I was saying to myself . . ." Or reflect desire: "yes I said yes I will Yes." Or express poetic yearning: "In the long, long darkness that has filled my life since, I have longed for the blackness of his eyes, and the blackness of his hair, and the blackness of his shadow on the door."

Whenever something is repeated, it is because the initial statement of it was not considered adequate. Perhaps it has been forgotten. Perhaps it does not give sufficient vent to the emotion. Perhaps the speaker does not believe the listener has heard. Perhaps he does not believe the listener is smart enough to get it the first time. Perhaps he is himself either stupid or obsessively purposeful. The playwright should always know what the repetition indicates about the character who uses it. Used well, repetition can be a powerful way of revealing character. Used poorly, it is by far the commonest cause of a play's seeming to be too long.

29. *Ecstasy.* People differ in their ability to enjoy life. One must feel his degree of enjoyment in each word that a person says. This need not necessarily be expressed directly, for many apparently cynical and ironic people enjoy life intensely, whereas many who insist that it is wonderful (mainly to convince themselves of the fact) really do not enjoy it at all. Also, ecstasy is not necessarily expressed through energy, for very energetic people often hate themselves, whereas quiet people often enjoy an inner peace. The expression of ecstasy is very subtle indeed, and there is probably no way to describe it. It may, however, be related to the degree of control a person feels he has over his life. If he feels that he says and does what pleases him, his words and his deeds will have a freedom that cannot be imitated by those who wish they were in other circumstances. Freedom of that kind is not dependent on external freedom. Many people brought up in almost total freedom suffer from so little ability to control their own impulses that they are always victims of their own whims. On the other hand, remember

the famous lines, "Stone walls do not a prison make,/Nor iron bars a cage."

30. *Weltschmerz.* The eternal pain of life, an agony from which there is no escape, is something of which some people like to keep reminding themselves. That sort of thing became extremely fashionable during the nineteenth century, predominantly among people who had lots of money and lots of time and very little responsibility. Characteristic of world-weariness is the feeling that high hopes have been dashed either by a single traumatic event or by a mysterious set of events that have deeply affected the personality. Weltschmerz is not very common among people under stress. It is usually found among people who have every external reason for enjoying life, but who hate themselves. The feeling of self-hatred is projected onto the world, so that every situation is interpreted in the worst possible light, and the speaker gives the impression of being down on everything. Weltschmerz is often expressed with a kind of cynical, satiric humor.

31. *Grotesquerie.* Occasional use of bizarre strangeness for its own sake may characterize a person who likes to escape from the rigidity of his usual personality or situation. Such behavior has a slight quality of self-intoxication. Such a character might make up words or distort existing ones. Writing in a grotesque style is easy to do and can be lots of fun. The playwright should avoid using it, however, unless he is sure of its dramatic purpose.

32. *Anxiety, precognition, and guilt.* Some people have a feeling that doomsday is just around the corner, or that because of their past guilt some terrible calamity is about to befall them. Such feelings are often expressed in fatalistic language that deals in large abstractions and uses symbolism. A character having these feelings usually has a hard time relating to other people and dislikes referring to himself because of his feelings of worthlessness. He is likely to be aloof and indirect in his expression.

33. *Fatuity*. The complacently stupid person uses language in a highly predictable way. He tends to say the obvious and to mouth moral precepts that are widely agreed upon. He is incapable of seeing anything erroneous in his own conduct and equally convinced that those he does not like are entirely in error. He is given to committing himself to things and refusing to compromise as a matter of principle. He is almost totally lacking in a sense of humor. He tends to repeat himself a great deal.

34. *Preciosity*. The overrefined person uses language affectedly. He tries to find big words where little ones will do, particularly big words that have more superficial appeal than sense. He is also fond of elaborate syntax and unusual figures of speech. He does not, however, use language very imaginatively, and is easily defeated at word play. One of the best examples of preciosity in literature is to be found in the character of Osric in *Hamlet*. In his scene with Hamlet he allows his use of language to be mocked without having any awareness of what is happening. Anyone capable of a great deal of preciosity is largely blind to the subtleties of human communication and settles for superficial sound patterns in their stead.

35. *Drive*. The overall energy level of a person is reflected in his speech. This is a physical matter relating to metabolism, and it is all-pervasive, though a given individual's energy level fluctuates from day to day. Energy level may be reflected in the way words move toward their culmination in a sentence. If one senses a need to get the sentence over with as quickly as possible and get on to something else, that indicates a strong drive. More often than not, men of action are men of few words. If, on the other hand, the sentence rambles and moves slowly, the drive is weak.

36. *Interests*. People indicate their interests subtly in their speech. Only a person who is so wrapped up in one thing that he can think of nothing else is likely to refer directly to his interest all the time. But in subtle ways interests will affect speech. If two people are conversing about the weather, it should be easy to tell which is the sportsman and which the bookworm. Two people meeting for the first time usually feel each other out, looking for common interests. Only when these have been found does their speech become really personal.

37. *DePersonalization*. People differ in how much they personalize their speech. One person may draw the conversation immediately toward himself, whereas another will try to steer clear of involvement. The former may quickly reveal his likes and dislikes and react strongly to other people. The latter may remain aloof and mysterious, so that one never knows quite where he stands. It is important for any two people to decide in their own minds how personal they want their relationship to be. If they feel at odds about this, they are likely to embarrass and irritate each other. Sometimes, however, the aloof person is so not out of choice, but out of lack of courage. He may really want to be led into a more personal relationship. The outgoing person who senses this often derives considerable satisfaction from drawing him out. The scene with the Gentleman Caller in *The Glass Menagerie* is an excellent example of such a situation.

Depersonalization sometimes occurs as a result of spiritual deprivation. The door-to-door salesman who has become so used to having a smile pasted on his face that he is afraid to look into his true emotions may become incapable of being really personal. Invited to do so, he will retreat into clichés. Arthur Miller's *Death of a Salesman* is a brilliant portrait of a man who has been thus depersonalized.

38. *Approach-withdrawal*. Closely related to but not synonymous with the above is the tendency either to approach or withdraw from unfamiliar situations. It is a question of the basic trust that a person feels in the world around him. The person who

habitually withdraws will tend to use language that is noncommittal rather than express himself positively. He is constantly afraid of what may happen, of what others will think, of what he might do wrong. The person who habitually approaches is also capable of backing away quickly and clearly. He is not afraid to say, "I don't want to," or "I hate him." The withdrawal-oriented person, on the other hand, may have to use indirect means of expressing dislike.

39. *Hostility.* In the handling of hostility in dialogue, the playwright faces a special problem that does not occur with any of the other categories. Everyone in our society suffers from a certain amount of repressed hostility, and writing plays is an effective and socially acceptable way of expressing some of that hostility. One can create the type of character toward whom one feels hostility and then cause him to suffer indignities at the hands of other characters. A high proportion of the dialogue in many popular plays expresses hostility, perhaps for this reason. The difficulty arises when the playwright abuses the opportunity to express hostility. When that happens, the play becomes unreal. Characters express themselves more quickly and more directly than they would in real life, and the feelings of the butt of the hostility are likely to be poorly accounted for. It is therefore very important that the playwright consider carefully the effect of each hostile remark on the character toward whom it is directed. He should further ask himself whether in a real-life situation the amount of hostility uttered in his play would be possible, and what would make it possible.

Because most people are afraid of facing conflict, the direct expression of hostility is relatively rare in real life. It is more often communicated by indirect means, sometimes without the awareness of the person communicating it. An excessively relaxed posture or tone of voice is one means of expressing it. A subtle putting down of the person one is talking to in a way that cannot be held against one is another. Expressions of hostility of this kind are quite common in our society.

When hostility is expressed directly, it is usually after lengthy repression, and it can then be cataclysmic in its effect. The feeling between two people that they are permanently rupturing the social amenities that have existed between them can be shattering for both, and is likely to make them further lose control of their emotions. Such shattering cannot occur on slight provocation; it takes a series of major incidents to bring it about.

Some people express hostility more easily than others. These people are generally of two kinds. Either they tend to fly off the handle easily and then forgive and forget, which can sometimes be a healthy approach to life, or they suffer from such generalized feelings of hostility that they antagonize everyone. The latter sort of person suffers from mild or severe mental illness, and if his behavior is carried to extremes he must be institutionalized. Such people usually have mercurial emotions, which means that they may be very friendly one moment and violently hostile the next.

Another and much rarer sort of hostile person is the one who seems friendly and deferential almost all of the time. He is, however, seething with a hostility that he can find no way to express. Under the influence of alchohol or a traumatic experience, or perhaps simply as a result of temporarily blacking out, he may become violently hostile, sometimes even committing a serious crime. When such a person gives in to his hostility, it is the most violent of all, for it is completely out of his control.

40. *Coercion.* Several ways may be found to force a person to do what one wants him to. The most obvious is the use of physical force. But remember Aesop's fable of the sun and the wind, in which both attempted to remove a man's coat. The wind tried to blow it off, but the man only wrapped it more tightly around him. The sun made him

too warm, so he took his coat off. Similarly, coercion can be more effectively accomplished by indirect, psychological means than by physical ones. Indeed, the only reason for undertaking direct coercion is to satisfy one's own sadistic desires, since it is either highly inefficient or totally ineffective in most cases.

When you get someone to do what you want him to by indirect means, you may either change his mind so that he wants to do it, which is not coercion but persuasion; or you may make life so unpleasant for him until he has done it that he prefers to do it to escape the unpleasantness. Tears are an effective means of doing this. So is the withdrawal of love. The technique may be reversed: Pretended joy may be expressed when the desired thing has been done; or one may offer love, renewed or increased. In relationships between adults, the use of such techniques of coercion often has undesirable results.

An interesting complication of the coercion phenomenon is the double-bind situation. It is possible to demand of someone two conflicting actions, so that no matter what he does he feels guilty and can be punished. If a mother asks her child to give her a big hug and then wonders how he can dare to hug her when his hands are so dirty, she has created a double-bind situation. Such situations are created by people who suffer from internal conflicts which they can express only by causing other people to suffer from the same conflicts. Much of the dramatic power of Arthur Miller's *After the Fall* lies in its effective use of double-bind situations.

41. *Condescension.* One of the decisions that must be made whenever two people relate socially is whether they are on the same level and meet as equals. If one person speaks to another with condescension, he thereby indicates that he believes he is superior in some way. The condescension may be genuine and desirable, as between a doctor and patient, or a teacher and stu-

dent. It may be genuine and undesirable, as between victor and vanquished. Or it may exist only in the mind of the person who is condescending, in which case the other person will either pretend to accept the condescension for the sake of politeness, or will change or abandon the relationship. Finally, it may exist only in the mind of the person who thinks he is being condescended to.

42. *Etiquette.* Often people depend on etiquette to help them handle unfamiliar situations. However, agreement is not always possible as to what system of etiquette should be used. This becomes particularly important when people whose social backgrounds are very different must meet socially, and is of crucial importance when value judgments are made on the basis of etiquette. Bernard Shaw's comedy *Pygmalion,* and the musical based on it, *My Fair Lady,* explore this question and provide many interesting examples of the relation between speech and etiquette. Etiquette becomes dramatically interesting whenever an individual cannot cope with the social situations demanded of him. Under such conditions he usually reveals much about his background and personality that would not otherwise be so clear.

Etiquette is just as important in subcultures as it is in high society, though there it is not usually referred to by that name. *The Silent Language* by Edward T. Hall discusses many ways in which people in various cultures communicate unspoken ideas by means of behavior and speech patterns associated with those cultures. It is a book that the aspiring playwright should study with a view toward discovering how the words of his dialogue must interrelate with the behavior patterns of his characters in order to suggest human relationships.

43. *Obsequiousness.* In many ways this is the opposite of condescension, though it tends to be more complex in its psychology. The obsequious person tries to make others feel that they are superior to him and that

he is at their service. He does so in the hope of some sort of reward from them. Obsequiousness may occasionally become so deeply ingrained in a person that he is uncomfortable acting otherwise. More often the obsequious person harbors secret contempt for those who take his obsequies at face value. The obsequiousness is a mask for that contempt, and a means of subtly manipulating the person at whom it is directed. The obsequious person behaves as if the other person were always completely right, meanwhile dissociating himself from any serious concern for what that person really wants. Exceptions occur when servants identify themselves so completely with their masters that they derive their own sense of achievement in life from their masters' achievements. That tendency is very common in societies with little or no social mobility, but it is rapidly disappearing in modern times. A servant's identification with his master's purposes has been carried to humorous extremes by P. G. Wodehouse in his delightful Jeeves stories.

44. *Euphemisms.* People differ in what they consider taboo subjects of conversation. Everyone has some taboos, but some have more than others. Even within an intimate group of people, differing tendencies to use euphemistic language will occur. Thus, it is important to observe when writing a play that some people swear a lot and others not at all, and that some people relate to slightly embarrassing situations easily and directly, whereas others would rather allude to them vaguely. In our society women tend to be more euphemistic than men, which means that a woman whose language is relatively relaxed becomes by that very fact dramatically interesting, and a man whose language is euphemistic also draws attention to himself as a character. Edward Albee's plays derive some of their impact from that kind of contrast in language behavior.

The use of taboo language presents special problems for the playwright, particularly at the present time. If he is himself repressed, he enjoys the release of having his characters swear a great deal. But because audiences react very strongly to taboo language, too much of it can detract significantly from the effectiveness of the play. If he is not careful, the playwright will get the audience more emotionally involved in the four-letter words he uses than in the dramatic content of his play. On the other hand, it is his obligation to use the language that would naturally be used by the characters he is portraying. The censorship problems that result from trying to achieve the proper balance in this matter are often complex, and tend to vary from one situation to another. The best guide for the playwright in the use of taboo language is this: When in doubt, leave it out. The playwright must also guard against the opposite tendency, which would be to burden his characters with his own personal taboos. They should not be more euphemistic than they naturally would be.

The category of euphemism is obvious when applied to four-letter words, but much more subtle when applied to situations that may be special to a given play. How openly can a character speak of a love affair that has ended unhappily? Suppose he meets a handicapped person for the first time: Does he refer to the handicap, or pretend it does not exist?

Personal euphemisms often derive from personal problems. An overweight person will be sensitive to the word "fat" and will have to adjust to the use of that word. He might do so by constantly alluding to his fatness in order to pretend to himself and others that he is not sensitive on the subject. He might systematically avoid all discussion of the topic and become very embarrassed whenever it is mentioned.

Those topics that are embarrassing are determined partly by culture, and partly on an individual basis. For example, it is a social liability to be fat, but not to be bald. Few people, therefore, would use euphemisms in relation to baldness, but an occasional character might have his own personal reasons for being euphemistic on the subject. Also, what is embarrassing changes as styles change. At one time, the word "black" when applied to a Negro was a word that caused embarrassment. Now it is used openly and with great pride. It used to be embarrassing to have it known that one was visiting a psychiatrist. Now many people talk openly about their "shrinks."

45. *Sense of humor.* One of the most important things to know about a person is the quality of his sense of humor. If he can stand back from a difficult situation and laugh at it, he can save himself much of the pain of life. If he can laugh at himself from time to time, he enjoys a great advantage. Some people are so rigid in their approach to life that they can laugh at nothing, and they are often types who unconsciously encourage others to laugh at them and play practical jokes on them. A character need not always be joking to reveal a sense of humor. In fact, people who have no sense of humor often tell jokes, though usually rather weak ones. Sense of humor is suggested by a relaxed, spontaneous approach to life. If nobody in your play has a sense of humor, things are likely to get rather dismal.

There is an important cultural factor in sense of humor. What is funny goes out of style more rapidly than what is serious. Moreover, humor is difficult to translate from one language to another. In addition, some cultures have a more highly developed sense of humor than others. For example, the English find it far easier to laugh at themselves than do the Americans.

Now that we have come this far in our examination of speech categories, you will probably derive the most benefit from beginning to apply them. Read a good play and place numbers here and there in the text, identifying the categories you find there as they are numbered above. You will not always be certain how to label a particular line, and you should not worry about that. It is not important that you have an accurate sense of speech categories, but rather that you sense the variety of them and the interplay between them. When you have analyzed parts of several plays in the way described above, write some of your own dialogue and analyze that. Then compare the numbers you find in your dialogue with the numbers you find in other plays. Are there some that you consistently avoid, others that you overuse? The exercise should help you to see your dialogue as others will see it. If you find that you are weak in important areas, practice them by writing long passages of dialogue in which you limit yourself to them.

So far the approach to writing dialogue discussed in this chapter has been rather technical. But good dialogue must be observed and felt, not imitated and analyzed. The purpose of the analytical exercises is to get you to increase your awareness of what is happening in speech. A good next exercise is to work with tape-recorded conversations, listening to the same conversation several times and seeing how many speech categories you can identify in it. This makes an excellent group exercise, for different members of the group will hear different things, and the discussion that results should increase everyone's awareness of what happens in speech. Bear in mind, though, that final agreement as to exactly which speech categories were heard is unlikely to result and is unimportant anyway.

So that you will not get too slavish in your approach to what we have written so far, you are encouraged to expand the descriptions of the speech categories that follow. In this way you will begin to think in terms of deriving the categories from observation, rather than hearing only what you have been predisposed to hear. Finally, you should add some categories of your own discovery to this list (we have purposely omitted some rather obvious ones), and write descriptions of those as well.

You should expect that as a result of doing this series of exercises a reorientation will take place in your thinking that will make you temporarily unable to write as well as you would like to. Once you have given yourself time to digest the results of your work, however, you will find that you can write much better than you formerly could because your awareness has been significantly sharpened. You will know that you have reached this stage when you no longer have to think about the different categories, but simply feel as if people were speaking inside of you.

Now let us briefly describe our additional speech categories.

46. *Egotism.* How obviously or subtly is the character concerned with himself?

47. *Heroic quality.* Is the speech larger than life in its suggestion of the greatness and power of the character?

48. *Dramatic quality.* Does the character dramatize himself?

49. *Lyrical quality.* Does the character want to sound like a poet?

50. *Paranoia.* Some people feel that everyone is out to get them.

51. *Narrow-mindedness.* People who have made up their minds on all subjects seem opinionated, and are difficult to converse with.

52. *Didacticism.* This occurs whenever one person feels he is teaching another something.

53. *Lecturing.* When a character talks at great length in a formal way, expecting others to listen quietly and not interrupt, he is lecturing, whether or not he is in a lecture hall.

54. *Narrative.* Often it is necessary for a character to tell a story. If you would like to know how many interesting forms of narration there are read *The Canterbury Tales.*

55. *Propaganda.* A character may have a vested interest in changing another character's mind about something.

56. *Domineering quality.* Some people expect everyone else to do as they say.

57. *Conflict.* Two characters may be in direct opposition, so that the action of each causes an equal and opposite reaction in the other.

58. *Group orientation.* Some people are introverts, others extroverts. You should know how comfortable your character feels in a crowd.

59. *Assistance.* Some situations demand that assistance be given. The way a person gives it will be revealing. Does he give it when it is not needed?

60. *Domesticity.* People feel differing degrees of comfort about being at home.

61. *Functionalism.* How does a person see himself as he is performing a task?

62. *Professionalism.* How does a person see himself in his role on the job?

63. *Materialism.* What is the comparative importance in his life of things and ideas?

64. *Logic.* Is he logical? Is he pseudological? Does he deliberately avoid logic? ("Don't confuse me with the facts.")

65. *Definition orientation.* How good is he at deciding what something means and agreeing with someone else about its meaning?

66. *Self-deprecation.* Does he seem to find fault with himself too frequently?

67. *Legal and moral orientation.* Some people care a great deal whether it is all right to perform a given act. Others worry about the consequences later, if at all.

68. *Motivation.* How great a sense of purpose does a character have, and how does that affect what he does?

69. *Significance.* The significance of what a person says and his awareness of that significance are two different things.

70. *Ambiguity.* Does what is said lead to two or more possible conclusions?

71. *Parallelism.* Are similar ideas expressed in similar patterns?

72. *Oxymoron.* This is a verbal device involving the juxtaposition of an adjective and a noun that are opposites. It is paradoxical in effect and often very significant in its implications ("loving hate," "gentle roughness").

73. *Positiveness.* Some people can see something good in almost any situation.

74. *Analytic and synthetic thinking.* Is the character more oriented toward taking things apart or putting them together?

75. *Consistency.* Most people are inconsistent. Some people think it is very important to be consistent. Bear in mind that "a foolish consistency is the hobgoblin of little minds."

76. *Tendency to catalogue.* List-making can include anything from stamps to spiritual experiences.

77. *Tendency to explore.* Does the character want to know what is going on in any situation?

78. *Fantasy.* Some people live more in the imagination than in the physical world.

79. *Mythopoesis.* Myth-making has fascinated certain modern poets and novelists. It could also be indulged in by a character in a play.

80. *Religion.* Is the character either genuinely or superficially religious?

81. *Romanticism.* Is the character fascinated by the extremely beautiful and the exotic, and does he try to see his own experiences in those terms?

82. *Love.* People who are in love have ways of talking to each other that are both special and universal. A person of generally loving nature uses some of these ways.

83. *Hyperbole.* A poetic exaggeration that goes way beyond the possible is often dramatically effective.

84. *Conceit.* A figure of speech may be extended so that various implications of the same metaphor are explored at length. You can find many examples in the poetry of John Donne.

85. *Alliteration and consonance.* Deliberate repetition of consonant or vowel sounds is sometimes consciously used by people for artificial effect.

86. *Tone.* Writers must indicate tone of voice by choice of words. Some people vary their tone more often than others.

87. *Mixed metaphor.* When a thing is compared to something else and the comparison is switched without warning, we have a mixed metaphor. It usually indicates disorganized thinking.

88. *Time orientation.* Does the character live primarily in the past, the present, or the future?

89. *Health.* Most changes in one's state of health are reflected in his speech patterns.

90. *Age.* Early childhood and senility have obvious speech patterns associated with them. In between, the differences are more subtle, but they are always present.

That completes our suggested listing of speech categories. As you reflect on what you have read, remember that each person has both an overall style of speaking and a characteristic style that he uses in the presence of a given other person. In other words, people adjust their styles of speech constantly as they talk to different people. The more rigid the personality, the less variation there will be in a person's style of speech as he shifts from talking to one person to talking to someone else. Such a character may find some people with whom he cannot communicate at all. On the other hand, a very unstable person may change his speech significantly as he speaks to various people. In a case of extreme instability, a character might even echo the exact words used by another person, indicating his desire to escape from the limitations of his own existence. Hamlet, one of the most unstable characters in all literature, changes his style rather drastically as he addresses the many people about the court. Polonius, on the other hand, shows his rigidity of thought and action by always talking in about the same way. Hamlet attacks Polonius' manner of speaking in an attempt to force him out of his rigidity; but Polonius, believing Hamlet to be mad, and therefore believing that his words are not serious, remains unmoved by the Prince's efforts.

Our approach to dialogue in this chapter has been entirely analytic. But your job is to put everything together into a play. Ultimately you will want to forget all about speech categories and just write as your newly strengthened imagination tells you to. You will want to be free of the artificial, analytical feeling you get about dialogue when you are first practicing speech categories. Rest assured that with practice you will achieve that freedom. Meanwhile, in the next chapter we shall consider some ways in which the larger patterns in dialogue interrelate.

Chapter XIII

DESIGNING THE DIALOGUE

One of the biggest differences between a play and a novel concerns the matter of shape. A novel may be of any length, and may ramble at the author's whim. A play must have a carefully constructed design that one senses as it unfolds. Critics will never agree on *how* a play must be shaped, but any play is certain to fail if its shape is unclear. We have already considered some of the ways in which the plot is structured, but shape also implies that every line, and indeed every word, must have a precise relation to the rest of the play. All of the lines are interwoven into a pattern like fine lace.

Among the first things that you notice about a pattern is that although all parts of it are necessary, they do not all make an equal claim on your attention. Some things leap out at you; others recede into the background. The same is true with a play. Nothing could be more tedious than a play in which every line had the same power. There must be some five or six that the audience will go away remembering. Do not try for too many; you will only get fewer. They are the high points, the things that the rest of the play is working up to and away from.

Perhaps the greatest fault of the amateur is overwriting. A good part of writing a play is holding things back, so that one is not too forceful or dramatic or even funny. An audience can take only so much, and the author must learn how much he may

give them. He is likely to feel that if a certain way of speaking is effective, an exaggeration of that way is even more so. Good dialogue, on the other hand, requires of its author a highly developed feeling for moderation. An audience will be more excited when it is doing part of the emotional work of the play, wanting the characters to intensify their reactions. Understatement can be very powerful.

Another common pitfall is lack of contrast. If the author has fallen in love with a particular style, he may impose that style on all of his characters. No play is helped by having two characters in it, no matter how interesting they may be, who are interesting in the same way. Contrast between speakers should be so clear that if the play is read aloud by one person who does not change his tone of voice and does not identify the names of the speakers, it is possible to tell who is speaking when. If you have doubts about your own play in this respect, you can easily put it to the test. Each character must contrast with the others and be consistently the same person in his own right. While shifting tone as he moves from one character to another, the author may temporarily lose sight of one of the characters and allow him to sound like a different person. This is hard to avoid, and even the best professionals need to revise carefully to get all of the characters sounding just right.

Still another pitfall lies in the author's

tendency to get bored with his own writing. If you are bored, your audience will be too. Boredom results from the fact that the desire to write a play often stems from a desire to write certain scenes or situations that the play contains. Getting up to those situations presents problems, and the author is likely to become overconscientious. He will have the characters saying and doing what they should to get where they are going, but he will not really be interested in what is happening. In a good play, every situation is interesting in itself. To conquer boredom, the playwright must keep working new material into his play. He will probably need many more situations than he started with.

This is an area in which a group of playwrights can be helpful to one another. After a synopsis of an act or the act itself has been read to the group, each participant can be asked to write out several subsidiary situations that might be added to the act to enrich its action. If the playwright examines the lists and finds he has a large number of ideas to choose from, he will not feel that he is stealing someone else's idea, as he might if only a few suggestions were made. Even if he uses an idea exactly as suggested, it is he who has selected it from the many available. More likely, the list of suggestions will spur his imagination, and he will think of ideas of his own that perfectly fit his original concept. The problem is to get into every moment of the unfolding of the action some twist that is itself dramatically interesting. When the young playwright finds out what a demand that places on him, he may feel inadequate. But once he has met the demand, his sense of accomplishment will be great.

Another concern for the beginning writer is the most basic rule in all writing: do not tell, show. Things must be made to happen, not narrated. Seldom is a long narrative acceptable in a drama. If events previous to the action of the play are to be narrated, information about them should be slipped in here and there, rather than stated in a long,

boring monologue. If such a monologue is necessary, it should be interrupted by other characters who want to know what is going to happen next. It might be a good idea never to let a character say anything in the way of exposition unless another character, for reasons understandable to the audience, drags it out of him. An exception to this rule is the soliloquy addressed to the audience by a character who takes on the role of a narrator. This storytelling technique may provide a framework for events that would otherwise be too episodic, and it is often a vehicle for theatre poetry that might seem too mannered if worked into the action more directly. In general, however, the playwright should keep our attention on what is happening now, rather than on what has happened in the past. Bear in mind the rule for getting the past into your play: focus attention always on its effect on the present. Some of Ibsen's plays, particularly *Ghosts,* provide excellent examples of how most of the important things in a play can have happened before the curtain rises, and yet our concern will consistently be with what is happening in the dramatic present.

If your play is a comedy, you will want to try to plan where the laughs are to come. Only a limited number can occur in a given period of time, and trying to add funny lines to a part of a play that already has its quota would only reduce the humor of some of the lines already present. It is also important to remember that a comedy should get funnier as it goes along, so that the laugh lines should be sparsely distributed near the beginning and more thickly distributed toward the end. The last five or ten minutes of a comedy should not be so funny, but should allow the audience to experience the warm glow of seeing all the characters work out satisfactory relationships with one another at the end of an enjoyable evening.

If your play is serious, you will still need some good laugh lines in it, to break the tension. These must be placed with great care. If you do not include them and the tension becomes too great, the audience will laugh at things that you intended seriously. This is because audiences can take only a limited amount of tension and eventually seek release in laughter.

Early drafts of your play are likely to suffer from excess verbiage. Much of the dialogue you have written will need to be condensed. Some of the conversation and events will prove irrelevant to what you are trying to accomplish, and those should be taken out. As you copy over a scene of dialogue, try as hard as you can to omit everything that can possibly be left out.

It is wise to keep early drafts very short because the essentials of a play will not have been fully explored in them as yet. In the chapter on deepening the implications we have indicated a number of techniques for getting away from the superficialities of an early draft. Do not be surprised at your own superficiality; you are merely human in that respect. Listening is a rare talent and must be developed. Because we do not know how to listen to one another, we are likely to write characters that do not know how to do so either. In an early draft they are likely to skim the surface of a situation and produce the superficiality that must be combated by careful revision.

But do not confuse depth with complexity. When you are writing a play, you are solving a series of artistic problems. You can solve these problems best by using the simplest solution open to you. Do not use an elephant to kill a fly. Do not have a major character murdered so that your lovers will have enough money to get married. Keep the plotting relatively simple and let the richness of your thinking go to explore the relationships between the characters. You will find that your characters develop their relationships as they become more attentive to one another.

An improvisation exercise will help you realize just what is involved in true dramatic interchange. Have two people carry on a conversation in which everything that each person says must be directly based on what the other previously said. Nothing new may be introduced except as part of the response to the other. Sounds easy? Try it. Time and again the speakers, after only a few lines, will want to skip on to something else. If they avoid doing so they are likely to find themselves discovering a rich and subtle relationship between them. Sometimes people who do this exercise attempt to avoid emotional involvement, so that their conversation becomes intellectual but not very exciting to listen to. If that problem arises, make an additional stipulation that everything that is said must have something to do with how the speaker feels about what is going on. The improvisation should be interrupted and started over whenever there is a failure to respond to the previous speaker's statement. It may take a long time before the two speakers begin to relate to each other effectively.

Now apply what has been learned to your playwriting. Are your characters interacting, or are they cut off from one another? (It is possible for two characters who are emotionally separated from each other to interact dramatically. They can communicate about their emotional separateness.)

We have explored in this chapter the importance of patterning the dialogue. All of the lines must not be of equal importance. Dramatic power is likely to grow out of understatement more often than overstatement. Characters must be in sufficient contrast with one another. Boredom can be avoided by increasing the variety of the material. The action that precedes the play must be handled naturally in the conversation of the characters. Laugh lines must be properly placed throughout the play. The playwright must be as economical with words as he can. The complexities of the play should grow out of the interrelationships of the characters. These observations summarize what the playwright should keep in mind as he works on and revises his dialogue. But simply remembering such rules will not produce good dialogue. The playwright should actually experience how an audience reacts to his work in order to develop a feeling for the subtleties that will be most effective in getting the response he wants. We shall discuss in Chapter XV some of the problems of working with an original play in production.

Part IV: PUTTING THE PLAY IN FINAL FORM

Chapter XIV

REVISING YOUR PLAY

We come now to that area in which it is most difficult to give advice. Everyone has, or should have, his own way of revising a play. Some writers revise as they go along, never proceeding from one scene to the next until each scene is perfect. Once such a writer has completed his play, there is little need for further work on it. Others write very rapidly and then rewrite many times, sometimes over a period of years. Revision is a very personal thing because it is your way of making sure that the total effect of your play is exactly what you want it to be.

In the early stages of working on your play you tend to put down whatever comes to mind, but while you are revising you must act partly as a critic of what you have written earlier. It is important, therefore, to come to terms with the process of criticizing your work. Beginning playwrights tend to experience three common difficulties with regard to criticism.

The first is the feeling that criticism implies that the playwright is inadequate. Many beginners think too highly of their work and feel shattered when any imperfections are pointed out. They are the victims of a false and vulnerable pride, which may develop in the following way: Having read or seen a few modern plays, one decides that they are overrated and that it should be easy to write something just as good. As the young hopeful begins to work, he determines to put into his play many of the imaginative qualities he feels other plays lack. Usually that means putting in more of something: more poetry, more excitement, or more unusual events or characters. Whatever else it is, the new play must not be commonplace.

While he works, the writer may sense that what he is doing is not really the best of which he is capable; but he convinces himself that it is rather good anyway. His masterpiece will come later, but here is a play that will shock or excite or provoke laughter as no play ever written before. He keeps these thoughts to himself, of course, and to others professes great modesty.

After he has worked on his play for a while, and perhaps finished it, he exposes it to some kind of criticism. Perhaps he shows it to a teacher or a friend. Perhaps it is discussed in a playwriting class; perhaps it is even performed. The young writer asks eagerly for criticism, but feels confident that he will receive only praise. The faults he was aware of in his work as he was writing it are not really so bad after all, and are not likely to be noticed by anyone else.

How great his chagrin when the response he receives is not the awed recognition of genius he had expected, but rather a lukewarm praise of some quality that is liked and a generous helping of suggestions about what could be done better! Disillusioned and disgusted at the insensitivity of the world and horrified at his own ineptness, the playwright declares inwardly that he will never write again. He quickly forgets all about the specific criticisms of his play and remembers only that it was unappreciated. Soon he is able to take solace from the belief that the world has lost a potential genius, and that the theatre will have to die without his assistance in reviving it.

It would be easy to abandon our young friend to his self-pitying woes, if it were not for the fact he may indeed be a genius. If one examines the early work of nearly every great playwright from Shakespeare to Tennessee Williams, one finds many sorts of ineptness. In his early tragedy *Titus Andronicus,* Shakespeare apparently set out to write the bloodiest, most horrifying drama ever written. His instinct was so true that even today that play can be made to work in the theatre, but it is a far cry from the great tragedies he was later to write. The early work of Ibsen, Chekhov, O'Neill, and Williams (to mention a few of the greatest modern playwrights) includes many bad plays containing raw material that was later reworked into masterpieces.

Furthermore, the play that has been exposed to criticism and found wanting is not necessarily as bad as it may have been made out to be. Several things usually go wrong when a beginner's play is criticized. People's tastes differ greatly, and a critic may condemn a writer for no greater fault than failing to appeal to his individual taste. Therefore, the difference between the value a writer places on his own work and that which another person may place on it is partly accounted for by legitimate differences in taste, and does not reflect a judgment of quality.

Secondly, most people are naturally prejudiced against anything that has not already proven successful. A play in manuscript form does not appear to be as good as a play that is out in paperback. Many confuse commercial success per se with quality.

A third factor that must be taken into account is jealousy. One does not begrudge success to persons one does not know nearly so much as to one's own friends. That sometimes means a classmate will judge your work more harshly than a stranger would. The classmate is not being mean; he is merely predisposed to notice the faults more than the virtues. Furthermore, the less sensitive he is to the intricacies of playwriting, the less able he is to recognize whatever virtues may be present, and the more prone he is to see a fault in everything.

It is possible that jealousy may take a more insidious form. Let us imagine a person who, sensing the playwright's extreme vulnerability (in that he has asked for criticism), sees an opportunity for exploitation. First he disarms the playwright by highly praising certain qualities that he admires in the play. That disposes the playwright to look favorably upon anything he says. He then proceeds to make suggestions as to how the play should be rewritten, in an attempt to express his own thwarted creative impulses. The budding playwright must at all costs extricate himself from the influence of such a fellow. Suggestions are fine, but they should always be made tentatively enough so that the playwright can easily reject them if they do not seem to him to fit what he is doing. Usually several solutions to a problem can be suggested, so that there is no danger of imposing a single idea. It is important that once a suggestion has been made, the playwright then be left to his own devices. The domineering fellow who weasels his way into becoming a collaborator can do nothing except diffuse the play. Collaboration is possible between people who have unusual rapport, but never under the conditions described above. Collaboration, to be effective, requires a sense of absolute equality between the collaborators.

A final source of distorted criticism is a little different from those mentioned previously. It stems from the reticence of the critic. Because he does not like the manuscript, he will not say what he really thinks about it. He may give no opinion, or he may give mild but insincere praise. He is anxious not to hurt the writer's feelings. Perhaps it is best that in many cases there be no communication about the play. The critic who dislikes it intensely may be completely blind to what the author is trying to accomplish, and the author is better off not knowing what he thinks. But in some cases the playwright could benefit immensely from a detailed point-by-point condemnation of his work. The experience may be shattering; but if he is to succeed at all, it is an experience he will have to live through. Certainly nothing can be worse than turning a deaf ear to everything except praise until one convinces oneself that one has had nothing but praise.

As a beginning playwright you must learn to seek good criticism and to respond to it unemotionally. It is more true in the theatre than in the other arts that maturity comes slowly. A beginning writer may sometimes achieve greatness in the novel or in poetry, but almost never does greatness come early to the playwright. If it did, it would not necessarily indicate a great career to follow. Sheridan, whose *The Rivals* provides the rare example of a first play that is also a classic, wrote only a small handful of plays in his youth and then gave up the drama altogether. It may be that success that comes too easily is not sufficiently valued.

So if our budding genius will take consolation from the fact that his early disastrous "work of genius" may in fact portend a long and successful career, he may develop the courage to write more plays. Soon he will learn that for success he must set his sights somewhat lower than on trying to save the theatre. He must learn, too, that the successful plays of our time were not written easily, and that even though they are not as great as Shakespeare's, they are far more subtle and valuable than they may appear to his first glance. He will write considerably better if he will develop love, rather than contempt, for such plays as *Death of*

a Salesman, The Glass Menagerie, and *Hedda Gabler.* His problem is not to write better plays than those, but to write plays that are almost as carefully thought through, whatever approach to the theatre he may prefer.

Another common difficulty that young playwrights have with criticism is that they ignore it. The young writer, having decided he is a genius, may also conclude that everyone else is an idiot; and he may retire to his study to write masterpieces that the world may never see. A tendency exists in some circles at present to regard any creative act as just as good as any other. Standards disappear in a revolutionary attack on the whole concept of standards. The artistic difficulty arising from that concept is that if all of one's own work is equally good, then there is no possibility of improving what one does. Throughout history most artists have derived great satisfaction from doing the best they possibly could at what they created. It is highly unlikely that in the near future human nature will change so much that nobody any longer wishes to do anything well. Charlatans have drawn crowds in every age, but interest in them is seldom lasting, and they themselves usually become bored with what they are doing. Furthermore, a playwright who does not demand excellence from himself will inevitably find that when and if his play is produced, it is a disaster. The writer who can improve his play before it is produced will save himself painful embarrassment.

One must, therefore, listen to criticism. If the playwright will not, let him give up writing plays, for the theatre is an art requiring the combined efforts of many people, and the playwright cannot stand alone. Some poets have done well to ignore the criticism they received and to leave their poems unpublished for later ages to discover. But playwrights are judged by the audiences for which they write. The romantic poets of the last century failed to write great drama because they often would not submit themselves to the rough and tumble of theatrical production. Shakespeare, who cut his teeth rewriting other people's plays, learned the hard way the relationship that can exist between poetry and the theatre. Most other great playwrights have also been practical men of the theatre, acting, directing, or producing their own plays and those of others, and indeed sometimes combining all these roles. Aeschylus, Sophocles, Euripides, Shakespeare, Molière, Goethe, Shaw, Ibsen, and Williams were all playwrights who were also versatile men of the theatre.

The third, and possibly the most disastrous, reaction to criticism is to embrace all of it. If a writer has too little idea of what he wants his play to be, he may take any suggestion that comes along and incorporate it into his play. Thus he will lose sight of the most important function of the creative artist, which is to express his own point of view as clearly and fully as possible. Criticism from friends, teachers, fellow writers, and theatre people should be given and taken with the understanding that it will be used only if it seems right to the playwright himself. The writer who is so insecure that he takes everyone's advice will soon care only about pleasing the public and the critics and end up producing what pleases no one. He should take the attitude that success is a fortunate accident that arises out of his having something to say that a given public finds important. If he makes enough attempts, the chances that he will be successful are increased, but when he begins to daydream about how he will spend his first million, he paralyzes himself as a writer. Keep in mind that many works that are considered great today were not particularly successful when originally produced. These include such classics of the modern theatre as *Come Back, Little Sheba, The Crucible, Summer and Smoke,* and *Porgy and Bess.* Work of genuine value will almost certainly find an audience eventually. Cheap work may achieve temporary success

and perhaps bring its author fame and fortune. However, in the long run it will be forgotten. Moreover, there can be little satisfaction in writing a play that does not represent its author at his best: There are easier ways to make money than trying to write something one does not respect. If one is merely trying to cater to the desires of some hypothetical mass audience, he had better write advertising copy. If, on the other hand, he doesn't care about his audience at all, let him devote himself to poetry. The playwright must find the ideal balance between the public and the private self.

Once he has come to terms with the problems of learning to accept and deal with good and bad criticism, the playwright must still face the technical difficulties of revising his work. His greatest problem will be to become objective enough about his own work to see it as others do. He must develop the capacity to divide himself into a creator and a critic. The two sides of the divided self must not work simultaneously—the creator must create, and the critic must decide what needs to be changed and created anew.

You can never know that initial awareness of your play as it is seen by an audience. As the play develops in your mind, you will tend to take for granted certain things that might not be clear to someone else. Furthermore, as you go over the same ideas in your mind, you will tend to repeat some things that have already been clearly established. Thus, one of your major problems in revision will be to clarify what is too obscure while omitting what is repetitious or unnecessary. You may find you need someone who from time to time can tell you how your play looks at the moment. Simple, honest opinions are what you want. If your reader will tell you such things as "I was bored here," or "I was confused here," that gives you a clue that something needs work. Watch particularly for the comment, "I don't think it would happen this way." These comments pose problems for you to solve. Your reader should not be concerned with how you should solve them—that is for you to work out. Simply listen to what he has to say, and then see what you can do about it. Avoid the temptation to answer his criticism with a justification of what you have done.

If, as you revise, you have before you a copy of your play in which someone has written the single word "no" beside every line that bothers him, you have a lot to go on. Those are probably lines you have not thought out very carefully. If you are sure you like the line, then leave it, but try to figure out what else in the play may have contributed to your reader's dissatisfaction with that particular line.

There will be some things in your play that you like very much and do not wish to part with. Be extremely wary of such passages. It may be that you like them for what they suggest to you, rather than for what they state so clearly that an audience will understand them. It is often true that one likes what he has done poorly better than what he has done well. That is because really good work often involves a great deal of preparation, so that the writer ends up with more ideas and materials than he can use. He feels frustrated by his inability to express everything he has in mind, even though he is actually expressing a great deal and expressing it well. On the other hand, hasty work may often seem very satisfactory to one who has done it, because it has made use of all that he has to say on the subject at the moment. Thus, a certain amount of frustration is involved in doing a thing well —the sense of what could have been done better, what is still left unachieved. But when an idea is not fully developed and its implications are therefore not particularly apparent, it may seem to be complete and fully stated. If you are extremely reluctant to take something out of your play, that may be a sign that it is what you most need to take out.

Beware of overrevising. Do not keep going over the lines, changing them simply for the sake of changing them. You may

just be making them less lifelike. Language in a play should sound natural, not beautiful. Too many writers want to polish every line until it has a musical beauty that makes it completely unreal and therefore uninteresting. Every time you make a change in your play, you should know exactly what dramatic purpose is accomplished by doing so.

So many things need to be adjusted in a play that the problem of getting them all to come out right can be exceedingly complex. Imagine that you have a table with twenty legs, and that all of them are uneven. It is your job to get all of the legs to come out the same length. The obvious thing to do would be to measure the shortest leg and then mark off that distance on all the other legs. But suppose that you cannot measure —that you must simply saw off part of one leg at a time and keep sawing off parts of legs until you have finally got all of them the same length. You have to keep setting the table on its legs and trying it.

If you were in such a position, your problem would resemble that of the playwright who has finished the first draft of his play. He will be aware of many things that must be changed. Each detail depends on all the others for its effectiveness, so that whenever a detail is changed, all the others are affected. When he polishes his play, the playwright is trying to make all the details fit together effectively. He makes changes and then watches the play in rehearsal. That is like sawing off some legs and then setting the table upright to see how it stands. He must keep changing things here and there, hoping that eventually all of the details will fit together in exactly the right proportions. If he can do this, his table will stand evenly on all of its legs. More probably he will succeed only in getting the table to stand up without being too wobbly. Some of the legs in the center will be too short, but the table will stand firmly enough to be satisfactory. Just so, a play will eventually be made to work well enough to please an audience, although its author may feel dissatisfied because of compromises he has had to make so that everything will fit together as a whole.

If he is lucky, the playwright may develop a feeling for the total effect of his play so that he is able to judge how each detail will work while he is writing his first draft. Almost instinctively he will make nearly everything come out right the first time. Perhaps Bernard Shaw and Oscar Wilde were such playwrights, and perhaps William Saroyan is also. Probably Shakespeare was not, and most of the playwrights of the modern American theatre have not been. It is very important, therefore, that the playwright learn not to be discouraged by the amount of revision that is necessary. No matter how bad his play may seem at the moment, there is always hope.

You will probably find that a good deal of your revision is done by your subconscious mind, if you encourage it to help you. Just as we suggested in the chapter on get-ting through a dry spell, you should put the play away between drafts and forget about it for a while, after you have made sure that you clearly understand what problems are afflicting it. When you return to it later, you may find that you know exactly how to solve the problems that have been bothering you.

Chances are you will spend considerable time and energy in this business of revising your play. You will experience frustration and misery, and your pride will suffer greatly. Is it all worth it? There are those who have been bitter about the experience and wished to avoid repeating it. Most writers, however, find that the satisfaction of a job well done is worth all the effort. In writing a play you are not merely creating an entertainment to help others idle away their time; you are telling yourself something that you need to know about life. If you have been honest with yourself in the process of revising, you should not only end up with a better play, but you should also deepen your understanding of reality.

Chapter XV

WORKING WITH YOUR PLAY
IN PRODUCTION

Because you can learn the most about your play by having it performed before an audience, it is a good idea for you to try to arrange a production of it. The possibilities range anywhere from a group of people sitting around a living room with scripts in their hands to a full-scale professional mounting. In this chapter we shall consider some of the problems that arise in producing an original play. You will gain a much clearer picture of these problems, however, from reading actual accounts by playwrights of their experiences in the theatre. Appendix B consists of just such an account. You may also wish to read *Act One* by Moss Hart and *The Seesaw Log* by William Gibson. These give detailed biographies of plays from the writing of the first draft to a successful opening night on Broadway.

Here are some guidelines for the young playwright who wishes to have his play produced. Get the best production you can, but do not wear yourself out trying to get a better production than is possible under the circumstances. Bear in mind that whereas professional companies are excited by new plays, amateurs would nearly always rather do established hits. They are likely to turn up their noses at your manuscript, wondering who you think you are for assuming that you can compete with Shaw and Shakespeare for their attentions. In fairness to the

contemporary playwright, it should be observed that great theatre is always a living thing, not a museum, and that far more is to be said for doing a reasonably good new play than for doing yet another performance of a classic. If it is the business of the theatre to hold the mirror up to nature, as Hamlet said, then let it hold the mirror up to its own time and its own place. Let audiences see what the playwrights in their own community have to say. Playwrights, like prophets, are too often without honor in their own land. So you will be lucky if someone takes an interest in your work and wishes to produce it.

Of course, you cannot expect anyone to want to do your play if it is unreasonably bad, or if you are not going to be cooperative in the venture of putting it on; so you had better make it as good as you can before you seek a production, and then admit what is so galling to playwrights to have to admit: that in the theatre the director is the final authority. Of course, it is the business of the director to serve the play, making clear whatever it has to say rather than obscuring its message. However, most directors are such creative people that they insist on going beyond the play and commenting on its meaning in ways other than the author had in mind. Since that is one of the conditions of theatre in our time, the playwright may as well accept the fact that any good director will probably do things with his play that seem wrong to him. That fact presents him with the challenge of making his play so clear that what he has to say will not escape the audience no matter what the director does.

You may wish to direct your own play. Indeed, some playwrights are very good directors. It is unlikely, however, that you will learn as much about your play if you direct it as you will if someone else does. It may be that you would cover up the faults of your play by effective directing techniques and never be aware of what you have done. The value of having someone else direct is that one is forced to see what his writing has actually communicated.

The first stage in the artistic work on your play will be casting it. In most cases you will have a small number of actors to choose from, and the chances of their exactly fitting the roles you have created are not great. That means that if you are rewriting the play during rehearsals, you will probably have to do some rewriting for the particular actors you have. You will have to simplify some speeches and change the characterization in others. It is important, therefore, that you get the most sensitive and flexible group of actors that you can.

As the director works on the play he will make suggestions for cuts, and may also suggest scenes that need to be amplified or added. Even if you do not like his suggestions, try them and see how they work. He may actually see values in your play that you have not yet seen.

During the whole process of rehearsal, it is very important that the playwright appear to like what is going on. So long as the actors feel they have his good will, they will be anxious to please him. But if he makes them feel he does not like their work, they will resent him and work even further from his intentions. It is the business of the director, not the playwright, to criticize the actors. Nothing frustrates a director more than to

have other people telling his actors how they should play their parts. Therefore, the playwright should make all his suggestions to the director—and he should make them tentatively and politely, showing that he respects the director's own creativity.

It may be that things will not go well in rehearsal, that emotional tension will flare up, and that the temptation to abandon the production will become strong. The playwright should resist the temptation. No matter how bad the production, he will learn something from it. It may be that he will learn how to become involved with better productions in the future. He should, at any rate, learn to think of himself as a practical worker in the theatre, not just a writer who works alone in his study.

As your writing improves, you should not hesitate to seek better productions and try to have your plays produced by established companies. Most large cities have many community theatre groups, some of which are willing to consider producing original plays. You should get to know the people involved with those groups and find out, through personal contact, whether there is any chance of their doing your plays. After a few community theatre productions, you should be ready to submit plays to the professional market.

In a high-school situation, the student playwright has an excellent opportunity to get his work performed in assemblies. A short play with a small cast can easily be performed for the entire school. A high-school audience provides excellent experience for the young writer, as it is a very difficult audience to please, but very appreciative when it is pleased. Realizing that an audience has been responsive to even a small part of your play helps you to understand and develop your strong points as a writer.

In a college or university there is almost certain to be opportunity for a polished production in the campus theatre. Most colleges have as part of their theatre program the production of student-written and

-directed plays. If your college does not have such a program, you may be able to get one started.

If the playwright can do no more than get a few friends together and have them read through his play a few times and work out some of the staging, that is what he should do. He should get used to hearing his lines spoken by actors, get over being in love with, or terrified by, the sound of his own words in other people's mouths, and discover the proper relationship between what he puts down on paper and what will eventually become a moment of excitement in the theatre. Even under the simplest conditions, seeing his play come to life before his eyes is the most exciting experience the playwright can have.

Chapter XVI

Most good plays can be adapted for radio or television with relatively few major changes. Special characteristics of radio, television, and films, however, make writing for them somewhat different from writing for the stage. We shall not dwell on those differences, as this book is intended primarily for playwrights who want to write for the stage, but it might help you to think briefly about a few of them.

Although the radio play must communicate entirely through the ear, it nevertheless has a visual element. It must do all it can to help the listener visualize in his imagination what is going on. Interestingly enough, people are likely to remember radio plays much longer than television plays because they are forced to create images of people to go with the voices they hear, and imagine an environment to surround them. Thus, in a way, they are actually participating in the creative process and may find that they therefore enjoy the radio play much more than they would have enjoyed the same play on television. In order to help the listener visualize, the dialogue must suggest whatever is necessary about the appearances of people and their reactions to things. It must also indicate more clearly than would be necessary on the stage when characters enter and leave. If a character is in a scene in a radio play, he should speak frequently enough so that the audience will not forget he is there; and when there is no further

need for him, he should be given an exit line. Furthermore, since the actors in a radio play cannot indicate their emotions with facial expressions, it is necessary for other characters to suggest what those emotions are. Lines such as, "Boy, do you look pooped," or "You certainly seem happy today," would be more necessary and more frequently used in a radio play than on the stage.

Since the radio play has no need for scenery, it is possible to shift scenes more frequently than in a stage play. A few words from an announcer or a short musical theme, and the scene has changed. Sound effects, too, are very helpful in indicating changes of scene. A situation that is commonly used in the radio play and almost never in the stage play is to have two characters walking down a street together chatting with the people they meet. It is a convenient way to introduce the major characters who live in a small town or a neighborhood, and avoids the artificial device of having to get them all into the main character's living room. The radio play also offers an opportunity to do what cannot be done in any other kind of drama at so little expense, namely to include violent and sensational action. Characters may go down in a plane crash and land on a desert island. They may be at sea, floating on a raft. They may be in the middle of a battle, or at the bottom of the ocean, or in a spaceship. Anything that can be visualized is possible, offering a wonderful challenge to the imagination. It also means that there is more need for self-discipline in the writing of a good radio play.

Another characteristic of the radio play that sets it apart from other entertainments is the naturalness of the announcer. When there is a visual representation of the unfolding of the drama, the announcer seems out of place, so he is seldom used on the stage and almost never in the movies. But he contributes beautifully to the radio drama, since we visualize what he is describing in exactly the same way as we visualize the characters whose voices we hear. This means that many portions of the story may be briefly summarized rather than dramatized, and it allows the script to concentrate on the highlights of the action. The announcer helps to make the radio play almost as free from limitations as the novel.

The one major limitation that applies to both radio and television plays is time. If the play is to be produced commercially, its length must be exact to the minute. That means the writer will have to tailor his work not to the requirements of his subject, but to the half hour or hour allotted to the broadcast. He will have to learn how to pad on the one hand and cut mercilessly on the other.

Two principal means are used to achieve variety in a television play. The first is frequent shifting of scenery. A television play can and should use more scenery than a stage play. For example, several of the rooms in a house should be used, rather than a single room. Most of the scenes can be quite short, so that the locale can be shifted frequently. Furthermore, the scene can seem to shift even more frequently as a result of using various camera angles. The second source of variety is the close-up, which the playwright should endeavor to use as effectively as possible. There should be frequent occasions when the story is told not by words but by the expression on a character's face, or by some bit of stage business

detailed enough so that it would be missed in the theatre, but just right for the screened close-up. If you watch a few television plays with these two things in mind, you should find many good examples of how they are used.

A screenplay differs from a television play in that the words are more secondary. If you doubt this, recall that everyone knows who the star of a film is, and many know who directed and produced it; but seldom does anyone know who wrote the screenplay. The most effective moments on the film are likely to make no use of dialogue at all, so the writer of the screenplay must train himself to think in pictures rather than in words. He must search for the telling image that will say far more than words ever could. He must study the careful way in which visual images are interrelated in the best films.

There is absolutely no point in writing a screenplay for Hollywood except for the fun of it, since no Hollywood producer will read an unsolicited manuscript. At the present time, however, there is increasing interest in student-made films, most of which are quite short and make no use of sound. The discipline of trying to write a script for such a film is a valuable way of training oneself to think in purely visual terms.

Two forms of theatrical entertainment that can be considered along with other media are the musical and the opera. Each of these is complex enough in its own right to require a separate volume to do it justice. We shall content ourselves with a few brief remarks.

The musical is related both to the opera, from which it is descended, and to the revue, out of which it more immediately developed. It is designed primarily for the sake of the musical numbers, utilizing a plot that merely serves to tie them together. It is made up of numerous scenes, in most cases alternating songs and dance numbers with dialogue scenes. It usually mixes humor, fantasy, and sentiment. Unless it is designed for an intimate theatre and uses only solo actors and a very small orchestra, it places great emphasis on spectacle and is very expensive to produce.

The songs are entities in themselves, appealing enough so that people remember them and want to sing them. The dialogue (sometimes called the book) should sparkle, but it does not carry the weight of character development nearly as much as the songs do. It should therefore be brief and somewhat sketchy, so that the audience is always waiting for the next song. Most musicals involve the collaboration of several authors. The music, the lyrics, and the book may all have separate authors, and sometimes several writers work on each of these elements.

An opera libretto is similar to a play, except that it must be much shorter. It is usually the work of a single author, and meant to be sung all the way through. Even if the music moves right along and does not repeat words over and over (and repetition is very common when words are set to music), it takes about four times as long to sing a thing as it does to say it. Because the characterization and emotional impact of the opera are carried primarily in the music, it often happens that bad plays can be turned into good operas. Good plays, on the other hand, may be so effective in themselves that nothing is left for the music to add. How-

ever, notable examples exist of good plays that have made highly successful operas. Among these are Shakespeare's *Othello,* set to music by Verdi, and Arthur Miller's *The Crucible,* set to music by Robert Ward.

The most successful composer of opera of our time (though he is not the greatest) is Gian Carlo Menotti, who writes his own librettos. If you are interested in writing an opera libretto, you should study some of Menotti's operas and see how effectively words and music complement each other. Separately, they would be relatively uninteresting, but when they are put together in a good production, the result can be very compelling.

We have not considered the multimedia productions that are popular with some avant-garde groups. Many of these reflect little observable artistic discipline. This does not mean that a multimedia production cannot be made into a mature work of art, but one should remember that the more materials that are used in a given work of art, the more discipline is required to control them effectively. The student should not expect to produce anything of value in a multimedia production until he has mastered separately each of the arts involved. When he has accomplished that much, he should need little guidance in interrelating them.

Appendix A

SCENES FROM STUDENT-WRITTEN PLAYS

The following scenes are meant to be representative of what eleventh-graders can accomplish within the framework and time limitations of a course in playwriting. These scenes do not represent the final, polished work of their authors, as most of the authors have expressed the intention of revising their plays substantially.

To Catch a Butterfly
by Sarah McClelland

Opening of Act 1

(*Living room of the apartment of Jim and Joan, a young married couple with a new baby. Jim and Joan are onstage. The baby is in his crib.*)

JOAN: Well, I guess it's time to buy a little food. The cupboard is bare.

JIM: Old Mother Hubbard's cupboard!

JOAN: Yes, old Mother . . .

JIM: What ya gonna get? Get something good?

JOAN: Could you help me out by telling me what you would like?

JIM: Certainly, certainly. How about peas and steak?

JOAN: Anything else?

JIM: I can't think of anything. Oh. Does old man over there—(*gesturing toward crib*)—rate steak and peas?

JOAN: Oh, you reminded me. I'd better buy some diapers and some more baby powder and baby—

JIM: Baby, baby, please don't leave me. (*Pause.*) Hmmmm. That ought to do it . . .

JOAN: Well, good-bye. I'll be back soon, and don't outdo yourself watching out for the kid.

(*Joan exits. Pause while Jim thumbs through a magazine. Baby starts to cry. Jim goes over to crib.*)

JIM: Hey, baby! Be quiet, how about it? (*Keeping distance from crib.*) Daddy— what a word—Daddy doesn't like it when you cry. Understand? (*Pause.*) Oh, well, why do I even try?! (*Still crying.*) Oh, here! (*Gives baby a pacifier. Baby stops crying.*) I'll remember that, anytime he gives me trouble. I'll stuff his mouth. He'll probably do that all his life—cigarettes—food—drink —oral things like that tend to be soothing. . . . Hey, pipsqueak! Get up and fight like a man! You shouldn't let anybody call you that—not even your—father! Well, what can I expect. Even I was like that once. Not *quite* like that, that's quite impossible. . . . I guess a lot has to happen to little Gregory in his lifetime, and a lot of the important things come from Joanie and me. (*Frowning, he sits down and pulls out a magazine*

159

and starts to read. Enter, Mrs. Hackshaw after a knock on the door.) Come in.

MRS. HACKSHAW: Oh, hello, hello. I just thought I heard the baby crying and I was going to see if he needed anything! You know I always like to help Joanie out. I had seen her leave, you see, and I thought maybe she had left the baby alone . . . just for a minute or so, of course, so I thought I'd come and see if I could help. There is nothing more terrible than a crying baby, now, is there?

JIM: No. Thank you for your concern. (*Rather sarcastically.*)

MRS. HACKSHAW: Well, I guess you took care of the crying baby now, didn't you? I always thought it was a real virtue for a father to be able to stop a baby from crying. Haven't you always thought that?

JIM: Yeah, I guess so . . .

MRS. HACKSHAW: Well, well, well. What a nice thing—a concerned father! That's very important, you know. Do you talk to your boy much?

JIM: (*Look of incredulity.*) Mrs. Hackshaw! Really! He's only two months old!

MRS. HACKSHAW: Well, it's always a good idea to start talking to them early— you know—it gives them a good basis for grammar in their speaking years. And you know it is very important to—to—to get along in this society as an a-accepted human being.

JIM: Uh-huh. Well, er, maybe you're right. (*Begins to concentrate hard on the magazine he has been reading. Mrs. Hackshaw has been standing with the door open all the while. Pause. Mrs. Hackshaw looks undecided and then plunges into speech.*)

MRS. HACKSHAW: Would you say that your wife leaves often like this—you know what I mean—just for a few minutes at a time? (*Jim looks slightly exasperated.*)

JIM: Not really, I shouldn't say that at all.

MRS. HACKSHAW: Are you sure? Of course you never can be too sure. Well, it may just start happening at first a little at a time . . . (*Jim looks exasperated, and then he slowly begins to smile.*)

JIM: Oh, well, maybe you're right. You never *can* tell about these things. It *could* be happening to me right now!

MRS. HACKSHAW: Oh, sir! That would be a pity, now, *wouldn't* it?

JIM: It most certainly would! What do you suggest I do about it?

MRS. HACKSHAW: Hmmmm—keep in mind that there is always a reason for things that happen like this—remember that, and maybe the first step to the solving of your problem is completed.

JIM: Yes, yes!

MRS. HACKSHAW: Just *how* do you *feel* about the baby?

JIM: Would you believe me if I told you something . . . ?

MRS. HACKSHAW: (*Delighted.*) Oh, yes, yes!

JIM: You know, it's something I don't usually tell anyone.

MRS. HACKSHAW: You can trust me —my lips are sealed!

JIM: It's something that's been bothering me for quite a while now.

MRS. HACKSHAW: Uh-huh!

JIM: Oh! I don't know if I should say it!

MRS. HACKSHAW: Oh, please do! It's a good idea to get it off your chest, you know.

JIM: Well, okay. (*Beckons to her—in a hoarse whisper.*) I think the baby is—is—is UGLY! (*He almost yells the last word. Mrs. Hackshaw jumps back and goes to the door.*)

MRS. HACKSHAW: Oh my, oh my! That is too bad—it will pass with time, of course. Yes, yes. I'd better be on my way! Watch after the Mrs. now. Good-bye. (*Steps outside.*)

JIM: (*Yelling after her.*) Now you won't tell anyone, will you? I trusted in you! (*She closes the door after herself. Jim chuckles to himself as he leafs through the magazine.*)

* * *

NIGHT OF PERILLUS
by Bill Swet

Act 1, Scene One

(*Guard walks onto stage, which is a dismal, concrete-walled room with heavy doors on both sides and an iron grid window in the center, about seven feet up the rear wall. People are huddled along the walls, a few sitting on the floor some distance away from the walls. They hardly move. It is the courtyard of an insane asylum.*)

GUARD: These cold walls are still here. I remember when there was more to the world than cold, gray walls; these walls that have never left my life, but have been dead for eternity. I would walk down the concrete corridors and glance up as my footsteps echoed past the clock on the wall. I would sometimes stop and listen to my footsteps as they whispered away from me. The lights above me would cast my shadows along the floor, each shadow stretching past the last, until the end of the corridor, the end with the door, would be a symphony of shadows in soft tones, etched on the dull bronze of the door. I would take the key off a peg on the door, unlock the door, then return the key. Then . . . (*Walks to the door, strangely lurching, stops, takes two slow steps back.*) I would walk into here, closing the door behind me. (*Pierre gets up from where he was huddling against the wall, stumbles a couple of steps, stretches and faces the audience.*)

PIERRE: Good morning, world. I suppose I said "world." World as usual, not mind. It's a perverse streak of reality in me that sees morning as light from a window stretching across the floor into my mind's eye. Morning isn't light from a window—it's me waking up to myself, my mind. Not that I mind myself, of course. Or is it myself that I mind? Myself. Myself. Good morning, myself. . . . World? Where is the world? (*Ponderously.*) Where is the world? Peek-a-boo? WHERE THE HELL IS THE WORLD? Anne? Where the hell is Anne-Marie? (*Wheedling.*) Gone picking flowers? Now, don't fall into the goldfish pond. (*Giggles.*) Watch the goldfish pond, pretty one. Anne, I love you, watch the pond. Anne? Anne? Aaaaa! (*Sobs quietly, briefly. Straightens up, surveys the ceiling with a sad smile. Looks around, sees the guard.*) Good morning, Jimbo.

GUARD: Morning.

PIERRE: What did you have for breakfast?

GUARD: Toast, coffee.

PIERRE: Did you? I forgot what I had for breakfast. I used to eat toast and coffee once. But not now. I can't stand the coffee here. Instant crud. Do you drink instant coffee?

GUARD: Yeah. I know what you mean.

PIERRE: Would that all would know what I mean. I intend them no harm, but to mean is to be mean to them.

GUARD: Come again?

PIERRE: You've got me coming and going, but we'll be friends yet. (*Cleverly.*)

GUARD: Thank you.

PIERRE: No need for thanks for a friend in need of service.

GUARD: No, I guess not.

PIERRE: Oh, Jimbo, I've got a kind of secret.

GUARD: Yes? (*Pauses.*)

PIERRE: (*Dramatically.*) I've got to get out of here.

GUARD: Yes, I know. You told me already.

PIERRE: Did I? . . . The toast here is soggy. I usually flush mine down the john. That's because cockroaches would come if I hid it under my bed. We have enough of them here, anyhow. At night, if I listen hard enough, I can hear them scampering under my bed and chittering, but I don't know. The way cockroaches eat toast these days. . . . Jim, why aren't you talking much today?

GUARD: I don't know.

PIERRE: Don't know what?

GUARD: Why I'm not talking much today.

PIERRE: Oh yes, you do.

GUARD: I probably do.

PIERRE: Why, then?

GUARD: I have a headache. I'm not feeling talkative today.

PIERRE: Oh, come on now.

GUARD: It's the truth. What do you want me to do, contrive a good excuse? A harmless alibi?

PIERRE: Yes.

GUARD: (*Easily.*) O.K. An excuse. Let's say . . . the Superintendent spoke to me yesterday. He said for me to stop talking so much.

PIERRE: He did? Why?

GUARD: (*Continuing the joke.*) Regulations? Hell, I don't know, Pierre.

PIERRE: Why do you have to do just what he says?

GUARD: Well, ah, if I want to stay here . . .

PIERRE: Want to stay here?

GUARD: I have to talk less.

PIERRE: Aw, come on.

GUARD: No. Actually I just have a headache, Pierre.

PIERRE: What the hell?

GUARD: (*Laughing.*) Wasn't that a good enough excuse?

PIERRE: Why are you so worried about leaving here? Don't you like it here?

GUARD: Of course I like it here.

PIERRE: You don't have to be here. I wouldn't waste my time here with these rejects of humanity. Like me.

GUARD: Why call yourself a reject?

PIERRE: Because nobody wants anything to do with me.

GUARD: But calling yourself a reject doesn't help matters any.

PIERRE: When even you won't talk to me?

GUARD: Now wait a second. That was just a joke. A game.

PIERRE: Do you call rejecting me a game?

GUARD: I didn't mean it personally.

PIERRE: Like hell.

GUARD: I'm sorry.

PIERRE: Sorry? Where's your backbone?

GUARD: Shut your damn mouth. (*Mildly.*)

PIERRE: So that's your backbone. Dangling from your lips.

GUARD: Shut up!

PIERRE: Good boy.

GUARD: Thank you. (*Both laugh relievedly.*)

PIERRE: (*Thoughtfully.*) I used to believe in God.

GUARD: I still do in a way.

PIERRE: Why?

GUARD: I don't know, really.

PIERRE: You mean you're not supposed to talk about it to me?

GUARD: Give me a chance, will you?

PIERRE: No, damn it! If you're playing a game . . .

GUARD: This is ridiculous. You know damn well I was only kidding.

PIERRE: Go on . . .

GUARD: Why?

PIERRE: Go on, damn it! You're not supposed to talk to whom?

GUARD: Please. (*Pierre goes into a tantrum.*)

PIERRE: With us. The scum of sanity. Our sweet society's Achilles heel. BUT YOU DON'T REALIZE. YOU DON'T REALIZE THAT WE ARE PEOPLE TOO!

GUARD: Yes, I think I do realize, Pierre.

PIERRE: Realize what?

GUARD: That you are people.

PIERRE: PEOPLE? What kind of people are those who are thrown into holes and covered with concrete? Who sit and sob and drool in their tomb, rotting their minds out? No, Jim, the only people there are are the ones who throw us in here for their own good, to keep the whole society from rotting to pieces. But they don't realize that they are too rotten to be people themselves.

GUARD: Not all of them . . .

PIERRE: THEM? Do you think you aren't one of them? Them are one and all is one! It was them, and you, who flushed me down the john, to sit and rot and twiddle my thumbs.

GUARD: Do you really think . . . (*Pierre barrels on, intensely oratorical.*)

PIERRE: I have crossed the River Styx and I know what it is to be Tantalus. I know what it is to sit and look out the window and see the sunshine choke to death in this dismal place. I know that the world is still out there, and that I'm more alone than anyone else has ever been. I know what it is like out there; it is autumn, and trees in fall, and strolls in the park with books under my arm. Books, Jimbo . . . are you listening? Books, I used to read books in the autumn on a park bench and the colors of fall, I was Daedalus and Icarus. I would see the sun and write about it, but I came too close to the sun, Jim. I saw the sun and fell, and the waters fell upon me as I hurtled down to here and my heart broke when they took my wings. THE MINOTAUR LAUGHED IN MY FACE! (*Sobs.*) . . . Jim? Jim, are you listening? . . . I am an artist. Yesterday I found a piece of soft stone, white and chalky. I ground it up and spat blood into it and took it and painted a picture on the wall with it. The painting was so beautiful I cried. THEN, ONE OF YOU CAME IN, *THE WASHER WOMAN,* AND CLEANED IT OFF! I could have killed her, but . . .

GUARD: But the washer woman didn't come in this morning.

PIERRE: So you are listening! Jimbo, you don't realize what a spineless bastard our guard is. He just stands there and says he can't talk. But do we care? Jim, do you think we care? Jimbo . . . GOD DAMN IT, ANSWER! (*Bitterly.*) Am I a person? Jim, AM I A PERSON?

GUARD: Why?

PIERRE: What a hypocrite. What a goddamn, spineless, guard, bastard of a hypocrite. But of course none of you realize what the word means.

GUARD: Why?

PIERRE: You have to be off your r-rocker—YOU HAVE TO BE CRAZY to know what the word means. I know truth. I've been to the Phoenix and back. And where is your Phoenix, man? Somewhere in Arizona?

GUARD: Please, Pierre, please. Must you do this every day? I'm a person too. I could have another job, but this is my own way of doing things.

PIERRE: What's this? Your own thing?

GUARD: Come off it, Pierre, please. Could you step off your pedestal for just a moment? Can't you believe that anyone can have sincere motivations?

PIERRE: Yes.

GUARD: Perhaps I shouldn't talk.

PIERRE: Go on, I'm sorry. I really am.

GUARD: I came here because I . . . I'm sorry, Pierre, I just can't say it.

PIERRE: (*Alarmed.*) Go on, please.

GUARD: (*Quickly.*) Sometimes I see you, or an old man, or a crying child in trouble, and I want to help. And it hurts inside.

PIERRE: Did you really say that?

GUARD: You don't understand . . .

PIERRE: Yes, I do. You've never said anything like that before. I suppose you really are a person. I feel confused and humble at the same time. It's seeing you through a new pair of glasses. I don't know why. You were a human being all along, one of us, and not a guard, a symbol. . . . It's partly my fault . . .

GUARD: I wanted to help, but my own feelings were too . . .

PIERRE: Tender, sensitive?

GUARD: I—I guess so. I don't know why. I guess I had pit . . .

PIERRE: PITY?!! (*Laughs wildly.*) So he's not only an altruist who sits and sobs in a murky corner when some sticky-fingered brat gets spanked, who boo-hoos and bally-hoos and then goes home to his favorite broad and a warm bed, who goes out to the movies and sheds a couple of tears over old Pierre and thinks he's fooled. Do you know where altruists end up! Huh? HUH?

GUARD: (*Long pause.*) How could a person be so cruel, so blind, so sick that he could do what you have just done?

PIERRE: Done what?

*　　*　　*

UNTITLED

by Gwynn Swinson

Act 1, Scene Two

(*The dining room. Anna is sewing at the table.*)

MARY: (*Off.*) Anna, Anna? Anybody here?

ANNA: Come on in, dear, the door's open.

MARY: (*Enters.*) Thought I'd be sociable for a change.

ANNA: Welcome to the bird's nest—

MARY: I'll fix some drinks.

ANNA: I could use one. A nice strong gin and tonic for me, dear. Do I need it!

MARY: By the way, where's the master? I'm sure he'd appreciate my visit.

ANNA: He finally fell asleep playing solitaire.

MARY: Whew! I wouldn't want to surprise him, you know.

ANNA: Got any ciggies on ya?

MARY: (*With drink.*) Right here. Let me light it. How are things, sweetie? You look pretty wrecked. . . . How you feeling?

ANNA: Like I look—like I look.

MARY: Then that *was* screaming I heard this morning?

ANNA: Damn right.

MARY: My friend George hasn't changed. Never did, never will.

ANNA: Mary, tell me what to do. I can't keep this up much longer.

MARY: We both know that, too, don't we?

ANNA: I don't have any money left.

MARY: Did you call Raymond?

ANNA: I can't.

MARY: Why not?

ANNA: Because George'll hear me.

MARY: No excuse, use my phone.

ANNA: But I can't leave George alone. Don't you see how trapped I am?

MARY: How many times have I told you—LEAVE HIM. Raymond'll pick up on everything. Especially you. What's your problem, sweetie? I'd be out of this dump and sailing the world on that beautiful yacht of his. You're crazy, Anna. You'll have to leave sooner or later.

ANNA: Sooner. Within the next three months, I'm afraid.

MARY: I take it you saw a doctor.

ANNA: Two months, almost.

MARY: Does Raymond know yet?

ANNA: Nope.

MARY: Call him.

ANNA: I just told you—I can't.

MARY: Then I'll call him. Look, sweetie, if I were you, I'd consider me a threat. I even admit to you how I feel about your lover.

ANNA: Then call him, take him, see if I care. It would solve a lot of problems for me.

MARY: Unfortunately, he wants you, sweetie. Another drink?

ANNA: Stronger.

MARY: I've known you for five years, Anna, and we've been through hell together —in nightclubs, beds—we know all about each other. You and Raymond, me and Marc, both of us married, both of us with kids and asses for husbands. Marc and I didn't last—but I swear to you, I won't spoil anything for you and Raymond. But you've got to get out of here soon—now that we know for sure.

GEORGE: (*Off.*) Anna! Who are you talking to?

MARY: I'd better leave.

ANNA: Take the glasses in the kitchen before you go. Don't forget the cigarette. I'll be over to call Raymond.

GEORGE: (*Off.*) Anna! It's time for my pills!

MARY: Ciao, sweetie. I'll be around. (*Exit.*)

ANNA: Coming, dear. I'll be right there. Would you like tomato juice or lemonade with your medicine?

GEORGE: Plain water. Hurry it up. I'm a sick man and can't even get service in my own home. Anna?

ANNA: (*Putting gum in mouth.*) Yes, dear. I'm just going out to get the mail. Then I'll bring you your medicine. (*She runs out the back way. Amy enters through the opposite door.*)

AMY: (*Putting mail on table.*) Mother? I'm here. (*Enter George, wheeling himself in his wheelchair.*)

GEORGE: She went out to get the mail, girl.

AMY: But—but—yessir. Can I do anything for you?

GEORGE: How was school today?

AMY: Mmmmm. Same as usual.

GEORGE: Tell me one thing you learned.

AMY: Well, I learned the quadratic formula. Let me see, that's . . .

GEORGE: Good enough. Just keep up the work, girl, and you'll make a fine woman. Daddy'll be proud of you. Is that the mail?

AMY: Well, uh—I guess. Why yes, that's the mail, sir.

GEORGE: Where's your mother?

AMY: I haven't seen her since morning. But I can do anything you'd like.

GEORGE: My shirts need ironing.

AMY: Yessir, I'll get on them right away.

GEORGE: Do the shirts at your leisure, girl. Here's thirty-five cents. Go buy yourself some pop. You're the only one around here who has any respect for my needs.

AMY: Yessir. Thank you, sir.

GEORGE: Go on, now. Before I change my mind. (*Amy leaves. George goes over to the mail.*) Light bill, water, Raymond Walters? Pretty fancy letter—smells like English lilac. "To Mrs. Anna Sherman." Well, that's her all right. And I'm Mr. Sherman.

ANNA: (*Enters.*) George! I thought you were reading.

GEORGE: I am reading. The mail.

ANNA: Y-yes, I-I, so I see. Did A-Amy get it? She must have.

GEORGE: Who is Raymond Walters, Anna?

ANNA: H-he—well, George, he's an insurance agent.

GEORGE: Glad to hear it. I suppose that means that you are taking out insurance on me out of my bank account.

ANNA: Well, not exactly.

GEORGE: Well, then?

ANNA: Put it down, George.

GEORGE: Where were you, Anna?

ANNA: I—I went to see Mary.

GEORGE: Who came to see you this afternoon. And with whom you drank a fifth of gin. I suppose you did go to see Mary, dear. How is she?

ANNA: George, Mary is a nice person. You always seemed to judge her at first sight.

GEORGE: First sight when I saw her get drunker than a fish in this house some five years ago.

ANNA: But that was a long time ago.

GEORGE: And Mary Bates has not changed.

ANNA: Neither have you, dear.

GEORGE: Nor you.

ANNA: George, I don't think we can last much longer.

GEORGE: You and me, or you and Raymond here?

ANNA: George! How can you . . .

GEORGE: Live with a woman I married only to find out that she would give birth to a boy who wasn't even mine? "How can I?" is a damn good question, Anna.

ANNA: All right, George. You found me on the street one night, you cleaned me up, took me in, married me of your own accord. You knew that I had a drinking problem.

GEORGE: But I did not know that you were pregnant.

ANNA: You loved me, George, and you loved André just as you love Amy now.

GEORGE: André is a foolish kid. As far as I am concerned he's dead. He isn't mine and I don't profess to own him.

ANNA: George, don't lie like that. Why, just this morning you told him that you brought him into the world.

GEORGE: I did. I paid for the medical help you needed all during that time, didn't I?

ANNA: Do you love me, dear? If you do, please don't . . .

GEORGE: Do you love this Raymond Walters?

ANNA: George, I know I don't deserve the love you have for me.

GEORGE: Then get out, Anna. Get out right now!

ANNA: All right, then, I will.

GEORGE: That's what you want, isn't it? You want to get out of having to nurse your invalid husband, don't you? You want to get out and be a social butterfly in the limelight; to be a real woman, isn't that what you want, Anna? You want to be the woman that I am not man enough to let you be. Am I right, Anna? Am I right? I'm no good. I'm half a man. I'm dependent upon you. Now you don't want me. Of course you don't. Any woman wants to live a decent life. She doesn't want a hardworking man with high blood sugar. She wants a strong, tall, suave insurance agent, huh, Anna?

ANNA: George, you know . . .

GEORGE: Forgive me for tying you down, my dearest. You are younger than I and you are not crippled. You are free to divorce old George here.

ANNA: (*Sobbing.*) George, I won't leave.

GEORGE: Make up your mind for once and for all, then. The boy is yours. He's almost grown, anyway. I want no part of him. Amy is the only one I have left to care for without fear of being hurt. Bring my dinner out on the porch. I'm tired. Here's your letter. I have nothing more to say.

ANNA: Do you really want me to leave, dear?

GEORGE: Do you think I want you to stay?

*　　*　　*

UNTITLED

by Stephen Frizell

(*Nighttime in the country by a bridge.*)

WISE GUY: How does it feel to cross that dark deep river at midnight?

PRINCIPAL C: If I had crossed the river when I was small I would be frightened. (*Pause.*) It looks as if there is something behind that bush on the other side of the river. Beneath me the water is gurgling dark and ominous. I reach the middle of the bridge, the town church bells chime twelve. I run in the other direction, back towards the safe side.

WISE GUY: You're not so small now.

PRINCIPAL C: I don't have the imagination to be frightened. I enjoy the dark calm, the somber whispering noises of night. I walk on across the river to the other side. I'd like to know if the grass on the other side is tall, if it is whipped by the breezes until it lies like a mat before me. I'll walk till night fades into the bright blue day.

WISE GUY: And when you're gray and

slow? You won't have the strength to walk.

PRINCIPAL C: No, but I'll be satisfied. I won't walk past this river. Beyond it is another river. But what a calm country to die in—the dark and cool. Pardon me, it is also good country to live in as well as to die.

WISE GUY: In!

PRINCIPAL C: That's very good, wise guy. You're really on your toes tonight. But wait, suddenly, I feel as though, as though we are dead. At least for the moment. At this river by the bridge at midnight we aren't here. We can see and feel, but we don't really exist.

WISE GUY: Conclusion?

PRINCIPAL C: There is no conclusion. That's it.

WISE GUY: The teacher said draw your own conclusions.

PRINCIPAL C: That's a rare coincidence.

WISE GUY: What?

PRINCIPAL C: I don't think we should forget that we are dead. Let's not waste our death hours worrying on conclusions.

FIRST LOVER: (*Enters. She speaks with a French accent.*) Principal, I never expected to see you here.

PRINCIPAL C: First lover, I'm glad to see you, even if you weren't looking for me. In principle you're right to think you wouldn't run across me on the black river.

WISE GUY: We're not usually here.

PRINCIPAL C: It is rare that anyone visits this secluded spot, and particularly not at this dark hour.

WISE GUY: We will admit only a rare sort of people visit this spot.

PRINCIPAL C: We are not rare. But I'll pretend to be. Perhaps I am an artist, a painter who will paint a somber canvas entitled *The Black River at Midnight*.

WISE GUY: You could be a writer. I will be the judge of your work.

PRINCIPAL C: Or a filmmaker. I write the scripts and direct the shooting. I am looking this spot over for a backdrop, for the part when the hero leaves the party to go for a walk and to think out his wild unruly past and confused future. He realizes that if he had stayed at the party he would have had the opportunity to make love to many beautiful women, but this thought means nothing to him. He has had enough of the wild aimlessness of partying life. He wants to be committed to something.

FIRST LOVER: Where do I come in?

PRINCIPAL C: You were his first love, whom he has long since forgotten. Now you appear on the scene. The sight of him makes you feel like Penelope on the return of storm-tossed Ulysses from the Trojan war. Tell me, love, were you the first love of many young men?

FIRST LOVER: Yes. I'm everyone's first love and no one's last. It's no way to live. When they all leave you to find another woman and all that is left of them is a fading memory, which I'd rather they had also taken, you begin to feel very old, a teacher whose pupils leave her to find their own destinies.

PRINCIPAL C: But here you have found me!

FIRST LOVER: But you no longer love me. Besides, I wasn't looking for you.

PRINCIPAL C: (*Eyes downcast.*) I can no longer love you. It would be impossible.

WISE GUY: (*To first lover.*) Aren't you looking for one of your old flames? Don't you desire the love of principal C?

FIRST LOVER: I know as well as principal C that we cannot return to those days. He has had many lovers since those days of his childhood.

WISE GUY: And all have faded to memory just as you were a memory.

PRINCIPAL C: A reincarnation.

FIRST LOVER: No, I've always been around. For a long time it seems.

PRINCIPAL C: Don't forget that I still have a future. When this night is finished, I'll find someone.

WISE GUY: That won't fade. It will be difficult.

FIRST LOVER: Like a needle in a haystack.

WISE GUY: A whale in a creek. Yes, very difficult.

PRINCIPAL C: Not too difficult.

WISE GUY: But difficult.

FIRST LOVER: To an extent.

PRINCIPAL C: You've changed so that I can no longer understand you. Do you come here often?

FIRST LOVER: Only rarely.

PRINCIPAL C: Be truthful to me.

WISE GUY: (*Speaking at the same time.*) You deceitful sloth.

PRINCIPAL C: Why do you want to deceive me?

WISE GUY: Tell us, woman.

PRINCIPAL C: Do you hate me or do you love me? Is it sport or contempt? Or is it boredom to lie to my face?

WISE GUY: Tell us, woman, tell us.

FIRST LOVER: What do you want me to tell? The words I spoke flowed naturally from within me. What are lies and what is truth? I don't know. Maybe I do visit the black river. Perhaps I live here. But does it matter? Should I be so positive to say that I have done this yesterday and that the day before? I consider what I told as truthful . . . more truthful.

WISE GUY: You're a clever girl, Claudia.

PRINCIPAL C: Claudia the clever, Juniper the jewel, Maria the maid. Violet the flower, Betty the bean, Leona the lioness.

WISE GUY: Alexandra the ape, and Electra the maniac.

PRINCIPAL C: (*Lyrical.*) My first love —and I can be fond of you for that!

FIRST LOVER: I don't care for your fondness. You old fool.

WISE GUY: (*To first lover.*) Cool fool.

PRINCIPAL C: (*Walks up and down, around first lover.*) You're looking as good as—ever. (*Has stepped behind. Slaps her on the rear.*)

FIRST LOVER: (*Not too serious.*) Thank you. You're so sweet.

WISE GUY: Principal C. (*He doesn't hear, wise guy repeats.*) Principal C, do you see someone coming?

PRINCIPAL C: Where?

WISE GUY: There.

PRINCIPAL C: Where? (*His eyes alight upon something in the distance.*)

WISE GUY: There, don't you see it? There!

PRINCIPAL C: (*Exasperated.*) I see it. I see it. A woman, painted black.

WISE GUY: Think of the time of day, idiot.

PRINCIPAL C: (*Still looking off in the distance towards the woman. He speaks mostly to himself.*) Who's the idiot? But here, she's coming.

WOMAN: (*Enters.*)

PRINCIPAL C: This is indeed a surprise. What do you expect to find here, my dear?

WOMAN: I am looking for—but there's no sense in telling. In any case I don't know. I can't put my finger on it.

PRINCIPAL C: Please don't evade it.

WOMAN: But I'm not—why should I? You're a stranger. What do I have to hide from a stranger?

WISE GUY: (*Making concession.*) She is beautiful.

FIRST LOVER: She wants to know him better.

WOMAN: Of course it is no concern of yours, and you shouldn't insist . . .

PRINCIPAL C: I won't insist. For tonight's sake. Because you have a beautiful face, a mysterious face, something unforeseen, unpredictable.

WISE GUY: Those lips, those eyes, that face!

PRINCIPAL C: I think we should reconstruct our lives on the grand scale. Mozart, Beethoven, Vivaldi (*conducting the symphony*) to Bach (*again conducts*).

WISE GUY: Oh, the fool.

PRINCIPAL C: I think I felt a few drops of rain. This is a lull before the storm.

WOMAN: Oh, I haven't noticed. The sky is black as tar.

PRINCIPAL C: And the wind is blowing in gusts. It's blowing in the South and being received in the North.

WOMAN: That's how I got here. I was blown from the South and received on the opposite end.

PRINCIPAL C: You're like Corrinna, being tossed by the wind. She was blown in circles for twenty years, until someone finally pulled her out of the wind's path.

WOMAN: Who pulled her out?

PRINCIPAL C: It was her lover.

WOMAN: Maybe you could call me Corrinna?

PRINCIPAL C: No, I don't think I should. Not now. Maybe later.

WOMAN: (*Nonchalant.*) But when?

PRINCIPAL C: Before the night is over. (*First lover rises and walks up to the couple.*)

FIRST LOVER: (*To principal C.*) What does the night hold for you, my boy? Is it going to give you gas?

PRINCIPAL C: Tonight something will happen. I can feel it.

WISE GUY: He can feel it in his bones.

WOMAN: What a horrible place to feel it.

*　　*　　*

UNTITLED

by Constance Stone

from Act 1

(*Scene: A living room with a large window on the left, sliding door to the kitchen at the back, and a door to the outside at the right. Next to the kitchen door is a bar. There is a large sofa left of center, and a table with a chair on each side of it right of center. The room also contains a record player. As the curtain rises, Arianna, Bernice, and Claude are discovered. Arianna is clearing the table.*)

ARIANNA: Excuse me for a few seconds. You two can, uh, do your thing while I clean this up and . . .

BERNICE: Oh, don't be ridiculous, I can help . . .

ARIANNA: I don't think it's ridiculous at all. Three's a crowd, and you two *must* have, uh, *plans* to make. (*Bernice is hurt by "three's a crowd."*)

CLAUDE: Yes, but they can wait . . . till I take Bernice home, anyway. Look, why don't you let us both help you?

BERNICE: (*Laughing.*) Claude, really! Ari doesn't want you breaking her dishes. (*Kisses him.*) You know how clumsy you are. (*To Arianna, pointing.*) *You* guard *him*, and *I'll* do these dishes. (*She takes the dishes from Arianna.*) I'm used to dishpan hands. (*Pushes them toward stage front and sofa.*) Go on, now, cooperate. (*Leaving.*) Flirt with him, Ari, and make him enjoy it. (*From off.*) I'll only be a sec. (*As she leaves, Arianna cocks her head at Claude, who is standing rather awkwardly. When Bernice leaves stage, Arianna winks and Claude jumps. Arianna is amused. Claude walks nervously over and sits on the sofa.*)

CLAUDE: You don't really have to bother, you know—flirting with me, I mean. I-I . . .

ARIANNA: Oh, it's okay. (*Walks over to window.*) Bernice and I are good friends. (*Turns to sofa.*) Practically family! Besides (*Sitting down beside Claude.*), I get a kick out of watching people in difficult situations. This is promising to be a goodie.

CLAUDE: I—see. Yes, of course. (*Loosens his tie.*)

ARIANNA: That-a-boy. Relax. I really don't bite.

CLAUDE: (*Leans forward, laughing, to pull over ash tray. Relaxing.*) I certainly hope not. You just don't impress me as the kind of girl who's a cannibal. (*Pulls out cigarettes and offers her one.*)

ARIANNA: (*Taking cigarette.*) Really? How come?

CLAUDE: Hmmm? (*Lights both cigarettes.*) Oh, I don't know. Somehow you just seem too delicate and refined. Besides, you cook too well.

ARIANNA: (*Laughing, grabs his knee.*) Best reason I've ever heard—and thank you. (*Jumps up.*) Hey, why don't you fix us some drinks. (*Points to bar.*) I'll put on some records and we'll make beautiful music together. (*Puts down cigarette.*) Okay?

CLAUDE: (*Puts cigarette down and rises.*) You know, the more you talk the better I like you. (*Goes over to bar.*)

ARIANNA: (*To herself, looking at records.*) Hmmm . . . something soft and sexily romantic. . . . Ah, yesss . . . (*Puts on Ramsey Lewis' "Since I Fell."*) How're those drinks doin'? (*Returns dancing to sofa, removes shoes.*)

CLAUDE: (*Returning to sofa with drinks.*) All done. Hope you like scotch and soda?

ARIANNA: (*Takes drink.*) Wouldn't keep it if I didn't. (*Sips.*) Mmmmm—good. (*Sets it down.*) Let's dance?

CLAUDE: Okay. (*Sets down drink.*) Wait a second. (*Removes coat and tie.*) Shall we? (*Proceed to dance. Arianna has her arms around his neck and her face near his. He is enjoying her nearness, but watchful for Bernice's entrance.*)

CLAUDE: What's keeping Bernice?

ARIANNA: (*Stops dancing.*) I'm really supposed to know! Look, love, go ask her! (*Raises voice, offended.*) Tell her you find me incurably dull and see how she likes that! (*Walks to sofa, sits and picks up drink.*)

CLAUDE: Hold on. (*Walks over to sit down. She rises and walks to window. He follows her and she walks to table and arranges flowers. He takes out another cigarette. This is during his line.*) I don't find you at all boring. You're rather fascinating at that, but I thought, since there were so few dishes . . .

ARIANNA: It does take pots and pans to cook with. (*Returns to sofa and sits. Downs drink.*) As you should know if you've ever had to cook. (*Slams down glass.*)

CLAUDE: (*Lights cigarette.*) Just 'cause I had sense enough to live with my parents until I matured is no reason to . . .

ARIANNA: Yeah. (*Gets up, goes to table, takes flower from vase.*) And you don't need to make sly cuts at me either. (*Turns suddenly.*) All right, so you know I got kicked out of my parents' house. . . . (*Sarcastic.*) That makes you special? (*Stamps foot.*) You're not so mature that you can treat me like a child!

CLAUDE: (*Smoking and getting angry.*) If you would, for once, act your age and take your own responsibilities instead of giving them to Bernice . . .

ARIANNA: (*Pointing.*) You shut up! What do you know about Bernice?

CLAUDE: (*Amused, crosses arms.*) I should think that I know her pretty well— I'm planning to marry her.

ARIANNA: (*Shocked.*) Oh. (*Pause. Frantic, but hiding it.*) Have you proposed to her yet?

CLAUDE: (*Furious as to why the interest.*) No . . . I will when I take her home tonight.

ARIANNA: I understand. (*Tearing flower apart deliberately, slowly.*)

CLAUDE: What do you understand? (*Uncrosses arms, sits on sofa.*)

ARIANNA: That she won't accept you. Not immediately. She'll ask me. Do you have any idea what I can tell her?

CLAUDE: (*Lowers cigarette to ash tray.*) You wouldn't. She'd not believe you if . . .

ARIANNA: Oh, but I would. And she would. She believes *me*—always—and I can tell her anything.

CLAUDE: What kind of person are you anyway? What do you get from this?

ARIANNA: (*Laughing.*) Don't tell me you forgot! I *told* you—(*Saunters over toward sofa.*) I enjoy watching people in difficult situations. It helps me find out what's inside, making them tick.

CLAUDE: (*Incredulous.*) You're crazy!

ARIANNA: (*Mocking. Leaning toward him.*) Absolutely. (*Goes to bar and makes another drink. Turns.*) I'm almost "inhuman," aren't I? (*Stands and drinks. Fixes another. Claude smokes angrily.*)

(*Bernice enters and stands looking from one to the other.*)

BERNICE: (*Astonished, nervous.*) God! The silence in here is thick as London fog. And not nearly as warm! Ari, you can't flirt with your back turned.

ARIANNA: (*Turning around to regard Claude with drink in hand.*) No . . . not unless you're walking away. But then, Claude doesn't like to be flirted with.

BERNICE: (*Looking at Claude, then sitting beside him, looking at him endearingly.*) What? Of course he does! (*No reply. Claude continues smoking, looking at ash tray and across room. Bernice curls up beside him, looking at him, then curiously at Arianna, who is picking up the shredded flower.*) Ah-hem! (*Cough.*) Why did the elephant wear green sneakers?

ARIANNA: (*Playing along.*) You tell me. (*Throws flower into trash can.*)

BERNICE: So he could hide in the tall grass! (*Arianna and Bernice laugh, Arianna feigning sickness at stomach. Claude looks up.*)

ARIANNA: (*Laughing.*) Your jokes are getting worse instead of better. Would you like a drink?

BERNICE: Yes, please, for both of us. There's another one like it: Why did the elephant wear white sneakers?

ARIANNA: So he could hide in the sand dunes? (*Fixing drinks.*)

BERNICE: (*Gleeful, squeezing Claude's hand.*) No . . .

CLAUDE: (*Smiling, interrupts.*) Because his green ones were dirty.

ARIANNA: (*Laughing, brings drinks over.*) Oh, GOD! When will I ever learn! (*Sits on other side of Claude.*)

BERNICE: Hopefully before I tell the next joke. . . . ummm.

ARIANNA: (*Holding hands up in surrender.*) Okay, okay. Enough! I'll be good.

CLAUDE: Promise?

BERNICE: (*Pinches his ribs.*) You hush!

ARIANNA: Yes, do—or I'll—(*laughing at him*) attack you! (*They all laugh. Bernice sips her drink and Claude takes out a cigarette.*)

ARIANNA: (*To Claude.*) May I have one?

CLAUDE: Sure! (*Gives her one.*)

BERNICE: (*As Claude lights them.*) I wish you wouldn't smoke so much, Claude—

CLAUDE: (*Coldly, smoking.*) Lay off, Bernie—we've been through this before.

BERNICE: Yes, dear. (*Pause. Arianna is amused, but hides it with a veil of smoke. Claude is annoyed at Bernice's meekness, and Bernice is miserable. She looks at her drink.*) What were you two—talking about when I came in?

ARIANNA: (*Gets up and walks to window, smoking. Claude clears his throat.*) We were talking about "us." (*Claude looks at Arianna, dismayed and shocked.*)

BERNICE: Us? (*Looks at Claude.*) Claude?

CLAUDE: The three of us . . .

ARIANNA: No, the two of us as related to you.

CLAUDE: (*Laughs bitterly.*) Ha! How right you are . . . us two *separately.*

BERNICE: Claude, you don't have to hide anything from me.

CLAUDE: I'm not hid—

ARIANNA: (*Finishes drink, interrupts.*) Bern, did you put away all the dishes?

BERNICE: (*Turning away from Claude.*) No, there were some left—I didn't know where they went.

ARIANNA: (*Rises and leaves for*

kitchen. Bernice looks back at Claude.)
Then I'll take care of that. My presence isn't
needed right now.

BERNICE: (*Pause.*) Will you talk to
me now? Can you? (*Claude gets up, walks
to window.*) Don't pull punches with me,
Claude. I can take a beating pretty well.
And I'd rather know now how you feel
about me. I have a feeling something's
changed. (*Claude turns angrily.*)

CLAUDE: How can you assume that
Arianna reads me like a book, too?

BERNICE: What does Ari have to do
with this?

CLAUDE: Plenty—everything. Why did
you bring me here?

BERNICE: Because I wanted you to
meet Ari. That's all.

CLAUDE: No . . . it's not. She asked
you to. Why?

BERNICE: Well . . . I—

CLAUDE: Do you tell her a lot? I mean,
did you tell her we were discussing marriage?

BERNICE: Of course. I tell her everything. I know she cares what happens to me.
You know, she—she can give me advice—
she can be objective—and I need that when
I get involved . . .

CLAUDE: Um—hmmm . . . and what
reason did you give for inviting me here?

BERNICE: (*Interrupts patiently.*) I
asked her to—for the same reason I've
asked before.

CLAUDE: What reason is that?

BERNICE: It makes no difference to
you! (*Clearly upset at his prying.*)
(*Arianna walks to the door and stands listening.*)

CLAUDE: You wanted to see if I could
be faithful to you! You can't trust anybody
who gives a damn about you!

BERNICE: I trust Ari!

CLAUDE: You actually think she cares?
Don't be absurd!

BERNICE: She's never failed me yet.
She's kept people like you from hurting me.

CLAUDE: Only because she took them
from you before they could prove their love
to you.

BERNICE: She never took anything
from me that I needed to keep! If I can't
keep it I didn't need it in the first place. If
she can take a man from me so easily, I
don't want him!

CLAUDE: (*Explodes.*) You fool! What
do you expect when you throw her at me
and leave. If you don't fight, you'll never
win! What do you want—a Superman?

ARIANNA: (*Walking in.*) No . . .
just a whole one . . . an all man:
steady, responsible, mature and . . . faithful. (*Walks up behind Bernice.*)

CLAUDE: (*Looks at the two of them.
Pause. Quietly.*) Then I guess I don't know
you after all. (*Picks up coat and tie.*) I
thought I'd found a woman—(*Puts on
coat.*) But you're still a little girl. (*Arianna
walks to table and watches. Claude puts tie
around neck and walks up to Bernice.*)
There just aren't any men like that, darlin'.
But—(*Lifts Bernice's chin.*) keep dream-
ing, little one. And don't ever wake up. I
don't want life to hurt you too badly. (*Kisses
her nose and leaves.*)

ARIANNA: (*Pause. She walks to sofa,
picks up ash tray and goes to empty it.*)
Well—

BERNICE: Ari—(*Goes and sits on
sofa.*) do you think he's right? I mean—
that there really are no men like that?

ARIANNA: No—he's not right. None
of them have been right. But the time will
come—you'll meet the right guy, honey.
Don't let him wrong you.

BERNICE: But—he seemed so—sincere.

ARIANNA: They always seem sincere.
Look—would it make you feel better if I
called him and asked him to come over
again? One more trial?

BERNICE: (*Doubtful.*) Do you think
he'd come?

ARIANNA: (*Confident.*) I think I could
talk him into it.

BERNICE: You don't mind?

ARIANNA: No, love—anything for you to be happy . . . you know that.

BERNICE: And you'll call me—

ARIANNA: 'Course I will—count on me. Okay?

BERNICE: Sure. (*Rising.*) I'll go home, I guess—can I do anything else?

ARIANNA: No, baby . . . you've had enough for one night. Do you need a ride? (*Stops Bernice at door.*)

BERNICE: I'll get a cab. That's easy enough.

ARIANNA: You have money?

BERNICE: Yes.

ARIANNA: Okay then . . . Take care, Bernie. (*Calls out door.*) I love you! (*Arianna enters, closes door and leans against it, concentrating. Then she walks over to the sofa, sits, picks up Claude's cigarettes and smiles smugly, taking one out. The lights gradually fade to blackness.*)

* * *

UNTITLED

by Carole Brooks

from Act 1

HARRIS: Do you mind my asking a personal question?

JOANNE: No.

HARRIS: How long have you been blind?

JOANNE: All my life.

HARRIS: Really, all your life—so you've never seen color or tall towering cities.

JOANNE: I've only heard them and smelled them, and of course I've felt them —I feel shapes and all the movement in a crowded city. Why did you never ask me before—that question?

HARRIS: Never thought to.

JOANNE: What made you think of it now?

HARRIS: I was watching you for a moment—you're very pretty. Do you even know your own face?

JOANNE: Oh, yes, I do—but not the same way that you do, I think. I know details; I don't know if they look good like that or not. My eyes and nose seem large.

HARRIS: You've never seen what an eye looks like, have you? You've never looked in someone's eyes.

JOANNE: Am I missing a lot?

HARRIS: But you are much wiser than I. Wisdom is not a thing you learn in school. I'm not trying to criticize you, I meant that you knew more than I about people.

JOANNE: How can I? I know so few people. *My* world is small. People are sensitive to me as I am to them and I can share with them some things which you will never know, but that is not wisdom, that is friendship. My life knows no in-between as yours does. Either people are close or they stay away, so all I know besides no relationship at all is an involved, understanding one. That is not wisdom, it's sentiment. I may have more sentiment than you, but then you have no great need for it and I do. Excuse me for running on so—I shouldn't.

HARRIS: What do you mean, you're not wise. You're wise because you know people—and that's more than I can say for myself and all my acquaintances. I think that because you care to know, you are wise.

JOANNE: Think what you will, but my life is simple and I've little experience. How can someone naïve be wise?

HARRIS: I see, you've not chosen the good, the good is all you know because you can't see the bad. If you were like the rest of us, then you'd probably run along also in the vicious circle between the two. What about your parents? I take it they weren't too hot. I mean—it doesn't bother you if I talk about it, does it? I don't know what they are like or even how you feel about them really, but I took it they really didn't care too much—didn't want to care.

JOANNE: You are right. (*Pause.*) I should love my parents, but I can't. They have no love for me. If they had tried to damage my life I would have been better off. I would have had something to fight or know or possibly change into love, but they didn't. They just didn't do anything, and because they didn't want to care they drove me to believe that I was nothing. I never knew until just these last few years that there were any other blind people in the world.

HARRIS: Have you ever been out anywhere—done anything? I know you walk to the park occasionally, and I guess you used to visit relatives or something, but have you ever been into anything—you know, like parties or—you know—stuff like that —sociable stuff?

JOANNE: My mother used to have parties at the house.

HARRIS: Yeah, but having a party with your mother, that's not really what I meant. See, like when I go to a party I like to . . .

JOANNE: I have no use for that, and besides my mother always locked me in my room.

(*Robin cuts in. She's standing at the top of the stairs.*)

ROBIN: Joanne—I thought you were going to take your nap.

HARRIS: Look, I'm sorry, Joanne—I was being pretty damn nosy. I wasn't thinking.

(*Joanne exits and closes her door behind her. Robin comes down the stairs and into Joanne's room with her. Harris is left alone on the stage. He looks then at the closed door, runs his hand through his hair. He gets up and walks to the couch, picks up a magazine and sits down. Robin comes back out, closing the door softly behind her. She goes over to the sink and begins to clean up.*)

HARRIS: (*Still looking at the magazine.*) Need any help?

ROBIN: No.

(*Another long pause.*)

ROBIN: I remember once when we were sitting in a hamburger joint—there was a man and a woman sitting in the booth beside us. He was saying something like,

"I'm fine when you're around, but when you're gone the bottle just takes over." We all heard him and we laughed. Of course, he heard us, so, with a frown, they left. I remember it—thinking—that poor man had wanted to cry, we were so cruel. We had laughed at his life, all his life. The girl with him didn't seem to care. I wonder what made me think of that?

HARRIS: You know, I really enjoyed that party last night, not so many people, good music, good booze.

ROBIN: It was just great to see some old friends again. Everyone's changed so.

HARRIS: What happened on Nineteenth Street? You know, the wreck we saw on our way back?

ROBIN: Yeah, it was pretty bad. There was an ambulance, and police. We couldn't see, and we were rushed on by the cops.

HARRIS: Remember those good old days, Robin, when we used to be in high school? My poor kid brother's going through that now.

ROBIN: Harris, please don't forget to call your parents. Joanne's really terribly bothered by them. That's all she could talk about last night.

HARRIS: I will, but I'm not going to get anywhere.

ROBIN: You don't have to get anywhere, just let them know you're still alive and kicking.

HARRIS: And then I'll have to answer to them about this and that—you know, there's one thing that gets me above all and that's their damned ignorance. Like when they argue with me about things they don't know about—and they never listen. All they know is the word *hippie*. And they keep saying it over and over like it's my name, or something—what did I ever do to deserve them?

ROBIN: I feel lucky. I also feel good. Let's not depress ourselves. It's a beautiful day and a nice quiet restful afternoon shouldn't be wasted by talk. What were you reading?

THE OTHER SIDE
OF THE FOOTLIGHTS*
by R. H. Gardner

A couple of weeks ago, while passing through *The Sun's* city room, I was hailed by David Kearse, the reporter who helps me out from time to time in covering the theatre.

"Tell me," he said from his typewriter, "if you think this lead is too flip."

In the jargon of journalists, a "lead" is the first paragraph of a news story. Mr. Kearse's stated that "Christabel tried crossing the Rubicon and sank in Olney Theater's premiere of a new comedy this week."

Too flip?

"No," I said, staring at the sentence thoughtfully. "It's a very good lead."

And it was. It always had been, since Alexander Woollcott used it for the first time back in the Thirties to describe Tallulah Bankhead's performance in a production of Shakespeare's "Antony and Cleopatra." It then read, if I remember correctly, "Tallulah barged down the Nile last night—and sank!"

I could not help, however, but be disturbed by its present application; for unknown to Mr. Kearse—a considerate and innately courteous young man—the play that he was annihilating with such enthusiasm was mine.

* Reprinted from *The Baltimore Sun,* September 14, 1969, by permission of the author, the drama critic of *The Sun.*

Policemen, they say, experience greater temptation to commit crime than people in ordinary occupations. And a drama critic, after years of watching inferior works become hits, may find himself similarly tempted.

Written on Vacation

I wrote "Christabel and the Rubicon" during a three-week vacation in the late fall of 1966. The thing that had finally triggered my decision was "Cactus Flower"—latest hit in a relatively recent series of formula comedies, which included "Come Blow Your Horn," "Generation," "The Impossible Years," "Barefoot in the Park," "Never Too Late," and "Any Wednesday."

By "formula comedies" I mean those conceived on the entertainment level of the Doris Day Show. All the above, that is to say, are mechanical in nature, frothy in substance, and generally unbearable to the "serious" theatregoer. But they have done wonders for their authors' bank accounts: and while money has never been a prime mover in my life, the older I get the healthier becomes my respect for it.

The job I hold would, I knew, be a handicap in my efforts to produce a commercially successful trifle. For some reason, the New York critics will accept something like

Woody Allen's "Play It Again, Sam" with amused condescension. But let Walter Kerr try it—as in the case of the 1958 disaster, "Goldilocks"—and they bring up their heavy artillery. The New York *Post's* Richard Watts, Jr., stated the matter as follows:

"Since drama critics and their wives are notoriously more brilliant than most people, a great deal is expected of them. And, when they are daring enough to challenge an envious world with a show of their own, nothing less than a masterpiece will satisfy the eager anticipation. Because 'Goldilocks,' the musical comedy for which Walter and Jean Kerr wrote the book and their share of the lyrics, and which Mr. Kerr directed, seemed, to put it conservatively, rather short of that status in its debut at the Lunt-Fontanne Theater Saturday night, it was a disappointment. What made the dissatisfaction all the more upsetting was that the weaknesses of 'Goldilocks' appeared to be chiefly in the writing contribution of the Kerrs."

The problem in my case was further complicated by a book, "The Splintered Stage," which I had published the preceding year and in which I had severely criticized the American theatre for not producing anything in the way of great drama. I could envision some sage leading off with "So this is what Mr. Gardner considers great drama!"

I did not want my thin little play judged on the basis of who had written it. Nor—and this was even more important—did I want to impose an additional burden upon those colleagues of mine who would feel embarrassed at having to pan it.

A nom de plume seemed the obvious solution. I chose H. J. Moorman, the name of my maternal grandfather, a highly respected man of Baptist persuasion, now, presumably, turning over in his grave.

My plot concerned a teen-age girl who, to the astonishment of her parents and boy friend, insists that she is pregnant by a 45-year-old novelist she has seen only once, on the night of their meeting in a New York discothèque. Summoned to the girl's home in Richmond, the novelist denies the allegation, and the question boils down to who is lying and why. In constructing the action, I utilized the "Rashomon" device of presenting several conflicting versions of the same story and a technique which, in its quick movement back and forth in time and space, is more characteristic of the cinema than of the stage. This was necessary to disguise the essentially simple nature of the story, and the method proved to be the thing that attracted most of those who, in the months that followed, became interested in the play.

Appeals to Number

And a quite surprising number did. For some people "Christabel and the Rubicon" seemed to have an instantaneous appeal. Alfred de Liagre, Jr., in his time one of the biggest producers on Broadway, showed great interest in it, and Pat Fowler—who optioned it almost immediately—said that, of the several hundred scripts she had read during the preceding year, only an unproduced work by Nobel Prize-winner Jean-Paul Sartre had impressed her as profoundly.

This, in view of my original purpose in becoming a playwright, worried me until I learned that Miss Fowler's previous Broadway involvement had been one of the worst, but at the same time most commercially successful, shows of the season—a two-character monstrosity called "The Owl and the Pussycat." "Christabel" had obviously found its proper level.

For six months, this producer held the play under option, while she strove to find a star for the title role. Unfortunately, the number of young ingenues with names big enough to mean anything on Broadway is rather limited. (Some time later, Hayley Mills, approached through her manager, Roy Boulting, expressed interest, but nothing ever came of it.) So, finally, the option was dropped, and Miss Fowler shifted her attention to something called "Leda Had a

Little Swan," which—though it did have a star (Michael J. Pollard) and a director (Andre Gregory)—never opened.

Then, for about a year and a half, "Christabel" went the rounds of the New York offices. Among those, in addition to Mr. de Liagre, who gave serious thought to producing it were an associate of the venerable Max Gordon, Leslie Odgen (co-producer of "The Man in the Glass Booth"), and a teacher of playwriting named Albert Zuckerman.

It was the last—for a while the most enthusiastic of the lot—who raised certain questions I felt could be answered only by seeing the play on the stage. Accordingly, I sent a copy to Olney, along with a plea to treat it like any other unsolicited manuscript. A week or so later, I received a call from James D. Waring, who said he liked the play and wanted to direct it.

I was delighted, having long regarded him as one of the best directors in the country, and I looked forward to discussing the script with him in detail. But his duties, as Olney's full-time designer and producing director, kept him so busy our meeting was postponed until two weeks before the start of rehearsals.

Our first real communication on the subject took place early one morning aboard the Metroliner on the way to New York to hold auditions. His opening remark came in the form of a grunt, as he stared gloomily at the script with eyes that obviously needed sleep.

"I see you've used a motion-picture technique."

"Yes," I said, pleased that he had noticed. "I know it's unorthodox, but, if the action is kept fluid, I'm sure it will work."

He nodded without conviction.

"You can do things on the screen you can't on the stage," he observed.

"That's true."

There was a pause. "Well," he said with another grunt, "we'll see."

And we did.

The auditions were held in a rehearsal room at Stage 73, a small off-Broadway theatre on Seventy-third Street. The walls were a leadened gray, and so was everything that transpired there.

Through this gray room, with its ghastly fluorescent lighting, passed a stream of nervous people—long-haired, miniskirted little girls; middle-aged women, with a look of patient desperation in their eyes; mopheaded young men in skin-tight jeans; older men, whose long, corrosive experience at this sort of thing gave them an air of defiance. They knew, before they entered, they weren't going to be chosen, and they were determined not to be destroyed by it.

My dialogue, in the mouths of these people, sounded flat and unfamiliar. There are at least six ways one can read a five-word line, depending upon which word, if any, one chooses to emphasize. It seemed to me that nobody who read my lines that first day put the emphasis in the right place.

This was especially true of the long monologue with which Christabel opens the play. Dull as this monologue now sounded to me, I knew it had a few laughs in it, which the young actresses were missing. They continued to miss, and the repetition gradually became unbearable—until I felt that, if another miniskirt said "I'm Christabel, and this play is about how I crossed the Rubicon," I'd collapse.

Knew She Was Christabel

Then one said it, and I didn't collapse.

It wasn't so much her delivery—which was on a par with the others—as the way she sort of glowed, infusing the room's gray atmosphere with vibrant pink. She was Rita McLaughlin, an 18-year-old student at Marymount Manhattan College who had appeared briefly in a Broadway turkey called "A Warm Body," and extensively on a network television series called "Watch Mr. Wizard." She had naturally red hair, green eyes, beautiful legs, and from the moment she entered, I knew she was my Christabel.

For Bobby, Christabel's unprecocious boy friend, we selected a young actor-musician named Jeff Conaway. Thus, having already decided to use Robert Milli, an Olney veteran of long standing, for the older member of this unlikely triangle, we had the principal roles cast. It had taken us three days, involving two separate trips to New York, during which time we had auditioned around 100 people.

For many reasons, it is imperative that the author of a new play attend rehearsals; and this, in view of my still fervent desire to conceal my identity—at least, until after the reviews were out—presented a difficult problem. Jim half-seriously suggested that I acquire a false beard and appear in all the hirsute splendor of a Henrik Ibsen or Karl Marx.

Emphasis Seemed Wrong

It was finally agreed that I would come at three-day intervals and watch—as unobserved as possible—from the rear of the darkened theatre. Afterward, Jim and I would compare notes and decide upon changes. In the interim, we would keep in close touch by telephone.

My first experience in this role, a three-hour ordeal which lasted until 6 P.M., was nothing if not traumatic. If my lines had sounded flat and unfamiliar in the gray room on Seventy-third Street, they sounded positively repulsive projected from the brilliantly lighted Olney stage. Always the emphasis—so crucial in comedy—seemed wrong. That night, Jim's and my session lasted until 2 A.M. The same thing occurred on the next visit, by which time I had begun to become aware of an even more ominous problem.

During the writing of "Christabel," I had anticipated that the numerous shifts in locale could be quickly accomplished by sliding mobile platforms containing fragmentary sets in from the wings. Monologues, delivered by one character or another, would help to cover these changes, the idea being that the action must be kept fluid and without pause.

The Olney stage, I knew, was constructed in segments that could slide right and left and backward and forward. I assumed that Jim would install a shallow, stationary set (representing the living room in Christabel's home) on the rear central segment and slide the other sets on in front of it. What I did *not* know was that, in order to slide a segment in from the side, the central segment first had to move back to make room for it.

Stage Had to Shift

From the standpoint of staging, this meant that every time the action shifted from the living room to somewhere else—say, the novelist's Manhattan apartment, down right —the portion of the stage bearing the living room would have to be pulled back (a feat requiring from 5 to 10 seconds) and then the side portion bearing the apartment set would have to be pushed on. The heavy stage, moving on its tracks, produced a deep rumble, like a subway train passing beneath.

During the afternoon rehearsals, the set for "Who's Afraid of Virginia Woolf?", the play then being performed at Olney, occupied one whole side of the stage, making it impossible to utilize the equipment as it would be used in production. As a result, I did not fully grasp the scope of the problem until dress rehearsal, the night before the Tuesday opening.

It was then I realized that changes, which I had envisioned could be made in a maximum of one second, would require a minimum of 15, much of which time the stage would remain in darkness. And the rumble made anything said, while it was going on, extremely difficult to hear. Jim had endeavored to bridge these pauses—which became increasingly irritating during all the jumping back and forth in the second act— with music, but the effect was jerky at best. The play lacked the substance to support all the trimmings, and the pace suffered.

Jim had been right. One cannot do on the stage what one can do on the screen. He had tried—because of the play, which he had originally liked, and, perhaps, because of a faith in me. Who knows? But, without wanting to, he had devastatingly proved his point.

And, painful though the proving was, I had benefited from it. I'd had the privilege of working with a real pro, whose ideas almost always turned out to be right. "Christabel" still has grave problems—the overlong monologues, the fragmented nature of the second act. But, because of Jim, it is a tighter and more actable script than it was three months ago.

Watching the actors become acquainted with the characters was enlightening; and, as time went on, the lines began to sound more and more as I had intended them to sound. Milli made a comic gem of the novelist, and Rita was a delight, whether on stage or off.

Valuable Experience

I had, in fact, received valuable experience that should deepen my understanding as a critic and stand me in good stead if— as now seemed highly unlikely—I should ever again be tempted to become a playwright.

One of the Washington reviewers, whose notice was both unfavorable and astute, criticized Olney for doing the play at all. I disagree. With all its faults, "Christabel" has as much substance and entertainment potential as "Never Too Late," with which Olney began the current season; and theatres should encourage new playwrights, even if they happen to be me.

Critical reaction was generally what Jim and I had anticipated. The reviews were, if anything, better than what I had expected.

Of the six daily papers in the Baltimore-Washington area that covered the play, three liked it (with reservations) and three loathed it. Fifty-fifty, in view of the fact that it was always the first-string critics who liked it and the substitutes who didn't, are not bad odds.

Oddly enough, I was not upset by the reviews. I had just learned that, from the standpoint of the playwright, the audience is the thing.

During that final rehearsal, before the opening night, which I, for obvious reasons (I would have been expected to review it) could not attend, I was haunted by one horrifying thought. What if the audience simply yawned?

Audience Liked It

To me, the play seemed lifeless and humorless. I could not imagine anyone's being entertained by it! Thus, the prospect of imposing it upon a large number of people appalled me. How could I do this to them?

It was, therefore, with a sense of unutterable relief that I learned, from Jim and others, that the opening-night audience had been extremely responsive, laughing consistently throughout and interrupting the action, on occasion, with applause. There had, moreover, been four curtain calls. A similar reaction, I am told, has occurred at all subsequent performances.

I have put in my order for a beard, and this evening—or, perhaps, the matinee—I shall go to see "Christabel" for the last time. This final communion will, I suspect, like all the others, be an ordeal—for I have yet to become accustomed to the sound of my own voice projected from a stage. And this time Jim will not be there to commiserate.

He has left the country.

Abel, Lionel (ed.). *Moderns on Tragedy.* Greenwich: Fawcett Premier Books, 1967. A collection of valuable recent theatre criticism.

————. "On Writing a Play," in Engle, Paul (ed.). *On Creative Writing.* New York: E. P. Dutton, 1964, pp. 205–242. One of the most intelligent short articles on the subject you can find. Abel will help you more in forming value judgments than in gaining specific pointers.

Allen, Walter (ed.). *Writers on Writing.* New York: E. P. Dutton, 1949. This book is devoted to poetry and the novel, but many of the generalizations in it about writing may prove useful. It is a collection of excerpts from the works of great writers on the subject of how they write.

Anderson, Maxwell. *Off Broadway.* New York: Wm. Sloane Associates, 1947. A collection of lively essays, most of them throwing some light on how Anderson has worked successfully as a playwright.

Archer, William. *Playmaking.* New York: Dover, 1960. Originally published in 1912, this is the first and, many think, still the best book on the subject. It is full of specific suggestions about how a play should be structured. Although many of them are now out of date, most of Archer's comments are still surprisingly relevant.

Artaud, Antonin. *The Theater and its Double.* New York: Grove Press, 1958. Although very enigmatic, this book has had tremendous influence on recent developments in the theatre.

Baker, George Pierce. *Dramatic Technique.* Cambridge: Houghton Mifflin, 1946. The dean of American playwriting teachers writes more technically and less enduringly than Archer, but his book is still full of valuable insights.

Baker, Samm S. *Your Key to Creative Thinking.* New York: Bantam Books, 1964. This book is *very* easy reading, and it may help you organize your approach to your work as a playwright, though it is designed to stimulate creativity in the solution to practical problems.

Bentley, Eric. *The Life of the Drama.* London: Methuen, 1965. This study of the elements and kinds of drama will help you think in terms of dramatic form.

————. *In Search of Theater.* New York: Vintage Books, 1954. Selections from the theatre criticism of one of the finest and most influential critics of our time.

————. *The Playwright as Thinker.* New York: Meridian Books, 1955. The ideas of playwrights in relation to their dramatic technique. Bentley's views on nearly every aspect of theatre are compelling.

Berne, Eric, M. D. *Games People Play.* New York: Grove Press, 1964. This half-humorous analysis of the psychology of human relationships should be of great value to the playwright in understanding how people interact, particularly in social situations.

Bogard, Travis, and Oliver, William I. *Modern Drama: Essays in Criticism.* New York: Galaxy Books, 1965. A good collection of penetrating essays on specific modern playwrights.

Breit, Harvey. *The Writer Observed.* Cleveland: World Publishing Company, 1956. Brief interviews with a number of modern writers, mostly novelists, shed occasional light on the creative process.

Brook, Peter. *The Empty Space.* New York: Atheneum, 1968. Observations by one of the most innovative directors in the world today.

Brown, Ivor. *What is a Play?* London: Macdonald, 1964. A readable analysis of all aspects of theatre.

Brown, John Mason. *Dramatis Personae.* New York: The Viking Press, 1963. A generous selection from the life work of one of Broadway's finest critics.

Cane, Melville. *Making a Poem.* New York: Harvest Books, 1962. One of the very few instances in which a creative writer has attempted to analyze the creative process at some length. It might help you to understand your way with a play.

Childress, Gagliano, Hirsen, and Perry, "On the Playwright's Condition," *Theatre Crafts,* Vol. I, No. 5 (Nov./Dec., 1967), pp. 30–37. Some contemporary playwrights who are on the way up chat informally about their problems.

Clark, Barrett H. (ed.). *European Theories of the Drama.* New York: Crown, 1947. This is a basic text in theatre study. It contains all the major authors on the subject of dramatic theory from Aristotle to the present. Most of these are abstract enough to be of little practical help, but you will also find such things as O'Neill's work diary on *Mourning Becomes Electra.*

Cole, Toby (ed.). *Playwrights on Playwriting.* New York: Dramabooks, 1960. An excellent collection from a large number of playwrights during the last hundred years. Although the value of their observations varies greatly, you should find a number of things here that will be helpful to you.

Cooper, Kenneth H., M.D., M.P.H., Major, U.S.A.F. Medical Corps. *Aerobics.* New York: Bantam Books, 1968. This book tells you how to maintain yourself in good physical condition. As your physical condition improves, so will your writing.

Egri, Lajos. *The Art of Dramatic Writing.* New York: Simon and Schuster, 1960. A good easy-to-read guide to playwriting.

Esslin, Martin. *The Theatre of the Absurd.* New York: Anchor Books, 1961. An excellent introduction to the work of many of the surrealist playwrights.

Fagan, Edward R. *Field: A Process for Teaching Literature.* University Park: The Pennsylvania State University Press, 1964. This book will help to make you aware of how information from such areas as physics, biology, and psychology is meaningfully incorporated in literature. Central to it is an analysis of George R. Stewart's novel *Storm.*

Fergusson, Francis. *The Human Image in Dramatic Literature.* New York: Anchor Books, 1957. Among many valuable essays is one on *Macbeth,* which makes very clear how analogous action works in that play.

————. *The Idea of a Theater: The Art of Drama in Changing Perspective.* New York: Anchor Books, 1953. An extremely important but somewhat difficult book that gets at the development of drama through the analysis of a number of classic plays. You will find in it the development of the idea of unity of action in drama. It also examines the relationship between drama and ritual.

Fordham, Frieda. *An Introduction to Jung's Psychology.* London: Penguin Books, 1953. Easier to read and more comprehensive than any of Jung's own books, this provides the playwright both with a good understanding of the human mind and also with some idea of how symbolism works in literature.

Frazer, Sir James George. *The New Golden Bough.* New York: Anchor Books, 1965. This great study of myth in many cultures might provide inspiration for both plot and symbolism.

Freud, Sigmund. *A General Introduction to Psychoanalysis*. New York: Washington Square Press. The best possible introduction to Freud's whole approach. Here again there is much on symbolism.

————. *The Psychopathology of Everyday Life*. New York: Mentor Books. This book will give you a deep respect for the significance of the casual utterance.

Fromm, Erich. *The Forgotten Language: An Introduction to the Understanding of Dreams, Fairy Tales and Myths*. New York: Grove Press, 1951. One of the best books on psychological symbolism. Extremely useful in understanding the whole psychological structure of the drama. The material on the relation between *Antigone* and its society is particularly interesting.

Fry, Christopher. *An Experience of Critics*. London: Perpetua, 1952. An important modern poetic playwright chats informally about his art.

Gallaway, Marian. *Constructing a Play*. New York: Prentice-Hall, Inc., 1950. A standard textbook approach, typical of many similar books in the field.

Gassner, John, and Allen, Ralph G. *Theatre and Drama in the Making*. Boston: Houghton Mifflin, 1964. An anthology of dramatic criticism through the ages.

Ghiselin, Brewster (ed.). *The Creative Process*. New York: Mentor Books, 1952. Creative people in many fields tell what they know about how they create. The collection includes not only contemporary thinkers, but ancient ones as well.

Gibson, William. *Two for the Seesaw* and *The Seesaw Log*. New York: Bantam Books, 1962. The trials and tribulations of getting a play produced on Broadway. This is one of the best studies of the professional playwright's life ever written.

Gordon, William J. J. *Synectics*. New York: Harper and Row, 1961. A systematic approach to the solution of technical and theoretical problems that some playwrights might find adaptable in improving their own creative writing.

Gorelik, Mordecai. *New Theatres for Old*. New York: E. P. Dutton, 1962. Perhaps the finest history of theatre yet written.

Gottfried, Martin. *A Theater Divided*. Boston: Little, Brown, 1967. A brilliant analysis of the problems the contemporary theatre faces. The split between conservative and radical playwrights is so great that we have, in effect, two theatres.

Granville-Barker, Harley. *On Dramatic Method*. New York: Hill and Wang, 1956. A collection of essays by one of the theatre's greatest directors, some of which have direct bearing on the playwright's problems.

————. *Prefaces to Shakespeare*. (2 vols.) Princeton: Princeton University Press, 1947. You can learn a lot about how a play is put together from a professional director's analyses of many of Shakespeare's plays.

Grebanier, Bernard. *Playwriting*. New York: Thomas Y. Crowell, 1961. An intelligent and detailed approach containing many valuable pointers and a large number of useful exercises.

Greenwood, Ormerod. *The Playwright*. London: Pitman, 1950. A rather difficult and technical approach, but still useful.

Hailey, Arthur. *Close-Up on Writing for Television*. Garden City: Doubleday, 1960. Actually, a collection of plays by this author, but the introduction provides a short essay on television writing with some useful pointers.

Hall, Edward T. *The Silent Language*. Greenwich: Premier Books, 1959. How people in different cultures communicate with one another through various unconscious devices that transcend words.

Hart, Moss. *Act One*. New York: Signet, 1960. Like *The Seesaw Log,* this tells the story of a play from the beginning to its final Broadway production. One of the best and most exciting ways to learn what the Broadway theatre is really like.

Hartnoll, Phyllis (ed.). *The Oxford Companion to the Theatre.* New York: Oxford University Press, 1951. One of the best reference books on all phases of theatre.

Hayakawa, S. I. *Language in Thought and Action.* New York: Harcourt, Brace & World, 1949. This book provides an introduction to semantics, a way of thinking about the implications of language use that playwrights should understand.

Herman, Lewis. *A Practical Manual of Screen Playwriting.* Cleveland: World Publishing Company, 1966. Complete details on the technical problems that arise in writing for television and the screen.

Hogarth, Basil. *How to Write Plays.* London: Pitman, 1933. This little old book may be hard to find, but it is surprisingly good. It is clearly written and filled with valuable pointers, only a few of which are out of date.

Hull, Helen (ed.). *The Writer's Book.* New York: Barnes & Noble, 1956. A collection of articles on all phases of writing, including radio, television, the film, and the dramatization of novels.

Ibsen, Henrik. *The Oxford Ibsen, Vol. VII.* (James Walter McFarlane, ed.) New York: Oxford University Press, 1966. This contains all the early draft materials and notes for *The Lady from the Sea, Hedda Gabler,* and *The Master Builder.* This volume is recommended because it includes a weak play, a great play, and a play in which Ibsen is attempting to move into a new area of playwriting. Comparing the two versions of *Hedda Gabler* should be extremely valuable to the playwright who is learning to revise. Although expensive, this volume should become a cornerstone in the playwright's library. No one can teach him more about technique than Ibsen.

Joos, Martin. *The Five Clocks.* New York: Harcourt, Brace & World, 1967. An enigmatic but fascinating little book that examines language use on five levels from "frozen" to "intimate." Its leading character, Miss Fidditch, is a woman from whose instruction we have all suffered.

Kernan, Alvin B. *Character and Conflict: An Introduction to Drama.* New York: Harcourt, Brace & World, 1963. Some of the elements of drama are given detailed examination. Included are the complete texts of a number of important plays.

Kerr, Walter. *How Not to Write a Play.* New York: Simon and Schuster, 1955. Complaining about the repetitiveness of the Broadway theatre in the 1950's, Kerr may have helped bring about the influx of new forms and techniques that has characterized the 1960's.

Kinne, Wisner Payne. *George Pierce Baker and the American Theatre.* Cambridge: Harvard University Press, 1954. This book may give you some insights into how Baker got his results. Among his students were Eugene O'Neill, Phillip Barry, and Sidney Howard.

Koestler, Arthur. *The Act of Creation.* New York: Dell Laurel Edition, 1967. Although long and complex, this book is brilliantly written, and it may help you better understand your own acts of creation.

Köhler, Wolfgang. *Gestalt Psychology.* New York: Mentor Books, 1959. This is somewhat tangential, but a play, like any other work of art, is a Gestalt, and one may learn from this book something about organizing its various elements.

Langner, Lawrence. *The Play's the Thing.* New York: G. P. Putnam's Sons, 1960. Out of the many experiences of the Theatre Guild comes a playwriting manual whose insights derive from extensive practical experience with success and failure in the commercial theatre.

Lawson, John Howard. *Theory and Technique of Playwriting.* New York: Dramabooks, 1960. Many consider this one of the best in the field, but it is rather heavy on philosophy and light on practical pointers.

Lederer, William J., and Jackson, Dr. Don D. *The Mirages of Marriage*. New York: W. W. Norton, 1968. Applying the principles of systems analysis to human relationships helps to produce a profound understanding of how people interrelate in marriage. Since marital relationships are very commonly dealt with in plays, such a book may be of considerable use to the playwright.

MacGowan, Kenneth. *A Primer of Playwriting*. Garden City: Dolphin Books, 1962. Not only does this book cover the field surprisingly well in rather a few pages, but also it quotes so liberally from a number of other writers that it will save you the trouble of locating them in the original.

Matthews, Brander. *The Principles of Playmaking*. New York: Scribner's, 1919. Brander Matthews was one of the leading lights in the American theatre, but this book is deadly.

———— (ed.). *Papers on Playmaking*. New York: Dramabooks, 1957. This collection is rather antique, including almost nothing from the twentieth century. Although interesting, it is almost no practical help.

Matthews, John F. (ed.). *Shaw's Dramatic Criticism*. New York: Dramabooks, 1959. The theatre's wittiest drama critic has a great deal to say to you if you follow his advice, which was not to take anyone's advice. He wrote on the assumption that all playwrights should write as he would later write. This is not true. Only Shaw should have written as Shaw wrote.

McLuhan, Marshall. *Understanding Media: The Extension of Man*. New York: McGraw-Hill, 1965. One of the most influential books of our time, this should help you better understand what has conditioned modern audiences, and how you can appeal to them.

Mearns, Hughes. *Creative Power: The Education of Youth in the Creative Arts*. New York: Dover, 1958. A great teacher of the 1920's discusses the means by which he stimulated his young students to think like poets.

Mosel, Tad. "Writing for Television," *Amherst Alumni News,* Vol. XXI, No. 2 (Fall, 1968). One of television's very best writers here writes cogently from his long experience, getting more into a magazine article than some can manage in a whole book.

Moulton, Richard G. *Shakespeare as a Dramatic Artist*. New York: Dover, 1966. Although originally published in 1885, this is probably still the best book on how Shakespeare handled plot and structure.

Muller, Herbert J. *The Spirit of Tragedy*. New York: Knopf, 1956. One of the most readable works of its kind. It is both historical and philosophical in approach.

Neill, A. S. *Summerhill: A Radical Approach to Child Rearing*. New York: Hart, 1960. In a completely permissive environment children gained many educational experiences, among them writing plays.

Niggli, Josefina. *New Pointers on Playwriting*. Boston: The Writer, Inc., 1967. A somewhat commercial approach to things, but very clearly written.

Polking, Kirk, and Deward, Marge (ed.). *Writer's Market*. Cincinnati: Writer's Digest, published yearly. This volume tells you exactly where you can market anything you write.

Postman, Neil, and Weingartner, Charles. *Teaching as a Subversive Activity*. New York: Delacorte, 1969. Anyone interested in organizing a class in playwriting will find invaluable information in this book on how to teach such a class effectively.

Potter, Stephen. *One-upmanship*. New York: Henry Holt, 1952. A humorous summary of the techniques that many people quite seriously engage in in maintaining the upper hand in a relationship. This book should be particularly valuable for writers of comedy.

Priestley, J. B. *The Art of the Dramatist*. London: Heineman, 1957. A surprisingly unhelpful book from a well-known playwright. It's readable, though, and quite short.

Raphaelson, Samson. *The Human Nature of Playwriting*. New York: Macmillan, 1949. This is delightful. Raphaelson taught a course in playwriting and wrote down everything that happened in it. As you read this book, you take the course right along with the rest of his students. You are bound to get some insights in the process.

Read, Herbert. *English Prose Style*. Boston: Beacon Press, 1962. The best book on the subject of style. If you are not sensitive in this area, study it.

Rowe, Kenneth Thorpe. *A Theater in Your Head*. New York: Funk & Wagnalls, 1960. This should help you visualize a play as you read it, a skill you will certainly need if you are hoping to be able to visualize a play as you write it.

————. *Write That Play*. New York: Funk & Wagnalls, 1936. A better than average manual of playwriting, though somewhat outdated.

Salerno, Henry F. (translator and editor). *Scenarios of the Commedia dell' Arte*. New York: New York University Press, 1967. This contains fifty of the scenarios on which the actors in the commedia dell' arte improvised their plays. You will find it a useful source of plot ideas for comedies, and you may wish to try improvising from some of the scenarios with your own group.

Schulberg, Budd (ed.). *From the Ashes: Voices of Watts*. New York: New American Library, 1967. What Schulberg achieved among the disadvantaged should be inspiring to creative writers everywhere.

Sedgewick, G. C. *Of Irony Especially in Drama*. Toronto: University of Toronto Press, 1948. A good but difficult study of dramatic irony.

Selden, Samuel. *An Introduction to Playwriting*. New York: Appleton-Century-Crofts, 1946. Easy to read and very useful.

Seyler, Athene, and Haggard, Stephen. *The Craft of Comedy*. New York: Theatre Arts, Inc., 1946. A correspondence between teacher and student that leads to informal but interesting speculations on what makes comedy work.

Shank, Theodore J. (ed.). *A Digest of 500 Plays*. New York: Crowell-Collier Press, 1963. Just reading through all these plot outlines might give you some ideas. These are the plays you should be familiar with so that you do not repeat what they have already done.

Shattuck, Charles H. (ed.). *Bulwer and Macready: A Chronicle of the Early Victorian Theatre*. Urbana: University of Illinois Press, 1958. Letters from a nineteenth-century playwright to the actor-manager who produced his plays shed some interesting light on how plays were gotten into shape a century ago.

Shaw, Bernard. *Complete Plays with Prefaces*. (6 volumes) New York: Dodd, Mead, 1963. If you can, read all of this.

Sorokin, P. A. *The Crisis of Our Age*. New York: E. P. Dutton, 1941. This discussion of three types of art and their progress through history should prove helpful to anyone trying to imagine what may be going to happen next in the theatre.

Spolin, Viola. *Improvisation for the Theater*. Evanston: Northwestern University Press, 1963. This approach is rapidly becoming one of those most widely used for training actors. The book contains dozens of theatre games and exercises.

Spottiswoode, Raymond. *A Grammar of the Film*. Berkeley: University of California Press, 1962. Familiarity with techniques of filming should be of value to anyone interested in writing screenplays.

Styan, John Louis. *The Dark Comedy: The Development of Modern Comic Tragedy*. Cambridge: Cambridge University Press,

1968. Probably the best book on recent developments in the drama.

————. *The Dramatic Experience: A Guide to the Reading of Plays*. London: Cambridge, 1965. A clear and simple explanation of many of the basic principles of drama, providing an essential background for the playwright.

————. *The Elements of Drama*. London: Cambridge, 1960. The best explanation of the subject to date.

Van Druten, John. *Playwright at Work*. New York: Harper, 1963. Perhaps the most readable and enjoyable of all the playwriting manuals. Van Druten writes out of many years of experience as a highly successful playwright.

Wager, Walter (ed.). *The Playwrights Speak*. New York: Delta, 1968. Wager's interviews manage to get about as little of value out of our most illustrious contemporary playwrights as anyone could, but still this book is not to be overlooked.

Watzlawick, Paul; Beavin, Janet Helmick; and Jackson, Don D. *Pragmatics of Human Communication: A Study of Interactional Patterns, Pathologies, and Paradoxes*. New York: W. W. Norton, 1967. Despite its formidable title and rather technical approach, this book can be of great value to the playwright. Much of it is devoted to an analysis of the communications techniques used by the characters in *Who's Afraid of Virginia Woolf?* This is psychology that the playwright would do well to understand.

Wellman, Francis L. *The Art of Cross-Examination*. New York: Collier Books, 1962. There is some common ground in the knowledge of human nature needed by the playwright and the trial lawyer, and this book may provide some insights the playwright could not get elsewhere. For one thing, you should know your characters so well that you could cross-examine them on everything they do.

West, E. J. (ed.). *Shaw on Theatre*. New York: Hill and Wang, 1958. Some of Shaw's best and least-known critical writings.

Wilde, Percival. *The Craftsmanship of the One-Act Play*. New York: Crown, 1951. Do not let the title mislead you. This is one of the best books on all types of dramatic writing.

Willett, John (ed.). *Brecht on Theatre*. New York: Hill and Wang, 1964. Much modern theatre technique stems from Brecht's theory of alienation. Here is where you can find out what Brecht was really trying to accomplish by it.

Williams, Tennessee. *Cat on a Hot Tin Roof*. New York: New Directions, 1955. Dissatisfied with the New York production of his play, Williams published both versions of the third act: his own, and what was finally produced. His comments on the production also make interesting reading.

Young, Stark. *Immortal Shadows: A Book of Dramatic Criticism*. New York: Dramabooks, 1948. Another leading critic whose views are worth your while.

Riordan High School
Library
175 Phelan Ave.
San Francisco, California 94112